THE BIG
BREAK

THE BIG BREAK

THE GAMBLERS, PARTY ANIMALS & TRUE BELIEVERS
TRYING TO WIN IN WASHINGTON
WHILE AMERICA LOSES ITS MIND

BEN TERRIS

12

TWELVE

NEW YORK BOSTON

Twelve
Hachette Book Group
1290 Avenue of the Americas, New York, NY 10104
twelvebooks.com
twitter.com/twelvebooks

First Edition: June 2023

Twelve is an imprint of Grand Central Publishing. The Twelve name and
logo are trademarks of Hachette Book Group, Inc.

The publisher is not responsible for websites (or their content)
that are not owned by the publisher.

The Hachette Speakers Bureau provides a wide range of authors for
speaking events. To find out more, go to hachettespeakersbureau.com or
email HachetteSpeakers@hbgusa.com.

Twelve books may be purchased in bulk for business, educational, or promotional use.
For information, please contact your local bookseller or the Hachette Book Group
Special Markets Department at special.markets@hbgusa.com.

Library of Congress Control Number: 2023932141

ISBNs: 978-1-5387-0805-7 (hardcover), 978-1-5387-0807-1 (ebook)

Printed in the United States of America

LSC-C

Printing 1, 2023

For Rachel, obviously

Contents

Prologue: Is Any of This Normal?   1

Part 1: The Players

Chapter 1: A Tale of Two Parties   13

Chapter 2: The Gambler   30

Chapter 3: Creature Comforts   37

Chapter 4: The Guy Who Left   41

Chapter 5: The Cowboy Diplomat   51

Part 2: The Doers

Chapter 6: Best Night of My Motherfucking Life   65

Chapter 7: Dear White Staffers   71

Chapter 8: The White Hat   78

Chapter 9: Scribe of the Subaltern   83

Chapter 10: They Know How to Run the Game   90

Contents

Part 3: Placing Bets

Chapter 11: The A-Bomb Kid — 99

Chapter 12: Betting Clears the Mind — 105

Chapter 13: New Money — 111

Chapter 14: Save the Swamp! — 121

Chapter 15: What Stinks in Building B? — 126

Chapter 16: This Is a Great Intentional
Smokescreen (Papa Bless) — 136

Chapter 17: Welcome to the Canceled
Hall of Fame — 143

Chapter 18: Trying to Transcend the
Morass of Shit — 152

Chapter 19: The Billionaire's Brother — 157

Chapter 20: Look at This Coalition — 163

Part 4: The Undone

Chapter 21: The Spiritual Chief — 173

Chapter 22: Police Unreformed — 177

Chapter 23: Your Allies on the Other Side
Are Allies Second and Opponents First — 183

Chapter 24: Nobody Saw What I Was Seeing — 185

Part 5: The Game

Chapter 25: The Original Big Boy — 191

Chapter 26: Chaos Is Good — 199

Chapter 27: The Tough Questions   204

Chapter 28: Another Crack at It   211

Chapter 29: I Will Spew You Out of My Mouth   214

Chapter 30: No, No, No, We're Doing Great   220

Chapter 31: The Turn   224

Chapter 32: Frank Luntz, Dr. Phil, and
Roe v. Wade   230

Chapter 33: Losing Traction   232

Chapter 34: Homeboy Does Not Cry   236

Chapter 35: Everything Is Not Okay, Dude   245

Chapter 36: If You Find Anyone Else
Like Me, Let Me Know   255

Part 6: The Breaks

Chapter 37: The Big Blind   265

Chapter 38: October Surprise   270

Chapter 39: Once You Go Down, It's Really
Hard to See How You Come Back Up   277

Chapter 40: Dark and Stormy Democracy   284

Chapter 41: What Side Am I On Here?   293

Chapter 42: Washington in Winter   299

Chapter 43: If People Think They've
Seen the Last of Me...   310

Epilogue   315

Acknowledgments   *321*

Index   *327*

THE BIG BREAK

Prologue: Is Any of This Normal?

I'm in the business of making Joe Biden's agenda look more popular than it really is," Sean McElwee announced to the poker table. "And business is booming!"

It was a July evening in 2021. Biden's presidency was six months old, his approval rating was hovering around 50 percent, and his agenda was on the move. Sean, the twenty-eight-year-old head of a Democratic polling group and think tank, was a few Miller High Lifes into one of his regular poker nights hosted at his bachelor pad in Logan Circle—a recently gentrified neighborhood in Washington, just north of downtown. In the living room, a big-screen television played *Rounders*, the 1998 Matt Damon poker movie that was canon among Millennial gamblers. A guest bed lay in the corner. Extra-large pizzas and cheap beer cluttered the counter in the kitchen, and tubs of protein powder sat on the shelves.

Sean was new to Washington—and splitting time with New York City, where he kept an apartment—but he had the vibe of someone who'd been around forever. He wasn't a pollster exactly (he hired experts to do the legwork there), and he wasn't a policy nerd. He wasn't a campaign guy either (although his nonprofit, Data for Progress, did do work for campaigns). He was *sort of* all of these things and also sort of none of them. More than anything, he was a political evangelist. He was in the business of making Democrats popular—figuring out what legislation to prioritize, what phrases to stop saying. And he was in the business of making himself popular too.

Since moving to town a few months earlier, Sean had managed to generate a gravity well, attracting other Democratic operators into his orbit. He hosted monthly happy hours that were well attended by professional progressives and establishment climbers. The boozy meetups were a way to see people and be seen, and it was hard to miss Sean. He was over six feet tall with a body type that fluctuated between lineman and linebacker. He had a signature look: translucent-framed glasses and black T-shirts—an outfit he deviated from just enough to avoid comparisons to Steve Jobs or, worse, Elizabeth Holmes. Sean knew everyone, and every few weeks he invited a rotating cast of his happy-hour crew over for poker.

Tonight's table featured: a spokesman for Facebook ("I work for our tech overlords," he said); a friendly former Senate staffer who now led an organization attempting (unsuccessfully) to end the filibuster; a former top aide to former Senate Majority Leader Harry Reid; a senior reporter who covered the Senate for MSNBC; and Gabe Bankman-Fried, the brother and political consigliere of the crypto billionaire Sam Bankman-Fried.

Like any effective Washington operator, Sean was good at getting close to people with money—or at least close to people who were close to people with money. Sean wasn't ultra-wealthy himself, but he did all right—his salary was $180,000 and he had started picking up lucrative consulting gigs on the side. He'd recently started doing work for Gabe's organization, Guarding Against Pandemics (GAP), which, backed by millions from Sam, was quickly becoming a powerhouse in Washington. One of Sean's main jobs for GAP was to hype their work at every opportunity.

"This pizza is good," someone said at the table.

"You know what else is good?" Sean said, looking at Gabe. "Pandemic prevention." *Subtle.*

The conversation bounced around, from Democratic Senator Kyrsten Sinema's habit of screwing up her party's legislative agenda (Sean: "She has such bad politics, but she's so hot") to the question of whether Donald Trump would be president again (Sean: "He's a cooked turkey"). There was talk, too, of the various recreational drugs used by different Democratic operatives (apparently Ecstasy was a popular choice for one well-known data guru). No one here was a particularly serious poker player. They bought in for $100 and bluffed when bored. Sean, especially, was prone to wild swings in chip count.

But Sean's biggest wagers had nothing to do with cards. They had to do with politics. Tonight, Sean had his eye on the upcoming Democratic primary in Ohio, where Shontel Brown, the establishment choice running with the backing of the Congressional Black Caucus, was up against Nina Turner, the former Bernie Sanders campaign staffer and progressive-wing favorite who once compared voting for Biden to eating "a bowl of shit." Political observers had been watching this race closely, since the outcome might hint at whether Democratic voters wanted to lurch left as the 2022 midterms approached (Turner) or stay the course (Brown).

Sean was betting it would be the latter. Literally. He had placed bets online and stood to win nearly $14,000 if Shontel Brown won.

"I make a lot of bets that would make progressives cry," Sean said.

"How many active bets would you say you have right now?" someone asked.

"My inbox is so full of bets," Sean said, "I don't even remember what I have money on."

"Do you make bets on races you're working?"

The question lingered as the players seemed to mull the ethical implications. Betting on politics while working in politics, betting on clients? Was this normal? Should it be?

After a few seconds, Sean laughed.

"Who can say?" he said.

* * *

What *is* normal?

That was a common question after four years of Donald Trump in Washington. "This is not normal," people would say when the leader of the free world raged at his own Justice Department, or undermined civil servants, or appeased bigots, or winked at conspiracy theorists, or palled around with geopolitical adversaries, or profited from his office, or told the American people blatant falsehoods over and over again. "Don't normalize this," admonished the admonishers. Nevertheless, Official Washington rearranged their habits around Trump's personality. The opportunists went on television to lobby a president addicted to cable news. They sucked up to a praise-starved man in hopes of avoiding a "mean tweet" that could sink their business prospects or political aspirations. They wore ugly red hats and changed their opinions about free trade. Florida Governor Ron DeSantis was spotted moving his hands around during speeches—as if playing an invisible accordion—just like Trump did.

When Joe Biden ran for president, he offered a selling point that was rare for political campaigns: a return to business as usual. After he won, Washington residents cheered from their balconies and banged pots and pans and honked their car horns. It was a catharsis, Victory Day for normality. But the war wasn't over. Two months later, Trump supporters led a violent siege of the U.S. Capitol to disrupt the peaceful transition of power. A coup attempt was thwarted, and Biden did assume his rightful office, but the odds of a return to normalcy were difficult to determine.

The future was a blind bet, and I spent the first year watching people place their wagers. I did interviews with President Biden's Covid response team as they prepared to declare "independence" from the pandemic on July 4th, and then watched the Delta and Omicron variants keep that mission from being accomplished. I met retiring Democrat Representative John Yarmuth for an interview in his Capitol Hill office, and the Kentuckian described to me a recent argument on the House floor—between the progressive Mark Pocan, of Wisconsin, and the more moderate John Garamendi, of California—that he said nearly turned into a physical fight. ("John was basically telling Mark to get his head out of his ass," Yarmuth explained to me.) Things were tense, he said. He drank a Dixie cup of whiskey during the interview; it was 2:30 p.m.

I watched Republicans take a step away from Trump after the insurrection, then watched them run back to him once they decided denouncing those lies was bad politics. I watched corporations stop donating to Trump allies who voted against certifying the election and then watched them start again. I heard MAGA diehards like Representative Marjorie Taylor Greene, the conspiracy theory fan turned bigoted blogger turned Georgia congresswoman, double down on the Trump election lies that had inspired the attack on the Capitol. I heard Dan Crenshaw, the Republican congressman from Texas, dismiss Greene as a performance artist who specialized in "self-inflicted controversy followed by claims of victimhood."

"She lucked her way into Congress," Crenshaw told me. "She says crazy things. And yet is looked up to. Why? What are we doing, guys?"

What some lawmakers were doing was trying to make federal legislation bipartisan again. The summer after Biden's inauguration, Senator Chris Coons, the Delaware Democrat, told me about how a group of senators who were trying to wrap up an infrastructure bill had bonded as party guests on Joe Manchin's houseboat, docked in a D.C. marina. Somebody else told me a story about Texas Senator Ted Cruz polishing off three beers in a matter of minutes while posing like Captain Morgan and chatting with a liberal colleague on Joe Manchin's houseboat. Another person told me an anecdote about Alaska Senator Lisa Murkowski bursting into a chorus of "God Bless

America" as she beheld the sight of the Washington skyline from the deck of Joe Manchin's houseboat.

Senators schmoozing: That was normal, right? So was intraparty jousting: Manchin eventually helped sink Build Back Better, the huge bill that Biden hoped would guide his progressive agenda through Congress. Meanwhile, there was a lot of hand-wringing about Biden's diminishing poll numbers and his advancing age. Trump and his lies had not gone away. Neither had the coronavirus. The pandemic had knocked the supply chain out of whack. Inflation was on the rise. For all his year-one wins—pandemic relief money, infrastructure, judicial appointments—Biden had failed to make things normal again. Even those who hadn't soured on him began to wonder whether it might be time to consider an alternative candidate for 2024, especially with Trump lying in wait to retake the White House.

In February 2022, I walked into the White House to talk to Jen Psaki, then Biden's press secretary. She had no reason to believe Biden wouldn't run again, she said. And yet it *had* been a topic of conversation in her own home.

Her brother-in-law had come over for dinner recently, and Psaki had joked that she hoped there was a secret meeting happening "in a basement somewhere" to figure out a plan in case Biden didn't run, she told me.

"And he looked at me," she said, "and was like, 'Should we be having that meeting now?'"

* * *

I was rarely the kind of reporter who chased The Big Story. I was more interested in the sideshow. When I started covering politics in Washington in 2010—first for *National Journal* magazine and later for the *Washington Post*—my job included writing about weirdos. People like Senator Jim Inhofe, the Oklahoma Republican and octogenarian climate change denier who forced me to consider my own mortality when he took me for a spin on his tiny airplane. And Brett Talley, a Republican speechwriter, who dabbled in paranormal detective work and took me ghost hunting in a cemetery near Georgetown. And Stephen Bassett, a registered lobbyist who represented UFO abductees.

When Trump descended from a golden escalator and became a candidate for president, he was just a sideshow. In fact, the *Post* didn't plan to send a reporter to cover his announcement in person. I lobbied to be there—I was the sideshow guy. It was quickly becoming clear, however, that the sideshow was moving onto the main stage. With Trump in the White House, it was boom time for weirdness in Washington. The president suggested nuking a hurricane. He said of Kim Jong-un, the dictator of North Korea's nuclear hermit kingdom: "He wrote me beautiful letters. And they're great letters. We fell in love." The coronavirus came and the president mused about injecting disinfectant and bringing light into the body. I reported a story about whether a recovered crack addict known as The MyPillow Guy represented the future of the GOP. Before it was over, a man dressed like a Viking would enter the chamber of the U.S. Senate.

Yes, Washington felt different under Trump. But what about once he left? Who was allowed to become powerful, and from where would they draw that power? What were the rules of the game, and how did you win? That's a big part of what this book is about. It's about the Washington that predated Trump, and the Washington he left in his wake.

Mostly, though, it's about people.

I wanted to explore these questions by spending time with people who were trying to make post-Trump Washington work for them. I wasn't as interested in the politicians themselves (boring, busy, overexposed) as much as the people whispering in their ears, or trying to. People like Sean McElwee.

Sean seemed to me like a type of person made specifically for Washington after Trump (brash, ideologically malleable, an outsider who wormed his way inside), while also being a type of creature that had swum this swamp for eons (brash, ideologically malleable, an outsider who wormed his way inside). He made big bets, big allies, and big enemies. He walked right up to the line of acceptable behavior, and kept walking. At my second poker night at his house, Sean showed off a new pair of pink high-tops he had bought with the money he'd made betting against Nina Turner's primary campaign.

"I was polling for Nina Turner's super PAC," he announced to the table. "So I knew Shontel Brown was going to win."

I couldn't believe he'd just admit that. Even Pete Rose had the good sense to *pretend* he didn't bet on baseball. What was even more surprising to me than the gambling was that, at the poker table, nobody seemed to think it was a big deal. By then it had already become clear to me that Sean was destined either to become the biggest thing in Democratic politics or to completely flame out. Because it was Washington, I also had to consider the possibility that both those things would happen.

Washington is a weird place like that, even in normal times—a place of change agents and stalwarts, strivers and survivors, wonks and wannabes, hustlers and true believers. Over the course of two years, I talked to as many of them as I could—an heiress to an oil fortune who got her start in politics at Occupy Wall Street; a cowboy diplomat who made his fortune as a fixer for foreign governments; the Republican shape-shifter who shifted his shape to thrive in Trump's Washington; and the exiled Republican spokesman who eventually decided he couldn't do the same. I talked to people working on Capitol Hill who were trying to figure out if Washington was the right place to be if they wanted to repair the country. I talked to a guy who left in order to repair himself.

In the course of reporting on their lives, I thought about how strange it was that they all ended up in the same city. They seemed so different. But in an important way they were similar: Politics was personal for them. The drama with their friends, the balance on their bank statements, the speeches they hoped people would give at their funerals, and the country they hoped to pass on to their kids—all were tied up in the livelihoods they had chosen for themselves.

America had gone through a big break, and in Washington people were sorting through the pieces—trying to put something together, or to keep something together. They were placing bets on the future, and hoping things would break their way.

Part 1

The Players

Chapter 1

A Tale of Two Parties

December 2021

It was the edge of winter in Washington, one year into the new-New Normal. Each day it grew darker earlier, people were getting sick again, and anti-democratic forces were on the rise. Maybe there was still time to turn things around. Or maybe it had been too late for too long and everyone was kidding themselves. But you had to do *something*, right? And so, with all signs pointing toward doom, Leah Hunt-Hendrix threw a Christmas party.

She had the perfect house for it, a $2.2 million brick Victorian. The cherrywood floors of the spacious living room flowed right into the open-concept dining room—ideal for dinner parties. And the expansive roof deck, overlooking Logan Circle, would come in handy for bigger occasions.

Not every thirty-eight-year-old progressive activist could afford such a house, but not every progressive activist was the granddaughter of H. L. Hunt, the late oil tycoon once believed to be the richest man in the world. H.L. lived a life as large as his bank account. He was a Texas gambler said to have won the money for his first oil leases at the poker table; a bigamist with two secret families; and a right-wing communist-hater who worshipped Joseph McCarthy.

H.L. was the kind of American about whom conspiracy theories were created, and he had been linked (without evidence) to the murders of John F. Kennedy, Robert F. Kennedy, and Martin Luther King Jr.

His granddaughter, on the other hand, had named her tiny white dog after Malcolm X.

"This is Malcolm," Leah said, opening the door to her home and motioning to the four-legged cottonball yapping at her heels. "He's my baby."

It had been nearly a year since Donald Trump departed Washington, and I was on a mission to figure out what, exactly, he had left behind. In mid-December, this meant checking out holiday parties. Washington is always awash in Christmas parties—the perfect excuse for organizations to boost morale and liquor up potential clients, and for power players to fill their homes with bold-faced names (an oft-used expression in Washington for "important people") in an attempt to bolden their own names by association. I've always found these parties to be awkward, like going to work after hours and without pay. But they are a good way to find out what people are gossiping or worried about, and so I attended two. They were only a few miles apart, but in completely different worlds. One would be at the home of Matt and Mercy Schlapp, two of the Swamp's Trumpiest creatures. But first, I was here, among the chic radicals of the left.

A fire roared in the living room fireplace as Malcolm the Maltipoo hunted for cheese crumbs redistributed to the floor by mingling socialists. There was Corbin Trent, Representative Alexandria Ocasio-Cortez's former communications director, surveying the crowd in the kitchen. Trent had come to work for the Democratic Socialist bartender turned champion of the left after cofounding a couple of progressive organizations dedicated to shaking up the House. But Trent eventually grew disappointed by how mainstream Ocasio-Cortez had become, and he left Capitol Hill and rededicated himself to being an outsider. He was now spending his days in Knoxville, Tennessee (with occasional visits to Washington), and had made it a personal mission to find a populist Democrat to run against Joe Biden in the next election. One time he drunkenly called Steve Bannon for advice.

In the dining room was Ryan Grim, the D.C. bureau chief of the lefty website The Intercept. He wore a T-shirt featuring a large photograph of Harriet Tubman, and chatted with Julian Assange's half brother, a film producer who had traveled to the States to advocate for the WikiLeaks founder's freedom. Grim was a regular at events like this. Faiz Shakir, a top strategist for Senator Bernie Sanders, on the other hand, was standing nearby telling guests he *never* came to these things.

"Sarah made me come," he said, pointing at his wife, Sarah Miller, a former Treasury Department aide who now worked at a think tank trying to break up monopolies. "And we have an au pair that lives in our basement, so I had no excuse."

Shakir may not have been a social butterfly, but he was a savvy navigator of the contradictions present in spaces like these. He'd worked for establishment figures like Speaker of the House Nancy Pelosi and Senate Majority Leader Harry Reid. He'd also started his own progressive media group called More Perfect Union, which produced slick videos boosting America's labor movement and economic policy. He was at once an insider and an outsider—a liaison between the Biden administration and the groups who were trying to pull the president to the left. He was something for Leah to aspire to.

People like Shakir came to Leah's party because they liked her, but also because she was an important person to know. There aren't a lot of progressive fundraisers who come from rich families and hobnob with multimillionaires. Leah had helped seed-fund lots of her guests' projects, including Shakir's More Perfect Union.

Since Hillary Clinton's defeat in 2016, wealthy, well-educated liberals had struggled with the idea that they were out of touch with the voters they needed to beat back right-wing populism. Leah's challenge was to be part of the solution while also being part of the problem. She was a rich White lady fighting inequality and working to help Democrats better appeal to an ever-diversifying working class. She had been an early financial backer of Black Lives Matter and was helping raise money for progressive congressional candidates all across the country—including many who had signed pledges to refuse money from the same fossil fuel industry that had propelled Leah's family into the donor class.

Leah was not the first woman in her family to try to make it in Washington. In the living room, standing underneath a peaceful painting of rowboats floating in a sun-dappled sea, was Leah's aunt Swanee, former ambassador to Austria under Bill Clinton. Of all the people in Leah's life, Swanee was perhaps the person she looked up to most. Swanee had an innate understanding of how "soft power" worked, of how to build out a network and use those connections for good. It was Swanee who had suggested that Leah move from San Francisco if she wanted to actually make political change. Swanee gave her approval for this house as Leah's base of operations (they both liked its hosting potential), and helped Leah decorate it with art Swanee had brought back from far-flung locales, including the seascape she stood by now. Swanee beamed as her niece—dressed in a floral skirt, brushing her blond hair out of her eyes—topped off drinks for thankful guests.

Leah seemed in high spirits, but she was in a bit of a slump. She'd thrived, politically speaking, during the Trump years. In 2018, she'd cofounded an organization, Way to Win, which had been a bright star of the #Resistance era, helping pump more than $165 million into Democratic causes. They had been especially important in places like Georgia and Arizona, helping fund on-the-ground organizations that worked to swing the Senate into Democratic hands.

Leah was hoping to keep energy levels up for the 2022 midterms, but was finding that difficult to achieve. Much of her focus was on the House of Representatives, but there was a Senate race that meant a lot to Leah: Mandela Barnes, the thirty-five-year-old Black lieutenant governor of Wisconsin, running for the chance to unseat Trump ally Senator Ron Johnson.

Leah had met Barnes years ago when they each spoke on a panel about economic populism in Miami and hung out together at the after-conference pool party. "He was riding on one of those inflatable unicorns," Leah said. "He was a lot of fun." The two became friends, and when Barnes was contemplating running for Senate, Leah promised him she would do whatever she could to help. For Leah, a Barnes win would be about a lot more than just having a friend in the Senate. It was a chance to prove that a progressive candidate could win in places deemed inhospitable—like statewide in Wisconsin—and a chance to help prove that Black candidates could win there too.

The Barnes race and the House races across the country were exhausting in a way that Leah wasn't completely used to. There had been something almost easy about doing the job under Trump: easy to convince people to give money to fight creeping authoritarianism, easy to build coalitions with fellow resisters. But now Leah was mostly involved in primaries, working to get the most progressive option through to Election Day. Dollars were harder to come by for this type of work. It also meant that many of her former allies were now adversaries. It took very little effort for Democrats to define themselves against Trump. But with him gone, Leah was struggling to rally people around a vision for what Democrats should be for, not whom they should be against.

* * *

Across town and over the river into Virginia, a yard full of Christmas lights shined upon the largest house on Mansion Drive.

A couple hundred guests mingled through the 10,000-square-foot home of Matt and Mercy Schlapp. They dressed in sweaters and houndstooth blazers, glittery cocktail dresses, and satin jumpsuits. They munched on canapés under the chandelier in the dining room, admired the cubist art in the living room, and posed for photos beside the lavishly decorated Christmas tree in a sitting room by the front entrance. In another era, many of the guests currently here would be little more than political wannabes, staffers for fringy Republicans or aspiring pundits. But they were more than that now.

"This is the White House Christmas party that should have been," Paris Dennard said over the din.

Dennard, the director of Black media affairs for the Republican National Committee, was standing just outside the kitchen by a table loaded with malt balls and chocolate chip cookies. He was talking to Hogan Gidley, Donald Trump's former deputy press secretary.

"You know what?" Gidley replied. "I think it actually *is* the real White House Christmas party."

Hosts Matt and Mercedes ("Mercy" to her friends) might not have been Donald and Melania, but they had come to resemble them. The Schlapps had once been the very picture of the old Republican establishment—stints in George W. Bush's White House, seats on corporate boards, lobbying contracts. But they were Trump people now. Matt was the chairman of the American Conservative Union, an organization that had become a top Trump-boosting operation, and Mercy worked there too, following her stint in the Trump administration. After Trump lost the 2020 presidential election, Matt flew to Nevada in search of fraudulent votes—or at the very least to be a part of a strategy, according to an email from a Trump official at the time, "to cause as much chaos as possible." When members of the administration got caught up in January 6th investigations, Matt created the First Amendment Fund to collect donations and help pay for their legal bills. Matt and Mercy shifted from their "compassionate conservative days" into MAGA warriors, but because their party moved with them, their place in the GOP hadn't really changed at all. *This* was now the Republican establishment.

Consider the Gidley.

A natty dresser whose current ensemble included a pocket square, tie bar, and monogrammed shirt, Gidley was one of those highly amenable Beltway Republicans who used to engage in slap fights with "mainstream media" while happily meeting with journalists for off-the-record drinks and appearing on MSNBC whenever he got the call. ("How could I not go on there?" he once said to me of the liberal cable news network. "They are my friends.") In a post-Trump Washington, Gidley was part of a growing cadre of lackeys tasked with giving Trump's election denialism the sheen of Washington professionalism. He had recently become the director of the Center for Election Integrity, a neutral-sounding body housed in the America First Policy Institute, a think tank stacked with former Trump administration officials. "The Center for Election Integrity has a simple goal in mind," according to its website. "Easy to vote, but hard to cheat."

In practice, this meant working with state lawmakers to address a nonexistent crisis—widespread voter fraud—under the auspices of good government. "Even Democrats used to talk about voter integrity," Gidley said to me, noting his belief that the system was broken. "Let's just fix it."

When he wasn't trying to "fix" elections, Gidley could be found doing the most Washington-guy thing imaginable: pretending he hated Washington. As he mingled his way through the MAGA merrymakers, Gidley told guest after guest that, yes, he was still living here, but that he was trying to get out.

"As quickly as I can," he said.

But no one here was really going anywhere. As was the case after every presidency, those who'd served the Trump administration had set up shop all around town: with their consulting groups, their lobby shops, and their think tanks. These were the professional Trumpists, not the amateurs who allowed their emotions to get the better of them and violently stormed the Capitol. The guests here had no real reason to be worked up into a frenzy. They had already gotten their big break when Trump became president, and had been collecting dividends ever since. Even though the Republicans had lost the White House *and* the Senate, the vibe at the Schlapp mansion felt merrier than at Chez Leah. They liked their chances at taking back power, and there was no real power struggle on the Republican side of the aisle—no identity crisis. The Republican Party was Trump, and so was the Schlapp party.

There was Stephen Miller, the thirty-six-year-old immigration hardliner, in a schlumpy sweater, standing in the dining room and looking like he wanted to disappear behind the yellow velvet curtains. Before Trump, Miller was just some twenty-something kid working for a backbencher senator. But now, having helped drive some of the former president's most nativist domestic policies, including separating children from their parents at the U.S. and Mexico border, he was a sought-after campaign adviser. These days, Miller was trying to help give hedge fund millionaire David McCormick a MAGA patina in his run for Pennsylvania's open Senate seat, a client he would eventually drop when Trump endorsed television presenter Dr. Oz instead.

Former White House Press Secretary Sean Spicer arrived at the front door.

"I loved you at the podium," a fan said, grabbing Spicer's micro-plaid blazer as he entered the house. "And I can't wait for your next book."

Spicer was a Washington Guy long before he was a Trump Guy. He had been spokesman for the U.S. Trade Representative under George W. Bush and then communications director for the Republican National Committee, advocating for free-trade policies and accommodation of immigrants; when Trump took over the party, Spicer had adjusted his politics accordingly.

I had first met Spicer when I shadowed him at the 2016 Republican National Convention for a story. Back then many GOP operatives were worried that Trump was going to be routed by Hillary Clinton. At one point during our time together, we ran into Jeffrey Lord, one of the first Trump surrogates. "He was like an early investor," Spicer told me at the time. "It's like being one of the first employees at Google, and seeing the stock go up."

Spicer had gotten in early enough to do pretty well for himself; he now hosted his own show on the MAGA news network Newsmax, along with writing books about how bad Democrats were. He'd love to see Trump run again, he told guests at the party, but even Trump's flirtation with the possibility was "good for business."

Guests here were mostly in Trump's business. Not the real estate business or the television business that had made Trump famous, but the culture war business that had helped make him president.

"I run the NRA, but for families," said Terry Schilling, president of the American Principles Project, standing with his wife beside the glowing Christmas tree in the sitting room by the front door. "It's transgender issues, critical race theory, pornography in school libraries. This year we raised $7 million. Next year we expect it to be $14 million."

Schilling was the son of Bobby Schilling, the late pizza shop owner turned Tea Party congressman from Illinois. Schilling had just enough facial hair to be described as both having and not having a beard and was one of those young conservatives who wished America could be a little more like he imagined it was before he was born.

"The other day I tweeted about how I wanted to have a Covid party for our kids," Schilling said. "You know, like parents used to have for the chicken pox? But someone who works for me told me I had to take it down, that if I wanted to get myself booked on Fox, I had to cut that out."

Like Schilling's beard, Trump seemed to be both here and not here at the same time. His name was on the lips of supplicants as they nibbled their appetizers and sipped their spirits. His face was on the television in the study, which was frozen on an ABC News promo for the first debate of the 2020 election. He was peering out from a framed photograph on the shelf. His name was scrawled on Alaska Senate candidate Kelly Tshibaka's business card, which had been abandoned on a table with half-drunk scotch glasses: "join me & pres. trump feb 10. Mar a Lago. Call Jenna."

"I was the one who came up with the term 'Trump Train,'" Billy Long, a Missouri congressman, said. "I even made it my computer password."

Long, a former auctioneer as large as two normal-size congressmen squished together, was watching the rain fall from the screened-in porch. He was running for the Senate in a Republican primary and proving himself to be a top-tier Trump suck-up. He had hired Trump's former campaign manager and White House adviser, Kellyanne Conway, to run his race; he had just returned from a Mar-a-Lago fundraiser where Long auctioned off a guitar signed by Trump; and here he was at the Schlapp party, making impossible-to-prove claims about inventing a pro-Trump phrase—like a MAGA version of Romy and Michele trying to impress people at their high school reunion by saying they invented the Post-it Note.

"I loved him first," Long told me, shaking me by the shoulders. I nodded. I backed away.

Whether or not the revelers on Mansion Drive actually believed Trump beat Biden in 2020, they were treating him like a winner. The fact that he was out of power only appeared to intensify the nostalgia for 2016, when Trump had run as a charismatic outsider rather than a battered incumbent. In this light, Trumpism was a promising investment—a blue-chip stock available at a discount. The more I made my way through this wannabe White House, the more it began to look less like a Christmas party and more like an investor's conference. Some were relative newcomers looking to buy Trump at his new low price.

Others, like the Schlapps, had invested early, and despite some recent volatility—a violent insurrection, another impeachment, a series of investigations—had way too much tied up in the former president to consider dumping their shares.

* * *

"How did you get an invite to this?"

Mercy had spotted me contemplating the malt balls by the dessert table.

She wore a ruffled green jumpsuit with a big bow tied at the waist, and looked like she just came out of a Fox News makeup room. Her auburn hair fell to her shoulders and she flashed her made-for-TV smile.

"I have no idea," I said to her. "Ask your husband."

There were days when the Schlapp Christmas party might have multiple non-right-wing journalists in attendance without anyone wondering how they got an invite. Tonight, it was just me, and as far as I could tell, Daniel Lippman, a human Rolodex of a reporter for Politico who seemed to show up to every event in the Washington area. Later this evening, Lippman would try to send a list of party attendees to the authors of Politico's morning newsletter, *Playbook*, for their "spotted" feature, but the newsletter would decline to flatter the partygoers by name-dropping them.

Life in a Republican-only safe space was a new development for the Schlapps, who had been in Washington for decades. Matt was a Kansas kid who arrived after running a winning House campaign for former Representative Todd Tiahrt. In 2000, Matt caught on with the Bush campaign. The race came down to a recount in Florida, and Matt and a group of fellow young operatives showed up outside the Miami-Dade County polling headquarters and clamored for an end to the ballot recount. The stunt became known as the Brooks Brothers riot.

Matt was rewarded for his campaign efforts with a job in Bush's political department. When the cute girl from the press shop came up to him after a meeting and suggested they discuss topics on which their portfolios overlapped, Matt thought she was hitting on him. She wasn't, but nevertheless Mercy and Matt eventually got together.

Matt left the White House in 2005 and began an establishment tour of Washington. He lobbied for Koch Industries, before he and Mercy started their own consulting shop that they called Cove Strategies. They picked up contracts with Koch, Big Pharma, and retail giants like Wal-Mart, and Matt—who also advised groups like the left-leaning Motion Picture Association—earned a reputation as the kind of Republican whom Democrats could work with.

In Washington, a reputation like that can earn a person a lot of time on television, and Matt became familiar enough with the rituals of doing TV that he developed particular tastes. Once, while waiting off-set before an appearance on *PBS NewsHour*, he gave me a rundown of all the green rooms across town ("Fox's is the worst"), and a former employee told me that Matt used to complain whenever his makeup brush was too soft.

People used to think that Trump's base consisted entirely of blue-collar workers in struggling industrial cities. But Trump's coalition had more than its fair share of elites—just maybe none as ridiculous about it as the Schlapps. Matt once stormed out of the White House Correspondents' dinner—an annual gala that often featured Hollywood celebrities dining alongside the Washington press corps—and tweeted about how upset he was with the evening's entertainment while in a limo on his way to an MSNBC after-party.

"I mean," he told the *New York Times* when they asked him about his own elite status, "I'm not trying to act like I drive a garbage truck in Des Moines."

Despite being the ultimate Washington Guy, Matt could claim a certain connection to Trump's actual base that most other Guys with jobs like his could not. As the chairman of the American Conservative Union (known by its initials, ACU), Matt was responsible for putting on the annual Conservative Political Action Conference (CPAC—as in "See Pac")—a must-stop event for pretty much anyone running for president in a Republican primary. It wasn't just a stuffy showcase of conservative ideas—it was a circus—and Trump had been a regular speaker there since 2011. The crowd didn't always love him there (he wasn't exactly a *conservative*). But Trump honed his entertainment-as-politics shtick on the main stage—and Matt was around to see what played.

When Trump first ran for president, he was a cause for concern.

After he announced, Trump's team had tried to strong-arm CPAC into certain allowances. He wanted a particular time slot, and more important, he didn't want to have to deal with the mandatory question-and-answer session to which all candidates had to commit. CPAC wouldn't relent (Trump was hardly an early frontrunner back then), and Trump backed out.

Trump was also a cause for concern in the Schlapp family. Mercy came from a family of Spanish-speaking Cuban immigrants. In 2015, she had predicted that Trump was "really going to struggle if he goes and continues to push a very strident immigration policy that doesn't show in any way that we can in fact find a legal path for these individuals who are here, for these undocumented immigrants that are here."

When an old *Access Hollywood* video surfaced before the 2016 election showing Trump bragging about how "when you're a star" you can "do anything" to women, even "grab 'em by the pussy," and they'll "let you do it," the Schlapps debated dropping their support for the sake of their five daughters. Unsure of how to proceed, they drove to their second home, Victory Farm—which sat atop a thirty-acre property in the Blue Ridge Mountains—opened a few bottles of wine, and decided that they would go all in with their support. They were crackpot committed. After all, if all Republicans—the disillusioned laborers, the evangelical Christians, the Wall Street libertarians, the green-room prima donnas, the Tea Party cosplayers in tricornered hats—had anything in common, it was a belief that Hillary Clinton would do nothing for them, and would likely mess with their worlds. This was gospel in the Schlapp home as much as it was at CPAC. When it came to the question of disavowing Trump over "grab 'em by the pussy," Matt told me that their thirteen-year-old daughter asked him why he would do anything to help Hillary Clinton. Ultimately, the Schlapps came to embody the constituency who actually tipped the 2016 election: people who saw Donald Trump as the better of two options.

And for Matt and Mercy, it was. She took a job inside the White House as director of strategic communications, and he was able to pitch himself to clients as having access to and influence over the president, which proved lucrative. The year before Trump became president, Cove Strategies had brought in $600,000. By Trump's final year in office, that number was $2.4 million.

In between they were making more than enough for the Schlapps to move to Mansion Drive, where, for a time, they hung an enormous Trump flag from a crane in their front yard.

*   *   *

"I probably have Covid," a woman said, plopping onto an outdoor couch. We're back at Leah's house, on the roof now. A man in a Santa hat threw logs on a fire pit. There were little plates of salami everywhere.

"Again?"

"I never had Covid!"

"What about in Vermont?"

"What were you doing in Vermont?" another guest asked.

"Oh, I bought a house online there during the pandemic."

There was no official theme for Leah's Christmas party, but unofficially it might well have been: Trying to Have Fun in End Times.

The first case of the Omicron variant had been detected in the D.C. area the day before, signs pointed to Democrats losing their majorities in Congress to an increasingly authoritarian Republican Party, and to top that off, Leah's oven had decided to quit right before her guests started to arrive.

"I have to get my party systems locked down a little better," Leah said, sighing, arriving on the roof with a plate of take-out Ethiopian appetizers.

It was an all-hands-on-roof-deck time for Washington's liberal coalition, so Leah was bummed that Ron Klain, the White House chief of staff, never showed up. And she didn't know how to feel that her neighbor and sometimes online combatant, the middle-aged boy wonder Matthew Yglesias, had turned down an invitation. Yglesias, a liberal blogger with a contrarian streak and a Substack newsletter that grossed him and his wife/editor close to $1 million a year, was a frequent object of scorn for the Online Left. "This feels like a trap," he had texted an intermediary about Leah's party. (He told Leah he had child duty.)

Still, Leah was happy to see a contingent from Cori Bush's office, and any party with her close friend and head of the Consumer Financial Protection Bureau, Rohit Chopra, felt like a good party to her.

Chopra was something of a hero to lefties in Washington. He had recently been confirmed by the Senate with a 50–48 party-line vote to run an agency, dreamed up by Senator Elizabeth Warren and created by President Obama in response to the 2008 financial crisis, that sought to protect people from predatory banks and various financial scams.

"I'm an executive branch asshole!" Chopra announced to the party.

He was standing on the roof with fellow Harvard alum Todd Schulte, the director of an immigration reform group.

"Do you talk much about your college experience?" Schulte asked.

"Not much, except to tell people about overthrowing Larry Summers," Chopra said. (He had been student government president in 2004 before Summers, an economist favored among establishment liberals and vilified in progressive circles, resigned the Harvard presidency less than two years later.)

"You overthrew Larry Summers?" an eavesdropper asked.

"Not me," said Schulte. "I just played a lot of water polo."

"You played water polo with Larry Summers?"

Leah enjoyed having people over to her house, but it was also part of a plan. Leah understood the power of bringing people together, her friend and party guest Adam Green, the founder of a progressive grassroots organization, told me. "When nobody is the most important person in the room, everyone who enters the room gains power and the convener gains influence," he said.

Over the course of the coming year she planned to host various "convenings"—parties, salon dinners, maybe a conference—to bring together the smartest Democratic voices to help chart a path forward for the party.

"Republicans have done a good job of clarifying their story about the economy," Leah said. "When we do this polling, everyone's main focus is on the economy, but if you ask voters what the Democratic message on the economy is, you'll get just a bunch of different answers."

What she knew was that Republicans seemed to love attacking her type of candidate (like Mandela Barnes) for wanting to "defund the police," while claiming the upper hand on economic issues. She was hoping Democrats could become the party of the working class again with a kind of "inclusive populism" that touted the importance of unions, minimum wage increases, paid sick leave, and making the rich pay their fair share in taxes. Was it a little strange for a New York City scion of great wealth to be the face of a blue-collar revolution? Sure. But it had worked for Republicans.

Still, Leah was starting to question her own life choices. She hated fundraising. The tensions within the Democratic Party were getting to her. And there was a part of her that worried that people were interested in her only for her family money.

Leah knew well that in politics, money and power are closely linked but not necessarily the same thing. This was a lesson she could have learned from her grandfather. As a billionaire, H.L. had the ability to get presidents and other world leaders on the phone whenever he wanted. He would have muckety-mucks over for dinner six nights a week. But as Swanee put it, he was "in that circle" but never "of that circle"—and as such, never really knew how to wield the political power he craved. In one story, memorialized in Hunt's biography, the billionaire was spotted at a Republican National Convention, late in his life, not walking into a smoke-filled back room with the powers that be, but rather walking the hallways, stuffing pamphlets of his writing under doors, hoping people might read what he had to say.

"People think of him as being this power, but I didn't see it," she told me. "He was such a country bumpkin."

In Washington, there can be real value being the kind of person who brings people together. Leah, no bumpkin, was showing that she could do that with her holiday party. But if she wanted to be influential, it was just a start.

As the night wore on, the bottles of wine went from half-empty to tapped out. No one here was naive enough to think that things had gone back to normal. Republicans had snatched an upset victory in the Virginia governor's race by riding a backlash to Covid restrictions and the teaching of "critical race theory"—a buzzy term that basically meant talking about how institutional racism persists in Western society—in schools. Democrats had spent the end of their first year in power bickering publicly about the size and shape of their policy agenda, and potential midterm voters didn't seem impressed. It was dawning on the party that things might only get worse—that the internal squabbles of a slim majority would seem like a blessing compared to a Republican-run Congress.

They had eleven months until the next election. Almost a year to take advantage of the congressional majorities to pass some legislation that could change lives and change their electoral odds. That was a small blessing. So was the perfectly cool breeze on Leah's deck, which felt like a gift after weeks of being stuck inside.

"Let's enjoy this," one of the partygoers said, taking in the view of downtown Washington. "Before the darkness settles in."

Chapter 2

The Gambler

December 2021

Sean McElwee stood on Leah's roof at the Christmas party, basking in the glow of the fire pit. Sean and Leah weren't exactly best friends, but they liked each other enough, and Leah had helped fund his non-profit polling organization, Data for Progress. Sean didn't have to go far to get to the party. His first-floor apartment was only a few blocks away, nestled into a neighborhood that had in recent years sprouted posh restaurants and expensive coffee options. It was a convenient part of town, filled with administration officials who enjoyed the straight shot down to the White House and big-shot *Washington Post* editors who could walk to the office. It was the kind of place filled with gossips and eavesdroppers.

I listened in on Sean, who was now deep in conversation with a criminal justice advocate about former New York Governor Andrew Cuomo. A few days earlier, the New York attorney general had released a trove of Cuomo and his team's correspondences—collected as part of a probe into alleged sexual misconduct that would ultimately lead to his fall from grace and resignation. There was a good lesson here, Sean was saying.

"I literally have a daily calendar alert that says: 'Don't put shit in texts,'" he said, holding up his phone for proof. His general advice for staff, he joked, was that "it's not illegal if you do it over the phone."

Sean might not put stuff in text, but he had said plenty of controversial shit. Earlier in the year, I went out to dinner with him and his organization's communications director, McKenzie Wilson. In a span of ten minutes he told me that Lee Atwater—the infamous consultant who had helped Republicans win elections by being racist without *appearing* racist—was his "political idol"; that he was a "Clarence Thomas Democrat," because, like the conservative Supreme Court justice, he believed untraceable donations—a top concern for progressives—were actually good for democracy (and good for both Democrats and the health of his own bank account); and that "no one understood the value of earned media better than Osama bin Laden."

After that last comment about "earned media"—political jargon for free press attention—Sean turned to his spokeswoman.

"You could learn something from him, McKenzie," he said—from bin Laden, that is.

McKenzie sighed and told me that journalists had in recent interviews declined to quote Sean because "so much of what he says is offensive."

Sean could get away with this kind of stuff because Democrats in Washington believed that he was a force for good—and an effective one. At Sean's polling firm and think tank, his staff seemed to genuinely like him, and instead of calling HR whenever he said something outlandish, they began keeping a secret document of the craziest comments he said: the time he got on a conference call and said, "Call me Armie Hammer because I'm going to eat you guys for lunch"; or the time he said he wanted to hire children to save the organization money. It was all in fun, an inside joke among a close-knit group of colleagues, but when Sean found out about the document, his staff stopped adding to it. The problem wasn't that Sean got mad, but that he liked it so much. He kept suggesting additional quotes. It got annoying.

Leah had found herself getting annoyed with Sean recently, too, but for different reasons. She had been an early backer of Data for Progress, back when Sean's values seemed to align more with hers. Back then, during the Trump era, she knew they were on the same team. But now she wasn't so sure.

"I think of him as my baby," Leah said. "But I worry about the direction he's going."

*   *   *

It's a common occurrence in Washington. An agitator arrives intent on changing the place, only to be changed by it first. Usually the process takes a little while. But not for Sean. He changed before he even moved to town.

"I sort of metaphorize like this," Sean said. "The progressive movement is someone who spends every day hammering onto a nail and someone comes up and says, 'You fucking idiot, that's a screw.'"

When Sean got his start in Democratic politics, he was a hammer-wielding lefty in New York. He was a young socialist who worked for a progressive think tank, called Demos, and hosted happy hours at a dive bar in the East Village called the Blue & Gold Tavern. The get-togethers were frequented by lefty media personalities and a crew of gleefully vulgar Bernie Bros (these categories were not mutually exclusive). For the most part, the weekly happenings were just a bunch of leftists bullshitting with each other and having their online arguments in real life. Eventually Sean would entice visits from mainstream guests like Pete Buttigieg, then still a Midwestern mayor, and New York Senator Kirsten Gillibrand. Sean held court most Thursdays, where he could be found wearing his Bernie Sanders—or Karl Marx—themed baseball caps. "He was the king of the castle," recalled Brendan James, a former *Talking Points Memo* staffer who used to go to the events.

The dyed-in-the-wool lefties didn't necessarily love Sean, who could come off as an operator.

"He had a way of always looking over your shoulder for someone more important," said Becca Schuh, a regular. "A lot of us would laugh about him. We'd be there to have fun, and he'd be figuring out the thing about you that could be most useful to him someday."

Sean seemed to some like he was at least as interested in promoting himself as he was in promoting a political cause. Which was why James laughed to himself in 2018 when he found out that Sean was on the board of an organization dedicated to safeguarding the country's fragile election systems. It was called the Secure Elections for America Now—SEAN for short.

In the early Trump years, Sean became Twitter-famous as the "Abolish ICE" guy. This was back when Immigration and Customs Enforcement, the federal agency tasked with enforcing immigration law, had become notorious for implementing a "zero tolerance" policy to separate undocumented migrant children from their parents. Sean hadn't invented the phrase, but he helped popularize it online and was happy to take some of the credit. "Abolish ICE" became a #Resistance rallying cry that had crossover appeal with mainstream liberals. Sean started keeping a spreadsheet of all the times politicians and pundits used the phrase. He grew close enough with the Gillibrand team that they would give him a heads-up if she planned to say it on television or on social media so he could tweet it out himself.

So, yes, he was an operator. And it was working. Sean was early to the Alexandria Ocasio-Cortez phenomenon, and had her on his podcast to talk about (what else) abolishing ICE—a move she agreed was a "commonsense call,"—and having her as a guest at his happy hour.

"Sean McElwee is part of the construction," the journalist Steven Perlberg wrote on BuzzFeed at the time, "of a New Democratic conversation that owes more to Noam Chomsky than Bill Clinton, more to Twitter than to white papers."

Sean was then in his mid-twenties and still under construction. He had grown up in a religious and conservative family, graduated from an evangelical college, became a libertarian intern for *Reason* magazine and then Fox Business Channel, and then took a hard left turn through the door of the Blue & Gold Tavern.

By the time I met him in 2021, he was twenty-eight and had tacked back toward the center of the policy spectrum. It was circumstantial. Back in New York during the Trump years, Sean had been an advocate for "moving the Overton window," or the range of "acceptable" government policy. Saying "Abolish ICE" wasn't necessarily about getting ICE abolished, but about expanding the leftmost limits of what Democratic policy goals could be considered. Once Biden won and Democrats held the White House and—by the narrowest of margins—the Senate and House of Representatives, Sean thought it was time to get practical. This wasn't so much a change of heart as a belief in using the instrument that worked with the current job at hand. With Democrats in charge, the goal was no longer about changing the conversation about what might be politically possible; it was to pursue an agenda that was politically viable.

Sean had started Data for Progress in 2018, and by 2022 had grown it to more than twenty employees. The organization's strategy was at once simple and revolutionary: It was a polling business that would help drive media coverage about the popularity of progressive ideas. If progressives needed some help figuring out which of their ideas were most popular, they could commission a poll from Sean's organization for a fraction of the price of bigger shops. And perhaps more important, if progressives wanted proof that their policies *already were* popular, DFP could publicize the data to help make the case.

"I like to joke that I gave Sean the idea," said David Shor, a friend of Sean's, who worked in Democratic politics.

Shor, like the new version of Sean, was famous for pushing Democrats to get and hold power by pursuing policies that were well within the Overton window. Shor's theory of winning essentially boiled down to: Talk a lot about popular ideas (bringing down prescription drug prices) and keep quiet about ideas that might turn off voters (like "defund the police"). You'd be hard-pressed to find a Democrat who advocated talking about "unpopular ideas," but Shor's approach had plenty of detractors—activists who believed in prioritizing moral causes over poll-tested ones, pragmatists who believed the best way to get voters was to excite the hell out of the base rather than offer tiny morsels of excitement to everyone. Some people started calling Shor's approach "Shorism," but Shor favored the term "Popularism."

Shor and Sean didn't agree on everything, but they did agree on most things, and Shor admired Sean's instincts.

"It's really easy to see Sean and make fun of him for being a Bernie person who then became a Warren person and then a Biden person," Shor said. "But I think he has a really good nose for seeing opportunities to bring people together and actually do things."

Sean had a particularly good nose for the power centers of the Democratic Party, and his instincts were serving him well. He was on regular calls with Majority Leader Chuck Schumer's staff. He kept in regular contact with White House officials and some bigwig journalists on a group Slack channel. His polls were getting tweeted out—sometimes multiple times a day—by Ron Klain, Biden's chief of staff. DFP's work had been mentioned in private conversations by Biden himself.

"I think they are arguably the most influential Democratic pollsters in America," Shor told me.

Other people looked at Sean and saw a turncoat, the guy who abandoned his Abolish-ICE-style convictions so he could follow power in Washington and become another ideologically flexible, administration-humping status guy. This bothered Sean.

"The irony of all the criticism of me is that of all the sellouts, I'm the least selly outty," he said. "I'm the worst-paid executive director in the country. I've worked in nonprofits all my life. I don't even take corporate clients."

He was, however, landing big clients as the Democrats positioned themselves for the 2022 midterms—and there was nobody bigger than John Fetterman, the 6-foot-8-inch lieutenant governor of Pennsylvania.

Fetterman was running for an open Senate seat that was being vacated by the Republican Pat Toomey. He was a strong candidate with appeal among voters who dislike politiciany politicians—a tattooed giant who wore gym shorts and a hoodie. Democrats saw Pennsylvania as crucial to their chances of keeping control of the Senate, and Sean had been brought on to help by Rebecca Katz, the chief strategist for the Fetterman campaign. Katz saw a lot of upside in Sean and DFP as a partner. His polls were cheap (around $6,000 a pop, where bigger shops might charge as high as $40,000), they were extremely fast, and credibly accurate. The campaign hired a different, more established pollster to do their internal work—the research needed to develop campaign strategy. The polling Sean and DFP would do would serve the purpose of "building a narrative" in the media—to tell a story about how Fetterman was crushing his primary opponents, and that his policy goals were popular.

Fetterman's main primary challenger in the race was Conor Lamb, a moderate Democratic congressman from the Pittsburgh area. Lamb had a lot going for him. He had the look (square-jawed Marine), the résumé (lawyer who won a district carried by Trump), and the implicit endorsement of establishment leaders—including President Biden, who had paid Lamb the highest compliment by saying he reminded him of his late son, Beau. Fetterman, whose vibe was a Tolkien character in Carhartt, was running on his everyman appeal and his progressive bona fides, like his early embrace of both cannabis legalization and gay marriage. He'd tried this before, when he ran for Senate in 2016. That year, Fetterman ran as a Bernie Sanders guy while most of the party was in the bag for Hillary Clinton. He ended up getting clobbered by former Bill Clinton adviser Katie McGinty, who would go on to lose a close general election to Toomey. Establishment Democrats hadn't taken Fetterman seriously at all back then. But after the election of Donald Trump, Katz believed they would. She believed he was the best chance Democrats had to win in Pennsylvania.

And Sean was willing to bet on it.

Chapter 3

Creature Comforts

December 2021

We've got to get over ourselves," Matt Schlapp said. "People die. It sucks. It's part of life. My daughter was telling me the other day she was sad because someone's grandparent died. And I was like, 'How old is the grandparent?' And she was like, 'Eighty.' And I was like, 'You know what? Not that sad.'"

A few weeks before his Christmas party, Matt had invited me to lunch at a private cigar club he frequented in Old Town Alexandria— a ritzy waterfront neighborhood of shops and restaurants not far from his house. He preferred coming to this quiet—and, oddly enough for a cigar bar, well-lit—club because he no longer felt safe going out in public as a result of his connection to Donald Trump.

"D.C. is a hostile place," Matt told me about life after the Trump administration. "D.C. can be the capital of Blue America and we will find the capital of Red America." He clarified: "I'm not saying we are going to have a civil war. I'm just saying you can't treat us this rudely and expect us to play ball."

Matt, whose ample belly, white hair, and whiter teeth made him look like the mascot for a football team called the Washington Lobbyists, had plenty of thoughts about the not–civil war that Republicans were willing to wage, and how the nation's capital was filled with out-of-touch and overly woke elitists. But first he had to figure out what to eat.

"How about the chicken Milanese?" the waiter offered. "We also have the veal ossobuco."

"I don't really ever love that," Matt said. "What's the Milanese?"

"It's a lightly breaded cutlet," the waiter said.

"What's it served with?" Matt asked.

"Arugula, onions, and tomatoes," the waiter said.

Matt scrunched up his face, like a frustrated toddler.

"How about the blackened salmon with kale?" the waiter suggested.

"I'm not a lover of kale."

"It's got bacon...How about a Caesar?"

"Is the salad cooked?"

"The lettuce is not cooked, sir."

"Ummm. Do you have, like, chicken piccata? How about chicken piccata? What does that come with?"

"Normally broccolini and roasted potatoes."

"What about green beans?"

"We don't have green beans."

"How about broccoli?" Matt said. "Not broccolini!"

Matt claimed to hate the Swamp, but in reality, he and Mercy had long been two of the ecosystem's best mudlarks—able to adapt and shape-shift to fit comfortably into whatever the environment had become.

Even now, with Trump out of Washington, Matt wanted me to know that he felt "more powerful" than ever. His CPAC conferences were getting the biggest names in Republican politics. Candidates were asking for his organizations' endorsements. He was in regular contact with an ex-president who maintained a firm grip on the Republican Party. Gone were Matt's days in the PBS green room—that lettuce was cooked. But there was always time for Fox.

"I saw you on *Gutfeld!* the other day," one of the few other patrons at the cigar club said, having spotted Matt, referencing a Fox News political comedy show.

"He got 108 million viewers!" Matt replied.

The waiter arrived with the food, placed Matt's dish in front of him, and walked away to grab some pepper.

"They still gave me broccolini," he said to me, dejected. "I guess they had to get rid of it."

The waiter returned a moment later.

"They still found a way to give me broccolini," Matt told him. "What, do they have a broccolini farm or something?"

* * *

Matt had been known to appreciate Washington's creature comforts. He was the person in the family who decorated their home and office, leafing through fancy catalogs at work. On a number of occasions, Matt tweeted complaints about having to be on a yearlong waiting list to get his preferred brand of dishwasher. He also took party planning seriously: curating the guest list and making sure everything was laid out just so. Once he had yelled at a subordinate because he thought the crab cakes at some event looked "too small" when on a platter near some jumbo-sized cookies. But at his Christmas party, the cookies were all the right size, and he was all smiles.

"How you doing?" Matt said, greeting an older ACU donor by the liquor cabinet.

"Getting better every day," she replied.

"Isn't it great how that's happening?" Matt said with a grin.

Matt grabbed my hand and shook it, while handing me a glass of whiskey with the other.

"There's lots of donors here tonight," he said to me. "Which is good."

The answer to Mercy's question of how *I* got here, as far as I can tell, was that I once wrote a profile of Matt and Mercy that they didn't hate. Yes, I pointed out that they had pawned their moral compass to cash in on Trump, but on the other hand, the headline (which I did not write) had called them THE COOL KIDS OF TRUMPISM.

Watching them mingle at their Christmas party, it seemed like a better description for the two of them would be MAGA parental figures. Young guests—many of whom held junior-level jobs in the White House—came up to Matt and Mercy throughout the night thanking them for their guidance, their mentorship.

As I mingled, I scanned the room for one of the first people Matt took under his wing at the ACU: his longtime spokesman and confidant, Ian Walters. I'd known Ian—a long-haired, jazz-piano-playing, fun-loving conservative—for years. I'd never seen Matt without him, and hoped to catch up with him here.

"You at the Schlappening?" I texted him.

I didn't get a response until the next morning.

"Naw," he texted back. "Was playing shows in Baltimore yesterday. Resigned back in September. A story best told over beers."

Chapter 4

The Guy Who Left

Winter, early 2022

In more than a decade reporting on politicians, I've had some strange interactions with press handlers (or "flacks," as they're sometimes called for some reason). There was the time a spokesman for Representative Aaron Schock, an Illinois Republican, tried to prevent me from writing about how the congressman's office had been redecorated (for free, by a company called Euro Trash LLC) in the style of the "red room" from *Downton Abbey*, the British costume drama. I did write about the Downton office, which generated some unwanted attention for both Schock and his spokesman. The flack resigned in disgrace just a few days later after other reporters unearthed some old, racist Facebook posts. (The congressman also resigned in disgrace, eventually, after reports that he had used taxpayer and campaign funds to fly on private jets owned by donors, attend a Katy Perry concert, and reimburse himself for car mileage he never actually drove.) A couple years later I was on assignment in Montana writing a profile of Jon Tester when the flat-topped, seven-fingered senator (who was also a working farmer) suddenly started relieving himself in an organic pea field next to his tractor without covering himself up. Later, a press aide (who, coincidentally, also had only seven fingers) popped out of a Subaru and posed to me a question as old as the federal government itself: "Can the senator's penis please be off the record?"

Still, none of my working relationships with flacks started out quite as bizarre as my relationship with Ian.

It happened right before CPAC's 2015 conference. I woke up that morning dreading the idea of making my way to National Harbor—an Epcot-like area outside of Washington made up of fast-casual restaurants, charmless pubs, a giant Ferris wheel, and the enormous glass hotel and convention center that was home to CPAC. Since I was a feature writer with a focus on politics, people often assumed I must love CPAC. It had provided fodder for political and feature journalists alike for decades—a place to catch presidential contenders give their stump speeches and to take the pulse of the conservative movement. It was also the place to go to see outlandish offstage happenings: seminars for people sick of being called racist and late-night debauchery from the college-age set.

For a journalist in search of a colorful story, going to CPAC could be like shooting fish in a barrel with a group of Second Amendment enthusiasts. But it always felt like a bunch of people who were desperate to be written about. I hated going. Still, my job required me to check it out, and so while still in bed that morning, I scrolled through the speaker lineup on the mobile website. I noticed something funny: A photograph of Senator Tim Scott, one of the GOP's few Black stars, appeared under the name "Ben Carson," one of the GOP's *other* Black stars. I took a screenshot and tweeted: "Whoops... Looks like the CPAC mobile app has confused @SenatorTimScott for @RealBenCarson."

I put my phone down and took a shower, not realizing that my tweet was going viral. Liberal websites picked up the story. Senator Scott himself tweeted out another error on the mobile site, this one featuring his picture under the name "The Hon. Ted Cruz."

"You missed this one from earlier this year," Scott wrote. Which was funny, and also suggested that this was a problem with the website, not a case of mistaken identity.

For Ian Walters, though, there was nothing funny about it. People were calling CPAC headquarters, seeking comment on the potentially embarrassing mix-up. The web vendor responsible for the page speculated that the screenshot I had tweeted must have been doctored. Ian passed this on to another CPAC flack, and that staffer told *Talking Points Memo*, a liberal blog, that my image had been Photoshopped.

It turned out that there was some kind of glitch on the mobile website. Nobody on the CPAC staff had confused Tim Scott and Ben Carson, and I (obviously) hadn't doctored the image to make it seem as if they had. Ian, to his credit, owned up to the mistake—quickly, and publicly. "It does not appear that Ben was sitting in his bed and Photoshopping this," he said in a statement given to the press. He also called me to apologize. We got a beer together and hashed it out. A year later, when I was assigned to do a profile of the Schlapps, Ian helped set up the interview. He seemed like a decent guy who understood that for all the adversarial posturing between the people who do politics and the people who cover politics, the game had rules that were worth respecting. For example: If you say something about someone that isn't true, you should feel bad about it. Better yet, you make it up to the person by giving them a story worth telling.

* * *

"I'm trying to figure out why I left," Ian said, resting his thumb on his lips to think.

We were sitting in the kitchen of his house in rural Maryland, about thirty minutes outside Washington. It was a temperate winter morning in early 2022. Wind chimes gently jangled from the porch. Three children, all under seven, shrieked gleefully while watching *Veggie Tales* in the living room. Half Filipino, with hair that fell below his shoulders and a goatee, Ian used to get mistaken for some kind of

Antifa troublemaker at conservative events all the time. It was easy to imagine that now, looking at him, with his jeans, his ripped Baltimore Orioles T-shirt, and his boots, muddied from an afternoon of yard work.

Ian's house was a simple four-bedroom rambler, with more than an acre of property outside for the three young kids to run around. On a neighboring plot, there was enough land for a second home, currently being completely gutted by a construction crew, where Ian's mother, Millie, a longtime employee of the National Rifle Association, planned to move later that year. The property was a refuge for Ian and his wife, Carin, who had both left jobs at the American Conservative Union—the organization behind CPAC—just a few months earlier. They had decided that Washington no longer felt like home. That was a hard change to swallow, especially for Ian—whose entire life since high school had been centered inside the nation's capital.

Ian had met Carin at CPAC. The two of them had grown so close to Matt and Mercy that they considered them family. He was in my phone as "CPAC Ian," and I wasn't the only one.

"When I quit smoking, a friend said it must have been hard for me because it was sort of my identity," he said, patting his pants out of habit for a phantom pack of Marlboro Reds. "But this really was my identity. I'm CPAC Ian."

Now that he'd left the place where he'd belonged forever, he was facing a hard question: If he wasn't CPAC Ian anymore, then who was he?

* * *

Ian was the son of a Washington newspaperman. Actually, he was the son of two Washington newspapermen.

His mother, Millie Bautista, met Colin Walters when they both worked for the D.C. government under the Democratic Mayor Marion Barry. Colin was a top budgetary aide for the city, and Millie ran the D.C. Commission on the Arts and Humanities. They were married to other people, but the chemistry was undeniable, and eventually they split from their partners. They had Ian together and they got married. After Colin exited the job amid a $28 million budget shortage, he became books editor at the *Washington Times*, an upstart conservative newspaper.

Millie left the D.C. government under a darker cloud: She got caught stealing $23,691 from the arts commission by writing a series of checks to fake recipients and keeping the money for herself. The punishment didn't end up being too extreme—she pleaded guilty and had to pay the money back—but the experience taxed a marriage that was already fraying, according to Ian. She and Colin called it quits, and Millie ended up with Ralph Hallow, another *Washington Times* journalist.

Ralph was a Syrian American raconteur who dressed with the panache of William F. Buckley and wore the umbrage of the politicians he covered like badges of honor. (George H. W. Bush, annoyed by Hallow's constant calls about the Iran-Contra Affair, referred to the journalist in taped diaries as "a horrible fellow.") Ian called him Dad, and Ralph became perhaps the biggest influence in Ian's life.

The work of journalism consumed Ralph. He returned home each night completely wired from the job. At the dinner table he'd talk about which politicos were screwing him over, which editors weren't giving him enough leash to pursue a big story, which other reporters were giving the profession a bad name. He had a temper, Ian said, along with moments of pure joy, and seemed to often be dealing with the highs and lows of a job, which was more than just a job.

"His religion was the church of journalism," Ian said, and Ralph's adoptive son was brought up in its traditions. Ralph brought Ian with him to CPAC events and the Republican National Convention. Ian watched Ralph interview presidential candidates. He still had photos from when his dad brought him along to Kennebunkport, Maine, where Bush—whose low opinion of Hallow was apparently circumstantial—let Ian grab the wheel of his cigarette boat.

For all the heartburn he gave Republican politicians, Ralph Hallow was also part of the club. He was known unofficially around town as the "169th member" of the Republican National Committee (which had 168 *official* members). This was a big ideological shift from his youth.

In the late 1950s and early 1960s, Ralph considered himself a leftist, a true believer that socialism could provide people with good healthcare and satisfy their basic needs. His political transformation happened after he became a journalist. The job gave him the opportunity to travel the world. One place in particular helped change his worldview forever: Romania under the authoritarian leadership of Nicolae Ceauşescu. Before he was overthrown and executed by firing squad in 1989, Ceauşescu was one of the most repressive communist dictators in the world—known for surveilling his people with secret police and starving them to death with rationing decrees. When Ralph finally left his assignment there and had his feet back on American soil, he kissed the ground.

Ian adopted his father's conservative politics. He spent hours listening to Rush Limbaugh. He loved the gruff voice, the call-it-like-I-see-it attitude, and found him hilarious. When Ian got a bit older, Ralph helped him get an internship with a conservative talk radio show, which eventually led to a job doing public relations for Radio America, a company that distributed right-leaning syndicated shows.

Ian had crossed into flack land. And as he looked for a new, bigger job, he found himself drawn to CPAC, a conference he had been going to since he was a kid. Back then, CPAC was a relatively sleepy affair—much more concerned with policy and defining what it meant to be a conservative than with entertainment. But Ian loved it: These were the people his dad wrote about, the people who ran the country and had ideas about how to run it better. He took odd jobs there over the years, making a few bucks an hour calling supporters to sponsor banquet tables at ACU dinners, or escorting VIPs from the valet parking stand to backstage. In the late '90s, Ian had planned and organized an event for World War II vets when he bumped into the new executive director of the ACU.

"I started spitting some game," Ian said. "And he decided he had to pick this kid up. Why? Because I was a kid. He could get a lot of work out of me and pay me next to nothing."

*   *   *

In 2009, Carin Hudson, a college student from Minnesota, was working CPAC as a volunteer. When a friend told her to keep an eye out for a cute guy named Ian Walters, she had rolled her eyes, picturing yet another young fogey in pleated khakis and a blue blazer. When she spotted Ian smoking a cigarette on a balcony alone, she reconsidered.

Ian saw her too, but was so taken by her that he avoided eye contact for most of the conference.

As the event came to an end, Carin found him on the balcony and said, "Are you going to keep ignoring me, or are you going to talk to me?"

The balcony was high enough that she knew he had two options: finally talk to her, or jump.

He talked, and she liked what she heard. Ian was passionate about conservative politics, and he was a Catholic, which would play well with her family, if it ever got to that point. He was also a piano player, just like her. Ian took her down to the lobby where there was a piano and a lot of "pretty lit" conservatives, according to Ian. Joe the Plumber was hanging out. People were riding high from Rush Limbaugh's closing speech, in which the host had lamented "sick" Democrats and the "drive-by media." The room had felt positively electric, and that feeling carried over to the lobby. At one point a member of the hotel staff came down to ask that they please limit the number of people standing on the piano to four. ("CPAC was a big account, they let us get away with a lot," Ian told me.) He rocked out on the keys and sang, feeling like he might actually have some game.

A few weeks later, Ian was in Minnesota to play a gig with a band he sat in on. He invited Carin out to see them. He was nervous when they met for lunch before the show—so nervous that he ordered the pizza topped with shrimp because he panicked and thought it was a normal thing to do. (Carin: "It wasn't.") But the spark was still there, and not long afterward Ian returned to Minnesota, sans band, to try and impress Carin's father. Carin had already laid some groundwork, explaining to her dad (a conservative in several senses of the word) that, yes, Ian was a long-haired musician eight years her senior, but that he agreed with them on the issues that really mattered: abortion, gun rights, lower taxes, Catholicism. Ian wore dress slacks and a button-up shirt, which was both uncomfortable and unnecessary. Ian and Carin's dad hit it off right away. People just seemed to like Ian when they got to know him.

"Come here," Ian told Carin over the phone from Washington after she graduated. "We'll figure something out."

Carin picked up a few jobs nannying and babysitting in town before she got a call from a friend asking if she might be interested in a temporary job helping with the events team that planned CPAC and other ACU events. It started to seem like she and Ian were sharing everything: their employer, their inside jokes, their friends, and eventually their home.

Carin got a permanent job at CPAC, and Ian eventually got the hint about the need to make their relationship permanent as well. In 2011 he took her to dinner at Billy Martin's Tavern in Georgetown. The old D.C. haunt was a favorite of his late father, Colin, who had passed away; it also happened to be where John F. Kennedy proposed to Jackie. The JFK table was booked, but Ian accepted the "Lyndon Baines Johnson" booth in the back.

"As long as it's quiet," he told the maître d'.

They ate oysters, drank bottles of beer and wine. There may have been a shot or two. With enough liquid courage, Ian got down on one knee and asked Carin if she would marry him. She didn't say anything, but she "nodded vigorously."

"I think I have to go to the ladies' room," she said, as much of the restaurant looked on.

While Carin dashed to the bathroom to vomit, Ian thought to himself, *What the hell just happened?* He was 80 percent sure, he said, that she had nodded yes to his question. But he couldn't swear to it.

Less than a year later in Dayton, Minnesota, their priest told the story of the Billy Martin proposal at their wedding and handed Carin a barf bag.

* * *

Not long after CPAC and the ACU had given Ian a wife, it would introduce him to someone he would look up to like a big brother: Matt Schlapp. Matt had been a member of the CPAC board for a number of years when he was offered the job of chairman in 2014. And it didn't take long for Ian to become a right-hand man to Matt, who had begun the job by publicly promising to make CPAC and the ACU more inclusive.

"The goal of ACU is not to kick all people out who might come from a different perspective," Matt told Politico the year he took the reins. "In its name, it's a union, to bring people together in a coalition. That's the goal."

It wasn't just a boilerplate sentiment from Matt. He risked alienating parts of CPAC's religious base by saying, "If you are a conservative who is gay, you have a right to be here."

Ian liked Matt from the jump, which wasn't exactly rare, since everyone seemed to like Matt back then—including TV networks from PBS to Fox, which made Ian's job that much more important. Ian felt incredibly lucky to have a boss that relied on him, and even luckier to have a boss that he enjoyed being around. And as Ian and Carin began to grow a family, he had a boss to emulate—as a father and as a husband.

"They were the kind of family we wanted to be like," Ian said. "We were looking up to them."

It wasn't surprising for the growing CPAC community to start to feel more and more like family to Ian and Carin. They were putting in long hours, and once they had children of their own, they were bringing them into the office more and more. Ian was spending so much time with Matt that he started to feel protective of him—both in the press and otherwise. Ian's text message inbox filled with notes between the two of them: Matt seeking advice on how to handle a press inquiry, Matt asking how he did on a TV hit, Ian making sure Matt got home safely and signing the messages "Mom" to poke fun at his maternal-like worries. The CPAC events started to feel like reunions—when Kellyanne Conway would show up backstage and coo at babies Violet and Hazel, Ian and Carin would refer to her in front of the children as "Aunt Kellyanne." And as the Walters family grew, they became closer to the Schlapps. They traded advice about the challenges they'd faced together: how to raise a large family, how to stay faithful to one another, how to give a lot to work but not have to tear apart the family. And so when Ian and Carin were on their way to having a third child, they discussed the possibility of asking Matt and Mercy to be the godparents. But that would never happen. A few months after their son Blaise was born in the spring of 2021, Carin and Ian would make a decision never to speak to Matt and Mercy again.

Chapter 5

The Cowboy Diplomat

Winter, early 2022

On December 24, 2021, I got a text from a man named Robert Stryk.

"Hey brother we don't know each other at all but Merry Xmas Eve," it began. "I have found myself thinking, lamenting and agonizing on the task you are about to embark on. It's one that you will struggle with to weigh both the Nobel and Righteous path if either truly exists in an environment where these pure human forms of Personality and Cult are embodied by a well documented rule of law. If nothing more I have become stimulated by our brief discussion and it has made me think about this whole environment in which we both feed our families... So for that I am thankful to you and I look forward to our future interactions. The one thing that has stuck with me since our last discussion is how those who believe they are Capitalists will sell the very rope to our adversaries which in turn will be used to hang us.

"Just food for thought," the text continued. "Again Merry Xmas Eve."

I knew very little about Stryk. I knew he was a lobbyist and a fixer for foreign leaders. I knew that he described himself as a bit of a recluse. He'd told me over the phone that he rarely left his farm in

51

rural Virginia. And I knew that in early 2017, he had been the focus of a *New York Times Magazine* article called "How to Get Rich in Trump's Washington."

Near the end of 2021, the Politico reporter Daniel Lippman had suggested I get in contact with Stryk after I'd mentioned that I was searching for characters who could help me figure out the ways in which Trump had changed Washington. Lippman put me in touch with Stryk in exchange for an acknowledgment in this book. (Thanks, Daniel.)

Stryk was interested, and on the one-year anniversary of January 6th, I headed out to Middleburg, Virginia, down a dirt road, through horse country, past a half dozen turkey vultures devouring a deer carcass, and up to the gate of Stryk's property. The sign said "Alibi Farm."

"The name came with the place," Stryk said after I'd parked.

Alibi was gorgeous. It had rolling hills, horses for Stryk's daughter to ride, and a 32-foot-deep pond for her and her brother to swim in. The Stryk family had pulled all sorts of treasures out of that water: a metal detector, a phone, bracelets, and even a sunken four-wheeler. Stryk's house was small and cabin-like, with just a couple of bedrooms. But there was more than enough outdoor space to require a Gator utility vehicle, which could shuttle Stryk and visitors to the nearby guest cabin, whose garage was filled with all-terrain vehicles and guns for shooting skeet. It was tranquil, too, the silence occasionally pierced by the sound of Stryk's down-the-road neighbor, an amateur pilot, taking his plane out for a spin.

"None of this could ever have happened for me if not for Trump," Stryk said. "I'm really not supposed to be this successful."

Stryk opened the door to his home and we walked inside. I was supposed to be there for a quick lunch around his fire pit. But lunch turned into a tall glass of bourbon, which turned into two more. It took him five hours to get through the story of his life—at least the parts that he wanted to tell. We didn't just sit beside one fire on my first visit to the farm; we sat beside three.

Fire One

A small fire crackled in the living room fireplace. Stryk offered me a BLT sandwich, and got right into it. From the start, he wanted me to know that he wasn't a *normal* D.C. lobbyist. He wore a cowboy hat, a sheep-shearing jacket, and ostrich boots—and said he didn't own a single suit. Unlike the palm greasers who bought their influence in Washington, Stryk said he didn't do political fundraising. He was allergic to schmoozing, uncomfortable in crowds, and unable to control a tic that caused his head to twitch when he got nervous. And the thing that really set him apart from the Washington cultured class?

"I don't have the pedigree," he said.

Before Stryk became a Washington fixer, he was a high school expellee from Scottsdale, Arizona. He was a political junkie even back then—a habit that got him kicked out of school after skipping too many classes to go volunteer in Senator John McCain's office. Even without a degree, Stryk made his way to Arizona State University. He didn't graduate from there either. First he took a break to work on Bob Dole's presidential campaign. Dole lost, but Stryk moved to Washington anyway. He was a staff assistant for Jim Kolbe, the Republican congressman from Arizona. At night he picked up desk shifts at a Capitol Hill hotel to make ends meet.

Despite his introverted tendencies, Stryk proved to be a capable networker. At twenty-one, he dropped out of college for good after getting a job offer with a fledgling consulting firm, the DCI Group, which would go on to help George W. Bush's presidential campaign and become a powerhouse in Republican politics. Later Stryk would set out on his own, first helping start a political job-listing website—which didn't make him any money, but introduced him to people all around town—and then starting his own lobbying operation. He called his shop the Sonoran Policy Group, named for the hottest desert in Mexico and one of the only places Stryk had been outside the United States (he went there on a motorcycle trip). He didn't have an actual office, but he pulled in some pretty good money over the years, mostly from companies looking to sell their products to the U.S. government. His first big contract came from a company selling flashlights equipped with audiovisual components.

"I don't have the education, I'm not a policy wonk or expert, I'm not the guy that sits and reads policy books all day," he said. "But I was pretty good, to be frank with you, at selling products."

With each success, he felt like he was kicking down doors, and proving to the elites that someone like him had every right to be there. He was a high school and college dropout, but he was also a successful Washington operator. But his luck turned in 2009 when Democrats took over in Washington, and Stryk lost many of his clients, right as he was trying to acquire a Maryland-based security guard business.

"I completely lost my ass," Stryk said.

Just like that, he was back in Arizona, living on his parents' couch. They drove each other crazy after about a week, and Stryk headed to California, first San Francisco and later Santa Barbara. He spent a chunk of his savings there, drinking Coronas and chasing women, getting by on the money he had coming in from a single lobbying client whose business he'd managed to keep.

He kicked around before moving to Oregon, where he did some consulting work for a man who owned a winery. The Pyrenees Vineyard & Cellars was located on a beautiful property, thirty acres of vines along the Umpqua River. In Stryk's telling he did so much work for the company that they made him a part owner before he took over the whole thing.

Stryk wasn't an expert on fine wine, but he was a hustler. And he'd recently met a young woman, a bartender at a fancy wine bar in San Francisco, so he had an extra incentive to make it work. The way Stryk told it, sometime in 2010 he had a realization that he no longer was drawn to Washington in the way he once was.

"The D.C. aphrodisiac is huge," he said, swirling his whiskey. "There is a very palpable powerful sexual power, men, women, it's there. It's very aphrodisiac. It's very…You know this, it's ruined the greatest men in the world. I mean, we had a former president that was giving blow jobs away. That's not a partisan statement…"

I took a sip of my whiskey. I was confused.

"Yeah, sure," I said.

I was finding that Stryk could do this—start up on a topic and veer away from it quickly. He always seemed to know where he was going with any story or aside, and it was up to me to catch up.

"One of the hard parts about D.C. is it really lacks authenticity," he continued. "I was tired of being somebody I'm not."

Washington's aphrodisiac had worn off. It was then that Stryk made the choice to give away all of his suits and ties to Goodwill—a symbolic act to show he was done with the Washington version of himself. He didn't sever all connections to the lobbying world, but he was getting further away from the life he used to want.

Still, he kept a finger in local politics. In 2014, he held a fundraiser for the National Rifle Association that featured Monica Wehby, a pediatric neurosurgeon who was running for the U.S. Senate against the Oregon Democrat Jeff Merkley. Stryk, who identified as a libertarian, liked her quite a bit even though she had little chance of winning; underdogs made life interesting. But Wehby's candidacy was plagued by stories about her nasty divorce and an ex-boyfriend filing a police report accusing her of stalking. She became known to some as the Sarah Palin of Oregon and lost badly.

Stryk saw potential in Wehby nonetheless. In 2015, he began running her political action committee, and with the help of a lawyer friend, Jacob Daniels, MonicaPAC quickly raised more than $225,000. The PAC's goal was to plot a resurgence of the state's GOP, but by 2016, MonicaPAC had stopped raising money altogether.

That was around when Stryk decided to help out with another underdog: Donald Trump.

Being a Trump Guy in the liberal state of Oregon wasn't a great business decision. But he appreciated how Trump was disrupting

American politics and promising to shake things up in the town that had chewed Stryk up and spit him out a few years earlier.

Since Trump didn't have much of a political operation, Stryk was able to get in direct touch with campaign manager Corey Lewandowski and offer his services as Trump's Oregon de facto state director.

It wasn't a high-profile posting. Nobody expected Trump to win Oregon. Stryk only ever saw Trump up close once. It was before a campaign event. Lewandowski had invited Stryk to join him backstage. The future president was spraying something into his hair and staring at himself in the mirror. The two men did not speak.

Still, Stryk did manage to make at least one important decision. He suggested the campaign hire Daniels as the only paid Trump staffer in the state. Daniels ended up becoming the Trump campaign's No. 2 guy in Michigan. Stryk didn't expect Trump to win, but he headed to Washington for Election Day just in case.

Fire Two

"Come on," Stryk said after pouring a couple tumblers of bourbon in his kitchen. "Let's get outside."

We loaded into a Gator and motored over a dusting of snow down to a covered outdoor pavilion with a chimney and fireplace, where Stryk's groundskeeper had lit a four-log fire.

"This is Jesús," Stryk said, introducing me. "He's my guy. His whole family works out here. His brother runs Robert Duvall's farm."

Stryk walked over to the enormous pile of firewood—at least a cord or two deep—and started throwing log after log onto the fire. The wood was wet from a recent snow, and so it took a while for the small fire to turn into a big one. But once it caught, the flames jumped six feet high and I worried that he might set the whole pavilion ablaze. Stryk told me he was a "pussy" about the cold, but he was also trying to make an analogy happen.

"I believe that capitalism will solve all the wars if it's allowed to burn like that fire—uncontrollable," he said, brushing his hands on his jeans once the fire was really crackling. "I understand the fight for justice and social things, but that burning fire of capitalism will change the world."

He told me the story of how it changed his world.

"I'm at the Four Seasons in Georgetown," Stryk said, taking a seat by the fire. "Religiously fucked up on whiskey and scotch."

He was smirking now. He'd told this story before, and was shaking his head as he spoke, as if he still couldn't believe what he was about to say. It was two nights after Trump had been elected president, Stryk said, and he had not stopped celebrating. He was out with his friend and business partner Christian Bourge, about five cigars deep on the hotel patio, when a chocolate Lab ran over and started sniffing Stryk's crotch. The dog's owner followed. She was "moderately attractive," Stryk said, and she spoke with an accent that he couldn't quite place.

"Oh, you're from England?" Stryk had asked her.

"Fuck off," she replied. "I'm from New Zealand."

Not only was she from New Zealand, she worked for the country's embassy in Washington. And part of the reason she was "so toasty" (Stryk's words) was due to the fact that the prime minister was having trouble getting Trump on the phone. For a top ally of the United States, this was a diplomatic embarrassment, but also not entirely unexpected; after all, New Zealand had been under the impression that Trump was going to lose the election and had spent all their energy setting up channels to the presumptive Hillary Clinton administration.

Now an act of dog had led her to this random drunk guy who was offering to help her country save face with the soon-to-be leader of the free world.

"What if I said I could get you the number of someone to call the president?" Stryk said.

"Who the fuck are you?" she asked.

Stryk was not, in fact, somebody who knew Donald Trump or had his phone number. But he was somebody who knew people in Trump-world. The next day, without any better options, the New Zealanders invited him to their embassy.

On the cab ride over to the chancery, Stryk called Stuart Jolly, a campaign official, and managed to score a cell phone number for Trump. He wasn't sure if the number would work.

"I knock on the door and the ambassador opens the door and I'm dressed like this," Stryk said, motioning to his cowboy attire. "And he's like, 'You're either the dumbest man or the smartest man I've ever met in my life. Come in.'"

Upstairs, in his office, Ambassador Tim Groser began punching numbers into his desk phone. Stryk's head and neck started to twitch.

And then Trump picked up. When the ambassador tried to patch through the call with the New Zealand prime minister, the line went dead, Stryk recalled. The call between the leaders wouldn't happen that night, but this was still a success. A connection had been made, and within days the call would happen. In the meantime, there was celebrating to do. So the ambassador and the lobbyist popped a few bottles of pinot that made Stryk realize the wine he'd been making back in Oregon "tasted like shit."

"Then he said, 'What else can you do for me,'" Stryk recalled Groser saying. "'Go get me a plan, I'll pay you for a plan.'"

Stryk woke up the next morning at the chancery. His head was pounding, his boots were still on, and his phone was dead. He opened the door to his room to sneak out, walk-of-shame style, and found a bottle of aspirin waiting for him on a platter.

"I don't take any drugs, including aspirin," Stryk told me. "Zero. Okay. I'm also not vaccinated."

He tapped his whiskey glass with his forefinger: "I don't put anything in my body except this," he said, taking a sip. "I've never even had a flu shot."

He skipped the painkillers and started walking in search of a pay phone, and despite this being the year 2016 and not 1986, he found one. He called his business partner, Bourge, collect.

"The fucker answered, thank God," Stryk told me. "And I said, 'Our world has just changed.'"

Fire Three

Stryk's whiskey glass had run dry, and so back into the Gator we went.

"I have wooden legs," he said, back in the kitchen. "I drink whiskey but I don't get drunk. I probably haven't been drunk in twenty years."

It was starting to get dark now, and with our glasses refreshed, Stryk motored the Gator to the top of a small hill, where Jesús had lit a small campfire. Stryk sat down in a foldable chair and clapped his hands together.

"People come to *me* out here," he said, motioning to the property. "I've had a foreign president land his helicopter right over that ridge."

Which world leader could he be referring to? Perhaps the former Congolese president, Joseph Kabila, whom Stryk represented despite the violence and corruption associated with his rule. Or maybe it was Nicolas Maduro, the Venezuelan leader whose attorney general hired Stryk to help lift U.S. sanctions. (Stryk told me that he considered Maduro a friend, and that he'd recently snuck into Venezuela to visit him.) Or could it have been the president of Albania, another former client?

Okay, *maybe* not them, since U.S. sanctions might make it impossible to sneak into Virginia. So, who?

"I'll never tell," Stryk said, sipping his drink.

It made sense that Stryk would be cagey about this stuff. His small lobbying shop had disclosed somewhere around $20 million in foreign lobbying work since Trump became president, for work that

Stryk referred to as private diplomacy—emphasis on *private*. (Stryk told me that there was probably another $10 million or so his shop brought in when you include contracts that didn't require disclosure.) But for all his talk about being uncomfortable talking about himself, Stryk seemed to be enjoying my company. He appreciated the chance to be taken seriously, he said. He had thoughts about Washington and about diplomacy, and there were few people willing to really hear what he had to say. He spoke quickly, and in full paragraphs—sometimes stopping only to apologize for rambling or to ask if anything he was saying was interesting. He had a habit of repeating himself—more than once telling me that he wasn't particularly educated and that "a fella" like him had no business being *this* successful.

During his first stint as a Washington lobbyist, Stryk had felt like his ability to amass influence and wealth had been stymied by the entrenched structures of the industry, which he described as being dominated by a "cartel" of influential lobbyists. Trump hadn't fundamentally changed the way the lobbying industry worked. The people with access to the administration and its allies were the people who mattered most. The difference during the Trump administration was that Stryk had been able to become one of those people.

New Zealand hired Stryk to put their embassy on the map in Trump's Washington. If people from the incoming administration knew Groser and his diplomats, their country would be better positioned to advocate for its interests.

Stryk decided to throw the highest-profile inauguration party the embassy had ever seen. He invited Trump campaign officials as well as Trumpy celebs like the actor Jon Voight. He got a sponsorship from the influential right-wing radio group, Salem Media, to help pay for the event.

"So this buzz starts happening—buzz, buzz, buzz starts happening," he said. "And the ambassador goes, 'Holy shit, like this is fucking turning insane.' . . . Secret Service had the street blocked off. We had cabinet secretaries. I remember, I'm onstage, I'm in the back . . . I look out and I see, like, Senator Shelby, I see, you know, all these—it was insanity—it was sea upon sea upon sea of people."

After the inauguration bash, Stryk kept the momentum going with a series of dinner parties at the embassy featuring Trump-aligned members of Congress like Representative Devin Nunes, the incoming chairman of the powerful Intelligence Committee. New Zealand offered Stryk a contract for $250,000. He moved his family from Oregon and began hiring people. He hired Daniels, whose stock in Trumpworld was high due to his role in flipping Michigan, and Jolly, who had come through in the clutch with Trump's phone number.

"They're deeply and closely associated with the Trump election campaign," Groser told Politico at the time. "Through their networking with the Trump people, they've been able to help us get in front of the queue."

People seemed to think that Stryk was more deeply connected to the Trump White House than he actually was, which was a boon to his business. But now, almost a year since the new administration took over, Stryk faced the challenge of being seen as a Trump Guy in Biden's Washington.

"I wanted to use the disruption and chaos to take advantage of Trump and do good for my country and myself, but I didn't care if I ever crossed his vision," Stryk said. "Honestly I've never even met the guy."

He told me that plenty of Trump-affiliated people opened up their own lobbying shops, but that they spent too much time touting their supposed friendships with the president, too much time eating and drinking at the Trump International Hotel to curry favor, and that hardly any of them are still in the business.

"I made it a rule not to set foot in the Trump Hotel," he said. "And I pretty much kept to it."

The distance Stryk kept from Trump wasn't purely geographic, and he wanted to make it clear that he had political disagreements with the former president. Stryk was, he said, in favor of tearing down all border walls and against arresting people who want to come to this country. He made it very clear that he was not one of those Trump Republicans who believed Democrats stole the 2020 election. He called the people who stormed the Capitol a year earlier a "bunch of morons and idiots."

He called Representative Liz Cheney, the vice chair of the congressional investigation into Trump's role during the riot, an "American hero," and Representative Marjorie Taylor Greene "a lunatic, a complete loony bird."

"I find fringe politics to be very disturbing," Stryk told me. "And I'm conflicted about Trump. I think he did a lot of important things in this country. The old guard needed to have a shake-up. But when people put deity status on a human being, it's scary."

Part 2

The Doers

Chapter 6

Best Night of My Motherfucking Life

He wasn't supposed to be there, but he was wearing a suit and he still had his congressional employee badge.

Jamarcus Purley. Staff.

He was ex-staff, actually, but the police officers guarding the entrance of the Capitol building didn't know that. They let him through.

It was well past midnight in the middle of February 2022. Jamarcus walked through the Capitol Rotunda, his footsteps echoing under the majestic dome. It was empty except for the statues of Presidents Eisenhower, Ford, Garfield, Jackson, Reagan, Grant, Truman, and Washington. He felt nothing but disgust for them, for his country.

He had a plan. He was going to expose the truth about what he'd seen, heard, and felt here, an experience he knew would resonate with other Black staffers. And he was going to do it in a way that people wouldn't be able to ignore.

He had been scared on the two-mile walk over from his apartment, but the psychedelic mushrooms he'd taken were kicking in, and his head felt clear.

He thought about his mother, who had grown up in Flint,

Michigan, where you couldn't even trust the water coming out of your faucet.

He thought about his family and friends in Pine Bluff, Arkansas, so many of them caught up in drugs and violence.

He thought about all this as he walked through a series of underground tunnels, a labyrinth he'd memorized over the past five years. Not a lot of kids from where he grew up got the chance to walk these hidden halls, and Jamarcus had to work hard to get here. Friends from his Pine Bluff high school described him as whip-smart, the type never to get in trouble. "Most likely to succeed," per the yearbook. Stanford for undergrad. Oxford for study abroad. Harvard for his master's in education. "Among the most intellectually curious and engaged students I've met," according to Karen Mapp, the senior lecturer in his master's program, per a 2016 article announcing that Jamarcus had won an award for scholars who "enhanced the academic life of the community and positively impacted their fellow students."

He had done his best to blend in at those elite institutions. The point wasn't just to learn things in the classroom; it was also to pick up things from the White students who surrounded him—the sons and daughters of some of the richest, most powerful people in the world. How did they think? How did they act? How could Jamarcus get some of that power and wealth? Not just for himself, but for the left-behind communities—the Flints, the Pine Bluffs?

He did a lot of drugs back then. He figured having a reputation as someone who liked to party would make him more popular with the mostly White college kids who would end up in the ruling class. He had sometimes felt like an undercover agent, pretending to like his classmates to blend in. Sometimes he began to like them for real.

The Capitol had been the next level in his mission, securing a low-rung position in California Democratic Senator Dianne Feinstein's office. It was another place where Jamarcus could be close to power and absorb some of it through osmosis. But the experience of tying himself in so many knots, pretending to be different versions of his true self, had been hard on him.

There were plenty of justifiable reasons for an unraveling. He'd agonized after the murder of George Floyd had led to a so-called "summer of reckoning" that hadn't amounted to any real structural change. The pandemic had only brought the country's racial injustices into sharper relief, as Covid killed a disproportionate number of Black Americans. One of them was Jamarcus's birth father.

Jamarcus didn't really know his father growing up, even though he lived nearby in Little Rock. For twenty-seven years of his life, this had fueled him with both a deep-seated anger and a desire to work hard and find a way to make his father notice him. In 2019, after the death of his paternal grandmother, Jamarcus ran into his father at the funeral and heard what he'd been longing to hear: His father apologized. He said he was proud of Jamarcus. A year later, Jamarcus's father was dead from complications with Covid.

This wouldn't have happened if he had the resources I have, if he had the healthcare that Feinstein has, Jamarcus thought to himself. *People in California are dying of Covid and they can't even reach our office for help.*

His original plan to change the system from the inside had failed. Before, he'd felt like his voice was getting stronger and stronger. Lately it seemed like as much as he tried to talk, no one was listening.

So Jamarcus had come up with a new plan to make them listen.

He walked into the Hart Senate Office Building with its nine-story atrium featuring an enormous aluminum sculpture of a jagged mountain range, and took the stairs to the third floor. At last he arrived at the door of his boss's office.

Feinstein was a political institution. At eighty-eight years old, she had served in the Senate for thirty years. She had come from San Francisco, where she had been the city's first female mayor; in 1994, she wrote the Senate's assault weapons ban; and after the George W. Bush era, she chaired the committee that produced the Senate's report on the use of torture during the war on terrorism. But by the time Jamarcus came to work for her office in the Trump era, there were questions about whether this giant of the Senate had lost a step. Or maybe a couple.

"My mind is fine," she said in a 2017 interview when questioned about the decision to seek reelection at an advanced age.

By 2022, the average age of a U.S. senator was pushing sixty-four years old, and the age of Democratic leadership in general was even older than that. President Biden was seventy-nine. Speaker of the House Nancy Pelosi was just about to have her eighty-second birthday, and her lieutenants, Representatives Steny Hoyer and Jim Clyburn, were both in their eighties. And Senate Majority Leader Chuck Schumer was no spring chicken at seventy-one. The Democratic Party had become a gerontocracy—old, wealthy, and, to Jamarcus, out of touch with the concerns of voters like him. Sometimes it could feel like the one thing Democrats had going for them was at least they weren't Republicans.

Jamarcus started his half decade of service in Feinstein's office as a staff assistant, and two years in had been promoted to legislative correspondent. The mid-level job involved drafting letters to constituents, and over time, Jamarcus grew frustrated with the work. The official language used in these missives felt patronizing and hard for normal people to understand. He'd begun responding to constituents using his own voice, writing in a way that he felt wouldn't "alienate Black people." At times, he said, his boss would tell him that his job was to "reflect the senator's voice," not his own. But Jamarcus didn't stop; instead, he started sending the responses without permission.

What led to his firing earlier that month, on February 8, was a matter of some dispute. In a termination letter, Feinstein's chief of staff wrote that Jamarcus had lost his job simply because he had stopped showing up to work and had repeatedly corresponded with constituents on behalf of the senator without first getting approval from his manager. Jamarcus, meanwhile, thought he was being punished for telling "hard truths" about Feinstein. It was obvious to him that her mental faculties were dimming, and that she might be going senile. He was sick of feeling like no one in the office wanted to work on, say, the issue of homelessness in Los Angeles because the boss "only cared about the Bay." Jamarcus thought the Senate office should be focusing more on their constituent services—casework like tracking misdirected benefit payments or providing help filling out federal forms. During a pandemic, this was the kind of work that Jamarcus felt could save lives—especially lives in hard-up communities of color.

Things had come to a head two weeks earlier. On a phone call with other members of the office, Jamarcus had let loose, airing concerns for what felt like ten minutes. He talked about the coworkers who had touched his hair while he sat at his desk, how the senator hadn't ever learned his name or spoken to him despite five years of service to her, how the chief of staff seemed to be operating as a shadow senator since the actual one was, in his opinion, no longer mentally there.

Perhaps most memorable to those on the call was his belief that the senator cared "more about her dog, Kirby, than she does about Black people."

After he'd finished speaking, Jamarcus said, there was silence.

"I wanted to say something in the moment but couldn't," one of his coworkers texted him after the call. "I didn't want to take up your space by relenting."

Jamarcus knew then that he wasn't long for the job. He'd ordered the mushrooms later that day.

Now, emboldened by psilocybin, he walked through the door into Feinstein's darkened office. His presence tripped the motion-activated lights. His heart rate quickened. But no one came.

He had planned to film a video where he would recite the injustices he'd seen and felt while working in the Senate. But on the walk over to the Capitol, he had changed the plan: Instead of using his voice, he would simply put on music and smoke a joint while looking directly at the camera. He believed this gesture would work like a piece of protest art, grabbing people's attention on a visceral level, and making them ask questions—about what could lead a person to pull off such a stunt—which he would then answer in detail.

He queued up his mother's favorite song, the 1982 R&B jam "I Like It," by DeBarge. Leaning back in Feinstein's chair, Jamarcus took a drag off his already lit joint. The horns hit, and his plan changed again: He was no longer sitting still, but dancing.

He waved his tie to the beat. He threw his hands in the air. He waved a finger, raised his arms out to either side, and swayed like an airplane.

He puffed plumes of marijuana smoke and hopped up on the chair, crouching and mugging for the camera.

Now he was taking off his jacket and tie and dancing around the office.

He felt free. *Best night of my motherfucking life*, he thought to himself.

The song ended. Jamarcus cut the video and scurried out of the office. He didn't know if anyone had heard the music, but if they did, he didn't want to be around for the police to arrive.

On his way out, he slid his ID through the hinge of a closed door. *Jamarcus Purley. Ex-staffer.*

He headed straight to the airport and booked a flight home to Pine Bluff.

He wanted to post the video from somewhere safe, far from Washington. He wanted it to go viral but was worried about what might happen to him if it did. But more than that, he was worried about what would happen if nobody cared at all.

Chapter 7

Dear White Staffers

Every year, hundreds of new staffers arrive at the U.S. Capitol—that majestic wedding cake of a building—to begin the prestigious honor of running the country from the seat of American democracy. And then, almost right away, many of them realize the same thing: These jobs suck.

Some members of Congress expect their junior staff to provide the range of service one might expect at a high-end resort: chauffeuring, dog walking, dry-cleaning delivery. The office buildings deal with regular rat infestations, and the workspace itself can often leave something to be desired. Once, a young House staffer on the fifth floor of the Cannon Building gave me a tour of her office that included a trip across the hall to a cage—meant for storage—which she said sometimes doubled as desk space for interns.

The senior staff might spend months working on a bill, only for the politics to shift at the last minute—at which point everyone moves on to some other legislation destined for a similar fate. When a bill *does* pass, it's their bosses who get the credit. The staff is meant to be neither seen nor heard, unless of course there's a bad tweet sent by a congressman, or a controversial letter accidentally sent around—in which case it's nice to be able to blame it all on "staff error." Also, the hours are long and the pay is bad.

"This is what radicalized me," Leigh Whittaker, a legislative director for Representative David Price of North Carolina, told me. In 2016, Whittaker was paid $30,000 a year, not nearly enough to live on in a city whose one-bedroom apartments were approaching $2,000 a month. To make ends meet, Whittaker took a second job, working at Kramers, a bookstore and café in D.C.'s Dupont Circle.

"It was a full year of working seven days a week," she told me. "And my friends are surprised I'm like an anarcho-communist now?"

Whittaker's experience was a common one, unfortunately. There are roughly 18,000 congressional aides working at any given moment. They are young (average age: thirty-three), and in 2021, entry-level staffers made around $38,000 a year, according to Issue One, a nonpartisan political reform group. The study estimated that as many as one out of every eight congressional staffers made less than a living wage, many of whom picked up second jobs, or relied on family money to subsidize their public service—which may help explain why more than 75 percent of Hill staffers were White. It also explains why it can be so hard to keep talented people working on the Hill, especially when there are lucrative jobs for the taking for anyone willing to do a little selling out and get a job as a lobbyist.

Whittaker had it good, comparatively. She liked her boss. She said she never felt abused in her workplace, and by the time I met her she was making a decent wage. But she wasn't blind to other people's horror stories. She'd heard the whispers and gossip from her friends for years. And now, thanks to a new, anonymous Instagram account, so could everyone else.

"Dear White Staffers has led to one of the craziest phenomena that no one was expecting," she said. "People are exposing the toxic and exploitative workplaces."

The account solicited and posted blind items about what it's like to work for members of Congress, the administration, and the various think tanks and consulting shops around town. Per its name, Dear White Staffers specialized in highlighting perspectives of non-White

Hill workers, but it was open to tips of all kinds. The account nurtured a solidarity that had to do with class as much as race. It featured "vibe checks" on members of Congress and their top staffers. It let potential employees know which places seemed chill to work for, and which ones to avoid.

The man behind Dear White Staffers named names but kept his identity concealed. I was able to figure out who it was, though. I had been interviewing a congressional staffer about Hill culture when the topic of Dear White Staffers came up, and I took a shot in the dark.

"You know," I said, wrapping up the interview. "Legally, if you're Dear White Staffers, you have to tell me."

"Legally?" he asked.

"Yeah, like how an undercover cop has to admit he's a cop if you ask," I said. I told the staffer I was kidding—cops can lie about that—which he told me he knew. But he seemed to take the underlying request seriously. "Can I tell you off the record?" he asked. I agreed. He admitted that he was, in fact, the guy behind Dear White Staffers.

Since I agreed to keep his real name a secret, we'll call him Dwight.

"The anonymity is important to the project," Dwight told me. "I think it's important to not centralize one person's voice or identity, you know, to democratize the platform as much as possible so that it kind of feels like people are yelling into a void."

Dwight told me he did some quality control on the posts. For example, he said he would not publish unconfirmed rumors about the sex lives of politicians unless one involved a member of their staff. But the material he did publish was rarely fully vetted, and always anonymous. This made Dear White Staffers journalistically problematic; it also made it powerful. A man without an identity can be easier to tell your secrets to, especially if he lets you do so without putting your name on the line. The account disrupted the balances of power within the congressional workforce, defying not only the going standards for reliability and discretion but also the decorous sensibilities of the Capitol. For example: Dwight once spent part of a week posting reports about a certain congressman who was known as a "serial farter" around the office. "He routinely farted in front of people with zero acknowledgement," said one tipster of a longtime Democratic congressman, via the account. "He was a huge mama's boy and his mother was EVERY-WHERE, including in the room when he hired new staff."

I talked to plenty of senior staffers who complained about Dear White Staffers. I heard a chief compare it to "cancel culture" for its ability to harm reputations without due process. I heard from others about how all the complaining would only make it less likely that people would want to come to work on the Hill—that it made it look more toxic than it really was.

"I used to think it was fun," one chief told me. "But now it's just too much whining." (They lodged this complaint anonymously. Go figure.)

I began checking Dear White Staffers pretty regularly starting at the end of 2021. The gossip was fun, even if it wasn't reportable. But there was also just something thrilling about there being a place to see unfiltered material from a normally buttoned-up institution. I'd been covering the Hill on and off for a decade, and it could be hard to get staff to open up about their experiences, even off the record. This felt like a sign that things were changing, that people were getting fed up.

"When you really start talking to people who work in Congress, that's when the realization sets in," Dwight told me. "Everyone here is very depressed and very underpaid and beaten down. That's when the shine starts to go away and it's like, 'Oh, these jobs are awful.'"

It didn't have to be this way. One of the underappreciated things about Washington is that most people arrive idealistic. There are better places to get rich (Wall Street) and better places to try and become famous (Hollywood). And so the type-A people who make their way to the capital often do so because—as corny as it sounds—they want to do some good in the world. But doing good takes time, which requires people sticking around. Dwight hoped his Instagram account could help with that.

Dear White Staffers was a kind of burn book, but that's not all it was. The account spoke to something deeper. The occupational hazards created by Covid had juiced an interest in labor organizing that had mostly been lacking on the Hill. Progressive politicians had made workers' rights a central part of their message following public reckonings—over sexual harassment and racism in the workplace. But somehow the organizing had never made its way into the Capitol— where there had never been a unionized congressional office. A group of staffers tried to change that in 2021, forming a group called the Congressional Progressive Staff Association. By 2022, the group included some 1,200 staffers and functioned in part as a sort of social club—they held happy hours and went on hikes. But the organization also brought an activist streak inside the Capitol. They organized a protest inside Senate Majority Leader Chuck Schumer's office, demanding action on climate change. They put pressure on House leadership to raise the minimum wage for staffers. They worked with Representative Andy Levin, a progressive from Michigan, to pass legislation to make a congressional union drive legal.

And Dwight was using his account to draw attention to all of it— an anonymous megaphone helping to give a voice to a group rarely heard from.

"This whole year has been so much about staffers speaking up," Dwight told me.

And then there was Jamarcus Purley, whose act of defiance included no speaking at all; just a blissed-out dance party in an empty office. In late February 2022, Dwight noticed a message in the Dear White Staffers account with a link to a video of a young Black man lighting up and grooving to an R&B jam in the office of a U.S. senator.

It was a bold video, and Dwight wasn't quite sure what to do with it. Jamarcus's caper was spiritually in tune with Dear White Staffers. It was a statement of fed-up defiance. But there was nothing anonymous about it. Jamarcus was making no effort to conceal his identity—he was trying to reclaim it.

The tip was from Jamarcus himself. He had already posted the video on his own Instagram account; clearly he wanted people to see what he'd done. Still, Dwight wasn't sure what to do. Would promoting the video help give a voice to the voiceless, or merely leave Jamarcus more vulnerable than he already seemed?

* * *

"I waited a week to post it," Dwight said.

He had agreed to meet up again, this time at a coffee shop near Union Station. Dwight still wanted to keep his own identity a secret, but he was speaking so loudly that I kept looking over his shoulder to see if he had accidentally blown his own cover on this highly trafficked sidewalk. He was in casual clothes: a corduroy jacket, jeans. It was a Friday, which meant Congress wasn't in session—members tend to have a three-day workweek in Washington, and that's *without* a union.

He told me he stayed in touch with Jamarcus for that week, checking in on him. Dwight wanted to make sure that Jamarcus really wanted the video to be shared, that it wasn't just a rash decision he'd regret the next day. Dwight worried about Jamarcus's mental health. "It sounded like years of instability were compounded by the loss of his father, all the stress at work, family stuff," Dwight said. "So I think like anyone, people just need a little stability."

Only a few hundred people had seen Jamarcus's video, according to his Instagram account. When somebody in the political press finally did take note of Jamarcus's stunt, it wasn't quite the audience he'd intended: FIRED FORMER DIANNE FEINSTEN STAFFER ENTERED INTO SENATOR'S OFFICE, SMOKED BLUNT IN SMOKE-FILLED INSURRECTION, screamed a headline from the right-wing website Breitbart.

Dwight saw in the video something more than trespassing and pot smoke. "I came to see it as one of the most beautiful acts of rebellion," he told me.

There were plenty of times when Dwight had been the only non-White person in the room, when he was looked at to speak for minorities everywhere. He'd experienced working long hours for little money. He'd been forced to use his own car for his first job (even though it paid only $30,000 a year) and had to chauffeur his boss around like a personal driver. The opportunity to drive around the boss was often sold as a perk to young staffers—a way to get valuable face time with the boss. Dwight found it a bit demeaning, and recalled being mistaken for a valet once at a fancy event. It felt a little racist, except that "they were right," he said, laughing. "But I wasn't *their* valet, I was hers!"

Jamarcus's wordless statement was a bit oblique. If you were a right-wing tabloid eager to apply the word "insurrection" to someone on the left, it was positively scandalous. But Dwight understood what Jamarcus was doing—or at least he thought he understood.

"When I saw that video, I was like, oh man, he's doing what all of us would love to do one day," he said. "That is insane. That is really out there. But it personifies what a lot of us feel to a degree."

Chapter 8

The White Hat

Jennifer DeCasper sometimes had a hard time relating to the stories of staffer oppression posted on the Dear White Staffers Instagram account. She was a Black woman on the Hill, but she also had the class privileges that come with being a senator's chief of staff.

"I always feel bad because I'm so high up," said Jennifer, who held the top job in the office of Tim Scott, the Republican senator from South Carolina. "I would walk into a room with all White dudes and I'd be like, 'What's up, fuckers?'"

Jennifer had busted her ass to get that high up on the Hill, and now that she had reached the top, she could go into any room and speak her mind and no one would treat her like she was "crazy."

"I would always forget that these junior staffers didn't have any of that," she said.

She was not one of the nightmare bosses getting burned in Dear White Staffers—one typical post called her "an absolute bad ass and wonderful human being." She was, however, one of the bosses who loved it for the gossip—at least at first. After a little while the gripes began to get tiresome.

"I appreciated how it started off," she told me, but before long, it started to seem to her like a "grievance party."

"I don't mind people being held accountable for actual things," she said. "But I would much rather if my staffers have a problem, they come to me and I promise we can fix it."

Not an altogether surprising perspective, coming from a boss. But Jennifer understood—better than a lot of staffers, especially other GOP staffers—how entrenched power dynamics could make an old club like Congress a messed-up place to work. She was, she believed, the first Black woman to become chief of staff in the Senate's history.

"Anytime somebody celebrated that, it upset me," she said. "I don't celebrate it. The fact that in 2013 when I became chief shouldn't be a celebratory mark. That's ridiculous. How is that possible in this country? I guess it's noteworthy, but it's a pathetic noteworthy moment."

I first got to know Jennifer when she was the legislative director for Scott, back when he was in the House. I had been assigned to profile him as a rising star within the Republican Party. There were two Black Republicans in Scott's freshman class. There was Representative Allen West, the retired military officer who was once fined $5,000 for simulating the execution of an Iraqi policeman, and who came to Washington as a lead figure in the rabble-rousing Tea Party crew that had been swept into Congress in 2010. And then there was Scott, the guy that everyone actually liked. He was the first (and only) member of the House whom I'd predicted (in print) might become a U.S. senator someday. He was also the first (and only) politician whom I'd asked about being a virgin. Earlier in his political career, Scott had gone on the record promising to abstain from sex until he got married; when I interviewed him in 2012 for *National Journal*, the magazine I worked for, he was still single at age forty-six.

"I'm not talking about my sex life with Ben Terris or anyone else," he told me at the time.

"The Bible's right," he continued after a supremely awkward pause. "You're better off to wait. I just wish we all had more patience."

A couple of years after that, he'd moved to the Senate and I'd moved to the *Washington Post*, and I interviewed him again. This time, we traveled to Greenville, South Carolina, where the senator spent the day "undercover" at a Goodwill store talking to volunteers and patrons. Back then, Scott was doing this kind of thing a lot: donning a baseball cap and jeans, riding on buses or taking a shift sweeping up burrito joints as a way to meet people on their level and have some connection to the working class. It was a bit of a shtick, but Scott hailed from working-class roots and had a common touch.

"Tim is a chameleon," Jennifer told me. "He can talk to third graders and billionaires and lead a church congregation."

She meant this as a compliment. Jennifer was devoted to her boss, and he trusted her in turn—even more than most senators trusted their chiefs. People in Congress knew she spoke for Scott.

"He calls me his best friend," she told me.

It took a while for them to find each other.

Her path to the top job in a Senate office started out typically enough with a lowly staff job in the office of Wayne Allard, a senator from Jennifer's home state of Colorado, before she went back to school for a law degree. She had hoped to use that degree to level up on the Hill, but finding a good job with good pay in Washington proved more difficult than she'd expected. Because law school loans wait for no one, she became a prosecutor back home. She rose quickly and became a deputy district attorney in Colorado.

"At first I enjoyed wearing the white hat," she said, using a saying originally used to describe the good guys in old western movies. "I really enjoyed justice. I liked giving people second, third, fourth chances—being creative with sentencing."

She was bothered most by the cases where there was no bad guy, per se, but rather ordinary people under pressure—the petty drug offenders, the people struggling to pay child support who got thrown in jail for driving to work on a revoked license. And then there were the cases that tore holes in her soul: stalkers, child abusers. By then she was a single mother, and one day she returned home to find her twelve-month-old-daughter crawling on top of a file of autopsy photos Jennifer had brought home.

"I was like, 'This is not my life,'" she said.

So she returned to Washington.

It was 2008. Good jobs were scarce in general, due to the awful economy, but especially so for Republicans who wanted to work in government after Barack Obama's hope-and-change wave had swept through the capital. Jennifer took the one job she could find: at Dulles International Airport.

"I was the gal with two orange glow sticks bringing in planes," she said. "At the time, it was not awesome."

She worked the late shift, coming home every night soaked in sweat and reeking of jet fuel. But Jennifer was a spiritual person, and when she talked about her life story, it could sometimes begin to feel like she was speaking in parables.

"The job humbled me," she said. "I found my faith. I wasn't a believer until I started working in the airport." Her coworkers at Dulles came from all over the world—people, she said, who truly believed they had reached the land of milk and honey by getting this job—and it made Jennifer realize how much of a spoiled American brat she had been to think she was too good for it.

"The minute I started finding joy was when things started to change," she said. "I had to be happy where I was to move on to the next phase. That's when someone handed my résumé to Tim Scott."

Jennifer bombed her interview with her potential boss. She'd cried when he asked her about her faith, and she cut the interview short. Neither she nor Scott were sure why she had gotten so emotional, but Scott decided to hire her anyway.

Early in the job, Jennifer decided to bring up her thoughts on criminal justice reform. She knew this wasn't exactly the kind of red meat conservative issue that Tea Partiers had come to Congress to fight about, but she felt like Scott might be in a unique position to get something done. He blanched at the idea.

"I remember him looking at me and saying, 'That is a hot button issue that I think people won't want us to handle,'" she said. This was code for: Let's not get pigeonholed as the "Black Republican."

Jennifer could relate to this. It wasn't always easy being a Black Republican for her either. She knew what it was like to work with people in Congress who were nice to her face but openly racist (she would not, however, name names). And in the Trump years, she knew the feeling of all eyes going to her and her boss every time the president retweeted a White nationalist or refused to disavow former Ku Klux Klan grand wizard David Duke.

"You have to do some calling out," she told me. "But we can't call out every racist thing; it's all we would do."

And yet instead of making her want to flee the party, it only made her more committed to it. She believed in Republican policies; she believed in tax breaks and limited government. Every time a Democrat accused the Republican Party of being nothing but a bunch of racists, it only made her "double down."

"It made me want to show people that's not who we are," she said.

A lot changed between Scott's freshman year in Congress and 2022. After the resignation of the hard-right Jim DeMint in 2012, Scott was appointed to his seat in the Senate and then won multiple reelection campaigns. He promoted Jennifer to chief of staff. And Black people kept getting killed in the streets, but little was being done in Washington to actually change that. Jennifer would help make it her mission, and her boss's mission. But she would find that legislating can be impossibly difficult, even when it seems like all the pieces have fallen in place to pass a bill.

She was an optimist by nature, but even she would come to find Capitol Hill dispiriting in many ways. She understood how Washington could make people snap. And so when the Jamarcus story crossed her radar, she was instantly fascinated by it. In fact, she was the one who sent me the story.

"Read with popcorn," Jennifer had texted.

It was coverage of Jamarcus's stunt. An article by a reporter whose name I didn't recognize in a publication I'd never heard of. *Pablo Manríquez, Latino Rebels.*

Chapter 9

Scribe of the Subaltern

When Pablo Manríquez told people what he did for a living, he'd often say he covered the subaltern.

"I like putting it that way because people have to look it up," Pablo said.

I had to look it up, and according to Wikipedia, "In postcolonial studies and in critical theory, the term subaltern designates and identifies the colonial populations who are socially, politically and geographically excluded from the hierarchy of power."

I'd come to meet Pablo at his apartment, a row house not far from downtown D.C., and we were sitting on his back patio—a sliver of fenced-in concrete right off the sidewalk. Pablo was thirty-eight years old, with close-cropped hair and a scruffy beard that couldn't hide his perma-smile. For Pablo—who was then the congressional reporter for the website Latino Rebels—covering the subaltern meant writing about the cafeteria workers, the custodians, the immigrants around the country waiting for reform, and the underpaid and overworked junior staffers who make legislation happen (or more often, not happen).

It was a beat Pablo felt uniquely qualified to cover. He was born in Chile, came to the United States as a kid, and worked his way into Notre Dame for college. He came to Washington after a stint on the Obama campaign, but was unable to land a job in politics. So he worked as a waiter and dishwasher at a couple of venerable Capitol Hill dive bars, the Hawk 'N' Dove and the Tune Inn. He made extra cash by selling weed to Hill staffers and killing rats for his bosses. It wasn't exactly *The West Wing*. One bar owner would pay a bounty of $8 per dead rat. Pablo would boot-stomp them in the kitchen, or bait them with cold cuts and snipe them with an airsoft gun.

The rats were big and dumb, which made for some easy money. Selling weed was even easier. The busboys were the ones with the product, but Pablo was the guy with the language and people skills to help connect them with customers—almost entirely White congressional and administration staffers. The bars he worked at were the dim-lit watering holes of Official Washington—off-the-record places, so to speak, where the normal rules didn't always apply. There were times that fights would break out and the cops would come, Pablo said, only to disperse once they had a few words with the Very Important (and very drunk) People involved.

Pablo used his spot behind the bar to observe power players who were off the clock. He knew which congressmen were good tippers (climate change denier Senator Jim Inhofe of Oklahoma and future dick-pic denier Representative Anthony Weiner of New York) and which were up for a good conversation over a cigarette (Representative Raúl Grijalva of Arizona). And then there were the journalists. It was cool for Pablo to be around when reporters he recognized from cable news would come in. Sometimes they'd even be at the bar while one of their previously recorded segments aired on the bar television. Pablo wasn't a reporter yet, but he'd wanted to be one since college. He eavesdropped on conversations that the young reporter Bob Costa would have with his sources, and listened in as the congressional reporter for a Hill newspaper (and eventual network television star) Kasie Hunt worked through articles with her editor, nursing a Coca-Cola for hours and still giving Pablo twenty bucks for a tip. When she asked if she'd given him enough, it took everything Pablo had not to tell her that she had no idea how much she had just given him.

One thing Pablo couldn't help notice, however, was how much some big-deal journalists complained about their jobs over beers and whiskey. Pablo was sure it was hard—spending hours staking out offices and hitting the phones to break news about, say, the Affordable Care Act (which was the big story those days). But Pablo paid his bills doing dishes until 3:00 a.m. and murdering rodents as a side hustle. If he ever got to sit on their barstools, he would never complain about the job.

Breaking into journalism was tough. But his campaign experience opened some doors to political flack work, and eventually he landed a gig as a booker for the Democratic National Committee, working with television and radio stations to get DNC chairwoman Debbie Wasserman Schultz and others on air. It wasn't a perfect job, but helping serve up stories to journalists beat serving them drinks. It was another quiet, anonymous job that hundreds of people do in Washington without anyone learning their name. But then, one day, everyone seemed to know his.

THE DNC EMAIL LEAK HAS A VIRAL HERO: PABLO, declared a July 2016 headline from *New York* magazine.

In what U.S. intelligence later determined was a Russian operation to undermine the 2016 presidential election, hackers had wormed their way into the DNC servers and passed a tranche of documents to WikiLeaks, which had dumped 19,000 private emails onto a public page. For the Russians, the whole thing was a smashing success. The emails, which appeared to show the DNC putting the finger on the scale for Hillary Clinton over Bernie Sanders, were embarrassing for Democrats. Wasserman Schultz lost her job, and her reputation took a major hit.

But Pablo came out of the whole scandal looking pretty good.

In one email exchange that made the rounds on Twitter, Pablo pushed back on a last-minute request to reschedule a 6:00 a.m. appearance by Wasserman Schultz on CNN.

"Can we move it closer to the 820 POTUS hit?" one of Pablo's colleagues asked. "If not we may have to pull the plug."

"They structured their whole show on that we'll make news in the 6am hour," Pablo had responded. "We told them a time. They took care of us. Now they are all asleep. Are we really going to screw them over on our mistake???"

In subsequent emails Pablo's colleague had told him to calm down, and later told him to "fuck off." Pablo told me he never took any of this personally—being a booker was really just being a middleman, and middlemen usually get treated like shit—but when journalists and curious citizens saw the back-and-forth on WikiLeaks, Pablo, who had left the DNC by the time of the leak, stuck out as a heroic figure. Maybe it was because people could relate to the idea of being treated like garbage at work, or maybe he seemed like a decent guy standing up to a bunch of Washington insider assholes, but #ImWithPablo trended on Twitter.

After the DNC, Pablo tried starting his own media booking company, then booked for the Capitol Hill newspaper *Roll Call*, and then took a different booking job for the Center for Investigative Reporting, which relocated him to California. That job lasted six months before he was laid off, at the start of the coronavirus outbreak. He called a friend, an undocumented immigrant who had a sort of halfway house in Northwest Washington, D.C., and from whom he could rent a bed for $500 a month while he looked for employment. Pablo moved into a house that was already home to twenty-three other people, mostly Latino immigrants, and swore to himself then that if he were to survive this pandemic, he would become a "fucking reporter." On January 6th, when Trump supporters stormed the Capitol, Pablo made the scene and freelanced his first-ever article about Congress, for a bilingual newspaper based in San Francisco called *El Tecolote*. Clip in hand, he called an old friend, Julio Ricardo Varela, who had founded a digital media company called Latino Rebels, and talked himself into a temporary gig covering the Capitol. Soon he had a one-month press pass—an ID he could hang from a lanyard and gain free rein to wander the halls of the Capitol, buttonhole the various members of

Congress who wandered those halls, and attend press conferences. He was officially a journalist, and had one month to prove his worth.

Pablo wasn't about to waste the opportunity. The first chance he got, he made his way to a press conference convened by Speaker of the House Nancy Pelosi, sat himself in a seat unofficially reserved for more established press, and asked Pelosi about a 2019 report from the Office of the Inspector General that detailed allegations of sexual harassment by members of Congress against night shift custodians in the Capitol. The issue was personal to him: His father had been a night shift janitor at a St. Louis hospital when Pablo was growing up. He had heard plenty of stories about the harassment, racial not sexual, that his father had suffered.

Just as Pablo was beginning to find his footing and learn to navigate the mazelike basements of the Capitol, he suffered a setback. His temporary press pass was not renewed. Decisions about who gets the privilege of covering Congress from the inside fall to a seven-person panel of journalists known as the Executive Committee of Periodical Correspondents—a group that over the years had granted credentials to publications including the *Washington Post* and something called Beeriodicals.com. But they had determined that because Latino Rebels was a nonprofit and not "chiefly supported" by ads or subscriptions, it didn't fit the criteria.

To Pablo and his Latino Rebels colleagues, it felt like just another example of established power structures determining who had the right to tell the story of Congress. They appealed. He spent six weeks unable to return to the Capitol. The committee reconsidered and granted him a pass.

"I gave myself the Underdog Beat," Pablo told me, lighting incense on the patio to cover the smell of car exhaust with patchouli.

One day in early 2022, Pablo caught wind that a group of Senate cafeteria workers had gotten layoff notices. It struck Pablo as a bullshit move, especially since senators had spent the past two years applauding the bravery of frontline workers during the pandemic. As one of the few fluent Spanish-speaking journalists on the Hill, Pablo had earned a lot of trust from the heavily Latino group of cafeteria workers. One of them texted him to let him know that a group of workers would be going door-to-door trying to get senators to agree that they shouldn't get canned. Pablo knew that he had a reputation as a "journovist" in the eyes of some—part journalist, part activist—so he tipped off another reporter, who would be able to cover the story herself as well, and also disabuse anyone who might assume Pablo was not merely reporting but also organizing the resistance.

Over the course of the day, the workers hit up about a dozen offices, but it wasn't until they bumped into Senator Cory Booker in the hallway that they struck pay dirt.

Booker listened to the workers. His chief of staff, Veronica Duron, started calling other offices for support. Booker called Massachusetts Senator Elizabeth Warren. Warren called Minnesota Senator Amy Klobuchar. Within a day, a group of six or seven senators were meeting with the person in charge of the cafeteria workers—the augustly titled Architect of the Capitol—and by the end of the week, the workers' jobs had been saved.

Pablo's days of slinging weed and killing rodents were long behind him. He was pulling in $75,000 a year, enough to split a nice apartment rental with a roommate, a fellow journalist named Eric Garcia. But he still had a side hustle to keep himself afloat, the evidence of which was strewn across his bedroom: oil paintings of various Hill personalities. During my visit I saw a grinning portrait of the CBS political reporter Ed O'Keefe next to Pablo's bed and a not-grinning-but-smirking (there's a difference) Senate Minority Leader Mitch McConnell on the desk. He told me he had promised it to one of McConnell's aides for fifty bucks—the type of transaction that traditional news outlets wouldn't allow, but which Latino Rebels didn't mind.

"It's not like me selling this painting is going to change how I do my job at all," Pablo said. As a matter of fact, his most viral moment of the year involved eliciting a gaffe from the Senate GOP leader.

Pablo had asked McConnell about legislation that would keep Black voters from being able to vote.

"Well, the concern is misplaced," McConnell had answered. "Because if you look at the statistics, African American voters are voting in just as high a percentage as Americans."

Oof.

It was, to be fair, a verbal miscue. Still, Pablo saw it as a kind of Freudian slip that elucidated an underlying truth that he had been trying to cover since coming to the Hill: The experience of Black people (and other people of color) here wasn't the same as it was for White people. On this, he and the man behind the Dear White Staffers account could agree, and they came to form a symbiotic relationship. Pablo would cover the kinds of stories Dear White Staffers cared about, and Dear White Staffers would promote Pablo's articles on Instagram.

Sometimes, the guy behind Dear White Staffers would even provide Pablo with the tips. One day in February 2022, Pablo opened Instagram and noticed a message from Dwight. It was a video of a fed-up Black staffer sparking up a joint and dancing in a senator's office. When he had become a journalist, Pablo had dedicated himself to covering the underdogs. And Jamarcus was the ultimate underdog, a prince of the subaltern.

He messaged Jamarcus right away.

A week later, Pablo and Jamarcus spoke by phone for over two hours. Pablo left that call drenched in sweat—partly because of how hot it gets in the little phone booths that still exist in the congressional press offices, and also because his heart was beating so fast from trying to keep up with Jamarcus's stream-of-consciousness style of talking.

"I recognized it right away as a story of struggle," Pablo said. "Struggle that I related to in so many different ways. I know how this town fucks you over, I know how this town likes to keep you down."

Chapter 10

They Know How to Run the Game

Shoutout to Dear White Staffers and Pablo," Jamarcus Purley said. "They were the only ones who really took this shit seriously."

We were sitting at an outdoor bar in Eastern Market, an upscale neighborhood not far from the Capitol, which, as Jamarcus pointed out, had, "like, no Black people walking around." It was early spring 2022 and Jamarcus had walked over here from his apartment in NoMa, a few miles that had left him a bit sweaty in his wool sweater, but not at all out of breath. He was talking a mile a minute.

"I might run for mayor at some point," he said. "It's something I've legitimately been thinking about for four or five years. It just hit me that there are so many ideas and so much energy that gets sucked out of you in Congress because you know bills aren't going anywhere. You need sixty votes for cloture. It's to the point where I'm realizing how important local politics is. I follow local politics more than ever now. I have about forty apps on my phone for news. I want a national platform to be able to talk. That's why I like entertainment. But realistically on a day-to-day basis maybe I could serve a bigger role just working on city council or mayor, because you are sort of hidden in Congress, whether you are a member or a staffer."

Talking to Jamarcus could be a bit of a wild ride. He was brilliant, but complicated, with so many thoughts trying to get out of his head at once that he could be hard to keep up with. Within minutes of meeting him, the conversation leapt from the time Jamarcus nearly beat a kid to death as an angry eight-year-old, and how he'd spent the rest of his life doing everything he can to never let his anger overwhelm him again; to commentary on how his public high school was being shut down and how his town of Pine Bluff was about to be home to a multimillion-dollar cryptocurrency mining operation that would displace poor Black families; to his thoughts on Feinstein's mental health; to his aspiration of applying to business school and eventually starting up a video production company that would feature Black artists.

Jamarcus's act of rebellion wasn't getting as much attention as he'd hoped. Pablo's article had been widely read, as far as Latino Rebels stories go, and yet the story hadn't really been picked up by the mainstream press.

Jamarcus had thought the *New York Times* or the *Washington Post* might come calling. Or at the very least Politico. The closest thing he got was a mention in Politico's *Playbook*, appearing in the newsletter's lighthearted "spotted" section alongside sightings of Jared Kushner having breakfast with Ye (formerly Kanye West) and an item about Joe Manchin walking across Constitution Avenue against a red light to avoid talking to a journalist:

"Jamarcus Purley, a former aide to Dianne Feinstein, talks about the time he took mushrooms and hung out in Feinstein's personal office smoking a joint and blasting DeBarge's 'I Like It.' He also made a video."

When I talked to various reporters who cover Capitol Hill, it wasn't entirely clear why Jamarcus's story didn't get more attention. Some thought it might have to do with the sensitivity of the allegations (racism, dementia) and the importance of the accused (she would soon become the longest-serving woman in the Senate). Maybe it had to do with the fact that Jamarcus was such a complicated whistleblower.

As sharp and thoughtful as Jamarcus was, he could also be pretty out there. In early March, after getting picked up by Dear White Staffers, he gave a series of rambling interviews to podcasts where he made unprovable claims about his boss being controlled by military companies such as Raytheon and Lockheed Martin who wanted to "keep her" in the Senate to "push their phony war in Ukraine." He said he used to stay at work late and read through memos on the senator's desk that proved this, but had no evidence and couldn't cite specifics. On his Instagram page, Jamarcus would post private messages he got from colleagues who appeared to be checking in on him, and would write openly about his sex life and drug use. Jamarcus could also be mercurial—excited to talk one day, and standoffish the next. Taken together, it all gave me pause—as it had Dwight—about whether I needed to worry about what giving him a platform might do to his mental health.

The fact that all these things could make him less credible in the eyes of a probing journalist struck Jamarcus as "bullshit." There were plenty of journalists, he said, who used to call him all the time as an anonymous source for other stories; now they suddenly wanted nothing to do with a story that had his name on it?

And he wasn't necessarily wrong about Senator Feinstein's cognitive decline. A week before we met up, Jamarcus pointed out to me, the *San Francisco Chronicle* had published a report—based on interviews with a handful of lawmakers and anonymous former Feinstein staffers—with the headline COLLEAGUES WORRY DIANNE FEINSTEIN IS NOW MENTALLY UNFIT TO SERVE, CITING RECENT INTERACTIONS. The article had related stories about apparent memory lapses where the senator on occasion would repeat herself or fail to recognize colleagues.

I had heard a story that fit the theme, from another Senate staffer. About a year earlier, Feinstein had approached Senator Tim Scott, stuck out her hand, and told him she had been rooting for him and was so happy to have him serving with her in the Senate. It was obvious to Scott and the staffers in tow that Feinstein had mistaken the South

Carolinian for Raphael Warnock, the newly elected Democratic senator from Georgia. Scott had played along. "Thank you so much," he had told Feinstein, according to the staffer who told me about the incident. "Your support means a lot."

When I relayed the story to Jamarcus, he leapt out of his seat, put his hands to his head, and crouched to the floor.

"This is what I'm talking about!" he shouted.

Some of the other Eastern Market patrons looked over.

There was an older Black woman sitting alone at the table beside ours. She was clearly a regular at the bar—she caught up with various other patrons and had an easy, familiar rapport with her server. She had been a mostly quiet presence during lunch, but she had overheard our conversation. After Jamarcus sat down again, she began speaking to him directly.

"I worked in the Senate for Strom Thurmond," she told him, referring to the South Carolina senator who had supported racial segregation and opposed landmark civil rights legislation, leading an unsuccessful 24-hour-18-minute filibuster against the Civil Rights Act of 1957. He moderated his racial politics later.

"So listen to me," the woman continued. "You have the opportunity to work in that building right there. Write them down. Don't confront."

"No, I like to confront," Jamarcus said.

"No listen, listen."

"I don't need that advice."

"You got to listen to understand the game."

"I do understand. I do."

"You could still be there journaling. I could read your journals and write them up from your insider experiences. The problem is too many young people are outspoken..."

"No no no," Jamarcus said. "I don't need that advice. I definitely don't need that advice."

It was hard for him to take this woman seriously. She had worked for a famously racist lawmaker. The woman would tell Jamarcus that Strom "wasn't perfect," but that even flawed politicians could accomplish a lot of good, and that there was value in learning to work with them.

"Listen to me, Jamarcus." Her voice was calm but stern. "They want to cut you off at the head before you get an opportunity to speak. They know how to run the game on you."

"Okay, okay."

"You understand the game. You're very intelligent. But they know how to run the game."

She wasn't telling Jamarcus something he hadn't thought of. He had essentially played her version of the game all his life—it was how he ended up in Feinstein's office to begin with and how he worked for her for five years. But that game had broken something inside him, and he just couldn't do it anymore. Over the course of the conversation, Jamarcus would try and get the former Thurmond staffer to say whether she thought her old boss was racist. She said he was a "womanizer" and that he was "patriarchal" and had once supported "oppressionist" policies, but she refused to call him a racist.

"You try to throw out a lot of buzzwords," she said. "Racism wasn't his main problem. It's deeper than racism."

Jamarcus was done tiptoeing around his own thoughts on matters like this. He was free to speak his mind. Though now the only place he could do that was from the outside.

"Jamarcus, next time you get an opportunity, because you're very smart," she said, "write it down. I would love to see the insider book, but for that, you need to be inside . . . You are a good observer, right? Journal it out. Because if they cut you off, we don't get to hear. How many people get to be in that position? You've got to slow down a little."

"That's real, I do be on 100," Jamarcus said, slouching in his chair. "I do be on 100 out of anger."

"You aren't really angry; you're trying to process some things."

"You're speaking fact," he said. "You're preaching right now. They won't trust anything you say, no matter what you do. You know better than anyone, as a Black woman."

"I didn't want to eavesdrop."

"I get angry quickly. I'm an intense person."

"I just don't want you to disappear."

Part 3

Placing Bets

Chapter 11

The A-Bomb Kid

Late winter 2022

Pennsylvania Avenue, just a few blocks from the Capitol. It was where Chuck Schumer's go-to hole-in-the-wall Chinese food joint was located, and the diner where former Speaker of the House John Boehner used to go most mornings for greasy eggs and sausage. It had the Tune Inn, where Pablo used to kill rats, and fast-casual lunch spots for time-pressed Hill staffers. And this heavily trafficked corridor was also home to a low-slung office building with a green-and-blue sign that read: "PredictIt: Let's play politics."

PredictIt was a website that allowed users to gamble on politics, and I'd come to its headquarters in early 2022 to meet with the cofounder, John Aristotle Phillips. After buzzing into the office, I climbed a creaky staircase and was met by Phillips—a handsome man in his mid-sixties, trim with graying hair. He invited me into a glass conference room, where I explained I'd come to talk about the pleasures and perils of political gamification.

"You know about the A-bomb, right?" he asked me with an impish grin.

Like, the existence of the atomic bomb?

"You don't know that I was the A-bomb Kid?" he asked.

I didn't. But Phillips was more than happy to explain. In 1976, while he was a junior at Princeton University majoring in physics, Phillips wanted to show how easy it was to design a weapon of mass destruction using publicly available information. He produced a thirty-four-page paper that he called "The Fundamentals of Atomic Bomb Design: An Assessment of the Problems and Possibilities Confronting a Terrorist Group or Non-Nuclear Nation Attempting to Design a Crude Plutonium Fission Bomb." He put together a plan for a beachball-sized explosive that weighed 125 pounds, would cost about $152,000 to build, and could explode with one-third the force of the Hiroshima bomb.

"It's very simple," Phillips said at the time. "Any undergraduate physics major could have done what I did."

Maybe anyone could have done it, but the fact that Phillips did turned him into a star. He did interviews with *People*, *Time*, and the *Washington Post*. WHAT'S A NICE KID LIKE JOHN PHILLIPS DOING WITH AN A-BOMB? asked a *New York* magazine headline. He appeared in a guest spot on *To Tell the Truth*—a game show where guests described their unusual-sounding lives and contestants had to figure out who was lying. He taped dozens of spots with nightly news television programs and got a call from Universal about the possibility of making a movie. He got mysterious calls, too, like the one from someone claiming to be a member of the Pakistani government looking to obtain a copy of his designs. After that, Phillips reached out to the FBI and to Senator William Proxmire, a Democrat from Wisconsin, just in case *his* government wanted to know about that sort of thing. The next week Proxmire and Charles Percy, a Republican from Illinois, both spoke about the incident on the Senate floor.

"Mr. President, recent attempts by foreign governments to obtain a paper describing a workable nuclear device are alarming," Percy said. "John Phillips hopes that his work will cause people to stop and think, and then do something about the dangers of nuclear proliferation. I sincerely hope so too."

Now known as the "A-Bomb Kid," Phillips decided to use his new-found fame to urge better safeguards against the theft or illegal purchasing of plutonium (if designing a bomb was easy, it better be damn hard to get the materials to make one). And then, after graduating from college, he used that same newfound fame to run for Congress in Connecticut. He lost. He tried again two years later in 1982. He lost again.

Phillips's second campaign was run by his younger brother, Dean, an MIT graduate, who invented a computer program that handled many of the arduous tasks of managing a campaign—most notably taking the lists of registered voters and organizing the data into a spreadsheet. At a time when campaigns were mostly run out of shoeboxes full of index cards, the program, which ran on an Apple II computer, was cutting edge. And so, to get out of the debt accrued by running two unsuccessful congressional bids, the Phillips brothers started selling the software at $199 a pop until it quickly became apparent that the more valuable commodity wasn't the computer program. It was the data.

Just as a nuke cannot explode without fissile material, it's next to impossible to win an election without a quality list of eligible voters. It's how campaigns get the signatures needed to get on the ballot; it's how they figure out where to send their campaign mail and which doors to knock on to get voters to the polls on Election Day. In the 1980s, those lists were controlled completely by the Republican and the Democratic Parties. That was until Phillips's company—Aristotle—began compiling and selling that data themselves.

Phillips was, once again, playing with powerful, possibly dangerous, material. And by 2007, he was getting media treatment of a different kind. Aristotle, *Vanity Fair* wrote that year, was now running a "shadowy" political organization whose data on American voters had been used by every successful presidential campaign since Ronald Reagan. Their voter lists were larger and more comprehensive than anything the DNC or the RNC had, offering everything from where voters lived to how much their house was worth, what kind of car they drove, what websites or churches they visited, whether they had ever been convicted of a sex crime or owned a gun.

"It's not that [Aristotle's] list is good—they're considered to have the only list," a conservative strategist told *Vanity Fair*.

Sitting in the Aristotle office now, I didn't exactly feel like I'd stumbled into the shadowy headquarters of some Big Brother operation. The stairwell had smelled faintly of mildew. The place was sparsely decorated with some political ephemera on the walls (an RFK poster here, a newspaper clipping there), and was mostly empty due to Covid. And there was a creature living inside the walls.

"That sounds way too big to be a rat," Phillips said after we heard a terrifying screech, followed by the sound of claws on drywall. "It was squeaking, wasn't it?"

We left the conference room and settled into another, where Phillips told me about the time he became aware of another phenomenon worming its way into the political scene. In the early 2000s, a website called Intrade was allowing users to make bets on everything from who would win *American Idol* to who would win the presidency. Sometimes the collective wisdom of gamblers allowed for accurate predictions: Intrade users were able to predict Saddam Hussein's capture in 2003 and the resignation of Secretary of Defense Donald Rumsfeld before it happened in 2006. Intrade was then reported to have more than 100,000 users and millions of dollars trading hands. But it was a sketchy operation. The founder, a larger-than-life Irish businessman named John Delaney, appeared to have pocketed millions of dollars in undocumented payments, and in 2011, Delaney took a hiking expedition to Mount Everest. He died fifty yards from the summit. Eventually his company shut down. Delaney's body was never recovered.

"There are people who Delaney took who are convinced he's on a beach somewhere, sipping drinks with the little umbrellas, with their $3 million," Phillips told me.

In 2014, Phillips decided to see if he could design his own version of the same thing. He found a prediction market being run out of New Zealand's University of Wellington, and got a letter from the U.S. government that promised not to prosecute as long as the betting limits were capped at $850. At first the website grew at a slow but steady pace. And then in 2016, it exploded.

"Trump was like nitroglycerin," he said.

With everyone watching the election, and with the election being more volatile than ever, hordes of people began flooding the site. They were making bets not just on who would become president, but on how many times Trump would say "Crooked Hillary" in a debate or the number of times he would tweet in a week. In early 2020, PredictIt offered a market on whether or not the World Health Organization would declare Covid a global pandemic. Later that year, after Trump lost reelection and PredictIt closed their market on the presidential campaign, Phillips says they received bomb threats from people who believed Trump still had a chance to be declared the victor.

Now even war offered the opportunity to make a few bucks. "Right now one of our biggest markets is whether Putin will meet with Biden by July first, and another was whether Putin will be in office by the end of 2022," Phillips said. "That's between 75 and 80 cents right now. It sounds a little high to me. I might buy that. Of course, I can't buy it because I run the company, but if I could, I might."

I asked Phillips if he worried that all this gamification trivialized world events, and might have a negative effect on democracy. Could it be that our politics had gotten stupider lately because we'd turned it into entertainment—just a higher-stakes version of *To Tell the Truth*, a game show riddled with imposters?

"It's a legitimate question," he said, leaning back in his chair and pausing for a long time. "I don't lose sleep over whether we are damaging democracy. But maybe I should."

In fact, Phillips thought maybe he was *helping* democracy. Here's what he knew: The people who bet on football games consumed "eight or nine times as much football statistics as the average person." Imagine the kind of political literacy voters would have if they just had some money on the line. Plus, there were dozens of colleges and universities, as well as West Point and the Federal Reserve, that received and studied anonymized data from PredictIt.

"Polling is broken," Phillips said. "Markets can be predictive."

Phillips believed that if you took the collective wisdom of the masses and made them actually put money where their mouths were, then maybe it could be predictive. Plus, it wasn't really just the masses Phillips was dealing with here. There was a special subsection of the PredictIt community with an outsized influence on the market. They often lived and worked in clusters around state capitals throughout the country, near Wall Street in New York, and of course, in and around Washington, D.C. They were often political practitioners themselves, whose jobs in and around government made them believe they could see the future better than your average citizen, and were just cynical enough to plow thousands of dollars a year into the site.

"They are," said Phillips, "our Super Forecasters."

I'd never heard the term before, but I knew what he was talking about. As it turned out, I'd spent the better part of the last year hanging around with one.

Chapter 12

Betting Clears the Mind

November 2021

Sean McElwee was not shy about his betting. Sitting with fellow political pros around the poker table, he'd make prop bets on everything from whether Kamala Harris would be the Democratic nominee if Biden didn't run (Sean said yes for $500) to whether the 2023 Congress would feature more than three self-identified new members of "The Squad" (Sean said no for $50). He'd sometimes end conference calls with other organizations by seeing if anyone wanted to make a wager with him about upcoming elections. He wagered tens of thousands of dollars a year on PredictIt, sometimes on contests as far-flung as the Seattle mayoral race ("I won like $6,000 on that," he told me). He told people he bet $20,000 on Biden's 2020 presidential campaign, and bet $100 on when Senator Ben Ray Luján of New Mexico would return to Congress after suffering a stroke. Sean once told me he would sometimes commission little polls here or there "mostly" for the purpose of getting intel that he could use to make smart bets.

Sean's girlfriend, Bobbi, told me that she used to worry about Sean's gambling habits. She said he used to play online poker so often and on so many screens at once that she talked to him about whether he had a problem. But when I asked Sean if he worried his clients might read him as some kind of "degenerate gambler," he said putting skin in the game forced a guy like him to be serious about his craft.

He was so serious about this that he encouraged his employees at Data for Progress to follow his lead. He held weekly wagering sessions. He called them "heuristics" classes. His staff called him—half mockingly—"Professor Sean." These courses didn't always involve real money, but Sean would sometimes Venmo members of his team small sums that they could use to place bets. The subject line of those payments was "DFP Stimmy"—a jokey reference to stimulus checks.

"I do want my staff to gamble," Sean told me. "People think it's silly, but I actually think it's very not silly. It is a really serious attempt to help them understand and engage with risk."

We're heading back in time here for a moment, back to November 2, 2021, the first election night of the Biden era—and the first proximal test of the president's political strength. I had come to Sean's apartment to meet his staff and watch returns come in from the evening's main event, the Virginia governor's race, where Democrat Terry McAuliffe was up against the Republican Glenn Youngkin. Sean had invited some of his employees over to his apartment to watch returns. He was bullish on McAuliffe's chances.

"If he wins by three, I break even," he told me early in the evening, splayed out on his futon sofa, murdering zombies in a video game while I waited for his team to show up. "If it's by two, I have a split loss, but that's because if it's over three, I'll make $10,000. I think it's going to be like three or four, maybe even higher."

Sean sat up in his seat and started mashing buttons on the controller to crush the skull of a zombie.

"If Terry loses by eight, I will quit politics," he said.

A McAuliffe loss would be a bad sign for Democrats and their odds in the midterms, still a year away. And it wouldn't be great for Data for Progress either. A week earlier, DFP had released a poll that showed McAuliffe winning by 5 percentage points. If there ended up being a big gap between that and the final margin, it would reflect poorly on DFP's ability to overcome the challenges facing modern pollsters. People didn't use landlines anymore. They screened calls from numbers they didn't recognize. Pollsters had to get more creative about getting people to participate in voter surveys.

"I like to tell my staff that the median survey-taker is taking your survey for Candy Crush tokens while taking a shit," Sean said.

The doorbell rang. Sean's staff had arrived. In came Danielle Deiseroth, the team's climate pollster; McKenzie Wilson, the communications director; Ethan Winter, lead analyst; and Marcela Mulholland, Data for Progress's twenty-five-year-old political director. Sean's bachelor pad wasn't exactly set up for company, but he put out the folding chairs normally reserved for the poker table, and the gang sat in a semicircle facing Sean on the sofa.

Marcela was already nervous. "This morning you were telling me to put my freaking life savings on the line," she said to Sean. "Am I fucked? Now am I fucked?"

Fortunately for Marcela, she had put only $10 on the race. Like much of Sean's young staff, Marcela had never made a political bet until she came to DFP. The gambling seemed a little strange to her, but Sean was so open about it and no one seemed to have a problem with it. So who was she to say otherwise?

"Sean will say, 'Gambling clears the mind,'" she said. "And it really does. I really felt it, you get a rush."

Marcela grew up in South Florida, Broward County, the daughter of a Venezuelan immigrant mother who taught Spanish and a White father who worked in the fossil fuel industry. They weren't a particularly political family. Her mom voted for Democrats; her dad tended to split his ticket. Marcela's older brother had done Hispanic outreach for Barack Obama's 2008 campaign, and Marcela thought that was cool. In high school, she did all the "normie" progressive things she could: Gay Straight Alliance, getting into the whole "Lean In" boss lady thing.

But then Trump won in 2016, and it felt like something broke.

Marcela, by then in college, needed to make a change. She went with her mother to a barbershop to get her head shaved—a statement of intent to be more radical—but the barber refused to cut her long brown hair, telling her she looked too pretty and would only be mad at him later. He agreed to do it if she cut off the first chunk. She grabbed the scissors.

She wore a poster around her neck to class that read "Climate Change Is Real." She got a fellowship with the Sunrise Movement—a new climate activism organization. She knocked on doors for Florida's gubernatorial and senate races. And in 2019, when the Democrats came to Miami for a presidential primary debate, she got an invite to attend as a guest of Jay Inslee, the Washington governor who had put climate at the core of his long-shot campaign. At a snack buffet backstage, Marcela proudly received "stink eyes" from Neera Tanden—a longtime member of the Democratic establishment who was disliked by much of the party's progressive wing. (Marcela thought that Tanden took issue with her "No More Fossil Fuel Money" T-shirt.)

Marcela moved to New York to take a job with a think tank working on climate projects, and one evening ended up at a Data for Progress happy hour, which was where she met Sean for the first time. Sean didn't leave a great impression. Marcela didn't know who Sean was, and Sean seemed confused by this. Months later, when she got offered a job at DFP, Sean didn't remember her.

Marcela's lefty friends held a dim view of her new boss. They thought he was a bandwagon guy, not a true believer. And Marcela had her own reservations, namely about the way he carried himself in the press, often saying outlandish things that made him seem like an "egomaniac." And yet he was great in the office—friendly, inclusive, encouraging. Marcela came to understand Sean's act as just that—an act, at least partially. Sean was one of those people who believed all attention was good attention when you're running an upstart business. There were people in Washington who talked about him like he was some sort of embryonic Donald Trump, but for good, or at least chaotically neutral—ideologically flexible, big mouth, but adept at drawing attention and able to use his skills to benefit the Democratic Party as well as himself. He had a way about him as a young leader of an even younger office. The staff looked up to him, and Marcela was no different.

"Did I tell you that Marcela and I are going to meet with Neera Tanden at the White House?" Sean said to me.

"I'm nervous," said Marcela. "Is she going to be rude or is she nice?"

"She called to say I should support the Build Back Better framework, and I was like, 'Queen, you don't even need to ask,'" Sean said.

Sean supported the legislation. He thought it was good policy. And he'd also placed a PredictIt bet on its passing.

The team settled into chairs around the television, nervously checking their phones. Ethan was especially jittery, having bet "just an obscene amount of money" on the race.

"I almost had a stroke when I saw the polls," he said.

Ethan was a native Vermonter and had the look—bespectacled, bearded, and trim—of someone who enjoyed skiing and hoppy IPAs. He had a big job at DFP, the lead guy running their polls. He was one of the longer-serving members of the team, and having been plucked right out of college, he felt he owed a lot to Sean. Sometimes Sean would remind him of that, joking about how he had "made" Ethan. Ethan didn't mind, though, at least at first. He was a key member of the team.

The crew that had shown up to his apartment didn't all look like Sean, but as I sat here listening to them, it *did* sometimes feel like they talked like him.

"I was on a call today with all these stupid fucking progressives," said McKenzie, DFP's communications director, breaking the silence while her colleagues checked election returns on their phones. McKenzie was herself a "fucking progressive." She had come to DFP after a stint working on Elizabeth Warren's presidential campaign. The call she had been on had been about a recent deal to lower prescription drug prices. It was a big achievement, but the progressives had compromised more than they wanted, and McKenzie had come to think of them as whiners.

"You just got a big fucking win on prescription drugs, fucking act like it," McKenzie said. "It's so stupid. No one ever wants to do a fucking victory lap."

It was important for Democrats to win where they could, McKenzie thought, and perhaps equally important to remind voters of their victories.

The polls in Virginia had just closed, and it would be hours before anyone knew that Youngkin was going to win, or by how much (2 percentage points). Data for Progress would whiff on the polling, like pretty much everyone else, but even before that picture came into focus, the DFP staff were talking about what Democrats needed to do in the future. To achieve progressive things, they needed to at least appear to be moderate. If the fence sitters thought the Democrats were a bunch of socialists, they would vote Republican.

Some members of Sean's staff had started feeling a little less progressive, or at least more practical about which progressive outcomes were achievable. Sometimes the staff would talk about being "mod-pilled," and every once in a while Marcela would ask Sean to remind everyone that they were in fact "libs." Looking around and listening to his team, I was having a hard time figuring out if Sean was responsible for promoting a young, diverse group of progressives who could someday bring their varying perspectives to positions of leadership within the Democratic Party, or creating a bunch of mini versions of himself.

"I definitely think I've become more moderate since working here," said Danielle, whose prior political work included a staff job on the 2020 Bernie Sanders presidential campaign.

"I look at so much data now that I'm like, 'Huh, maybe this policy I really used to like isn't as popular as I once thought,'" she continued. "I'm more pragmatic. Yeah, in my heart of hearts, of course I want everyone to have access to healthcare. But is Medicare for All the most popular thing in the world? No."

"We drank the Kool-Aid," Marcela said.

Chapter 13

New Money

Late winter 2022

In my family you have to find your thing and do it excellently," Leah Hunt-Hendrix said.

Leah's family did big things. Her half uncle Nelson Bunker Hunt was one of the biggest funders of the right-wing, conspiracy-minded John Birch Society. Nelson's brother Lamar was a founder of the American Football League (which merged with the National Football League in 1970) and owner of the Kansas City Chiefs—which he passed to his son Lamar Jr. Leah's aunt June was a successful Christian radio personality in Texas. Leah's sibling Hunter led a metal band with a cult following. And Leah's mother, Helen LaKelly Hunt, was a prodigious fundraiser (National Women's Hall of Fame Class of 1994) who was also a bestselling coauthor with Leah's father, the psychologist Harville Hendrix.

"There were days when we came home from work too tired to listen to what she was saying, too distracted to give her our full attention," Harville and Helen wrote of their daughter in their *New York Times* bestseller, *Getting the Love You Want*. "Regrettably, we also wounded her by unwittingly passing down our own childhood challenges, the emotional inheritance of generations. We either overcompensated for what we didn't get from our own parents or blindly recreated the same painful situations. We call this the *legacy of wounding*."

Leah had a complicated inheritance. Her oil tycoon grandfather H.L. left a fortune to his kids and their kids, but he wasn't much of a family man—even if he did have three separate families and a total of fifteen children. Leah's mother, Helen, and Helen's sister Swanee were daughters of H.L.'s mistress (and eventual second wife). During the early years of their childhood they didn't know who their father was, or that they had secret siblings, despite growing up in a modest brick house just a few miles away from H.L.'s mansion, which was built to resemble George Washington's Mount Vernon estate. When Swanee and her family eventually moved in after H.L.'s first wife died, the first thing she remembered her father asking was, "Which one are you again?"

Swanee remembered H.L. as strict, unkind, and with political pre-occupations that were all-consuming. "He thought there was a communist everywhere," Swanee told me. He wrote about the communist threat in newspaper columns, and sponsored a conservative radio show called *Life Line*, which he would play at dinner, demanding total silence from his family at the table.

"He was absolutely fanatical," Swanee said. "I don't mean he was interested. I don't mean he was passionate. I mean it was over the line. It was all he talked about. I don't think he ever said to me, 'How was your day?'"

Swanee and her sister Helen grew up and worked to unwind the kinds of projects their father cared about. Swanee made big political donations to Democrats and their causes—most notably to Bill Clinton's 1992 presidential campaign. Helen started foundations that sought to raise money from an otherwise untapped natural resource: rich women.

When Helen got together with Harville—a second marriage for both—they blended their families. And when they became coauthors, they blended their professional lives too. There was a time when Harville had a recurring role as a marriage counselor on *The Oprah Winfrey*

Show and was given, Leah said, the opportunity to play the role of Dr. Phil before there was a Dr. Phil.

"My mom said he couldn't," Leah told me. "My parents were having marriage issues at the time, and my mom was like, 'It's not fair for you to go around being the guru when we're miserable at home.'"

Harville and Helen nearly split up, but the two worked through their differences and used the experience to create a new kind of couples therapy, called Imago. Imago Therapy was tuned in to the unconscious tendency of couples to look to each other to "satisfy the unmet needs and emotional needs" of their respective childhoods.

Leah's material needs were met. The Hunt-Hendrixes had a Fifth Avenue apartment and a yacht on the Hudson, and Leah went to Convent of the Sacred Heart, a private school rumored to have been the inspiration for the TV show *Gossip Girl*. "Leah was very interested in socializing with the daughters of wealthy people," Harville told me of his elementary-school-aged daughter. "She had socialite interests."

During Leah's middle school years, though, her parents—burnt out on New York City and work—relocated the family to New Mexico, where they lived on a ranch in what Harville described as "one of the nation's poorest zip codes." They were still rich, but now instead of being ensconced in Manhattan wealth, they were surrounded by poverty, and Leah, in her own words, became "obsessed" with inequality. By the time they moved back to New York, when Leah was finishing up middle school, she was more conscious than ever of her privilege.

"In my experience of her," Harville said, "it was the end of her becoming a socialite."

Leah agreed that living in New Mexico had been formative for her. But so too were other sojourns. After getting her bachelor's degree from Duke University, she moved to Egypt for a year in 2006, followed by a stint in Syria. While getting her PhD at Princeton, she spent summers in the West Bank, where she picked up the idea for her thesis: a philosophical study of "solidarity." Three years into the Obama administration, roiling frustration with income inequality boiled over in the fall of 2011 with a protest movement that sprung up in Zuccotti Park, in New York City's Financial District. As part of her studies—and to show her own solidarity—Leah began showing up to the tent encampment known as Occupy Wall Street. The online magazine *Salon* dubbed her "Occupy's Heiress."

Where H. L. Hunt might have seen a bunch of dirty communists squatting in a private park, Leah saw something energetic and essential to the future of the country. Leah was twenty-seven years old, and her various inheritances—the wealth of her oil magnate grandfather, the organization of her philanthropist mother, the empathy of her psychologist father—were beginning to mature as she prepared to transition from being a child of the ruling class to a vested member who could start pulling levers. It was Harville who used to tell her to find her "fulcrum"—a point of leverage—with which she could create the most change.

After finishing her thesis (which one of her advisers, Dr. Cornel West, told me was "brilliant"), Leah came to realize that she possessed a golden fulcrum that most people at Occupy Wall Street didn't, and that the best way to use it wasn't among the tent dwellers of Zuccotti Park. It was to organize the 1 percent and turn them into "class traitors."

First, she started the Solidaire Network—an organization that helped rich people figure out what progressive causes to donate to.

"When we look at the history of social movements, we find that individuals with wealth have often stepped in to quietly support the ability of activists to organize and mobilize," she had written in a 2012 pitch for members. "They bet on David vs. Goliath struggles."

Leah had her own struggles running that organization. She was a bad manager back then, she said, too young and too overwhelmed to be a steady hand at the helm. By the time she left in 2018, things were tense with the staff, and she moved on to help run her new organization, Way to Win, which had more of an electoral focus.

* * *

A few months after her Christmas party, Leah invited me over to her house to catch up. When she answered the door, she was finishing up a video conference call with a donor.

"I'm pumped up," Leah said, shutting her computer and taking a seat in her living room. "We just made a million bucks!" she said. "That was... That's good."

She didn't sound so sure.

As part of her goal to help elect the most progressive candidates in various open-seat primaries around the country, Leah's Way to Win organization had a PAC that had so far raised about $3 million—not bad for a first quarter of fundraising.

"It's probably the most on the progressive side," she said. "But it's not a lot compared to the other side."

In this case, the "other side" wasn't Republicans, but moderate Democrats, engaged in the struggle to determine the makeup of the Democratic Party. It wasn't a new fight—progressives and pragmatists were always "battling for the soul" of the party. Now that battle was being waged in a fog, and the sides were not always clearly delineated: Was Fetterman in Pennsylvania the same kind of progressive as Barnes in Wisconsin? Would a candidate be considered a progressive if they used to say things like "Defund the Police" but then distanced themselves from it? Was Sean McElwee on the side of progressives or corporate Democrats?

Sometimes Leah didn't know who her allies were, but she knew her opponents had the cash advantage. Whenever one of her candidates would start to do well, Leah said, a cavalry would come in to try and destroy them. Often that meant lots of money being spent by the American Israel Public Affairs Committee (AIPAC), a pro-Israel nonprofit that had in recent years taken a particularly conservative turn, and Democratic Majority for Israel (DMFI), a left-of-center version of the same thing. But AIPAC and DMFI weren't the only groups Leah felt like she was contending with. There were plenty of Democratic operatives who believed the path to victory was best paved by centrist candidates. Dmitri Mehlhorn, the powerful "donor adviser" who told the billionaire Reid Hoffman how to spend his political money, had recently sent an email to a group of progressive activists he had supported in the past saying Democrats would have been better off if they had "simply taken a long nap" over the past year. This had really pissed off Leah, who had gotten the email. When her organization, Way to Win, had begun drafting a response, the team titled their Google Doc "FUCK YOU DMITRI."

There was also the problem of new money—and Leah, a product of old money, was at odds with the newest money around: cryptocurrency.

The main culprit was Sam Bankman-Fried, the thirty-year-old billionaire and newly anointed political kingmaker. Bankman-Fried was the founder of the crypto exchange FTX and had an estimated net worth around $24 billion. In 2020, he donated $5.2 million to super PACs supporting Biden's campaign. Now he was looking to expand and refine his influence in Washington. Over the course of the midterms, he would give more money to Democrats than anyone other than megadonor (and favorite boogeyman for the right) George Soros.

Bankman-Fried had enlisted the help of his younger brother, Gabe, to serve as a political consigliere. In 2020, Gabe had started a nonprofit, Guarding Against Pandemics, whose stated purpose was to prevent future pandemics, and whose practical purpose was to carry his big brother's purse. Due to campaign finance laws, Gabe's organization could give only *so much* money to political candidates. But the organization had a super PAC affiliated with it, Protect Our Future, which could spend much, much more to shape the political landscape. Sam gave that group $27 million.

The Bankman-Frieds adhered to a philosophy known as "effective altruism," which promoted a data-centric approach to achieving maximum positive change through philanthropy. The idea was to give with your head, not your heart. It was popular among the large-brained, big-money set in Silicon Valley, givers whose generosity came with an entrepreneur's devotion to return on investment. (An organization called GiveWell, for example, rated charities on their cost effectiveness and helped funnel millions of dollars to malaria prevention groups— which GiveWell had determined saved the most lives per dollar.)

Effective altruism was also big among the Sean McElwees of the world—in particular Sean McElwee. Sean had recently picked up a side hustle consulting gig for Guarding Against Pandemics, having been connected to the Bankman-Frieds by a mutual friend.

Data for Progress had been hired to do some polling for Guarding Against Pandemics, but Sean's work with Gabe Bankman-Fried wasn't all done under the DFP umbrella. His freelance consulting work included giving advice on political and media strategy. He knew a lot of people in Washington, he could make introductions, and he could evangelize the hell out of Guarding Against Pandemics.

"I've been paid a couple of times for my ability to bring things up at happy hours," Sean once told me about his work for Gabe.

Sean was a good messenger on behalf of effective altruism, but Sam Bankman-Fried was the poster child. He flexed his commitment to pragmatism by cultivating a persona that appeared uninterested in the trappings of wealth: He drove a Toyota Corolla, always seemed to be wearing shorts, lived with roommates, and supposedly slept on a beanbag chair. (He and his roommates lived in a luxury penthouse in an exclusive resort in the Bahamas, but whatever.) Journalists compared him to Mr. Spock on *Star Trek*—a fundamentally good guy who didn't allow emotions to cloud his judgment.

Nobody ever called Leah Hunt-Hendrix a Vulcan. She wanted to be effective, but her orientation was solidarity, people, connections. She wanted to bring a lot of people to the table, and she didn't want to offend anyone. Sometimes this approach wore on the patience of her political advisers. When she planned a small conference to talk about economic populism, for example, a consultant had advised her to limit the guest list—maybe leave off a few of the most outspoken groups—so as not to let any critic paint the event as a gathering of "police defunders." She ignored that advice. When she hoped to get Hakeem Jeffries, the New York congressman who would likely succeed Nancy Pelosi as the Democrats' leader in the House, to come to dinner, she was told that the best way to entice him would be to raise some money on his behalf. But because Jeffries had some moderate tendencies and was seen as an establishment guy, Leah declined to fundraise. Doing so might have upset her friends in the movement.

She was a movement person, not a data person. She was also a scholar with a PhD in religion, ethics, and politics from Princeton who didn't think effective altruism was an adequate framework for thinking about addressing societal problems.

"The problem with EA is they don't have a power analysis," she said. "They are like, 'Let's try and save as many lives as possible,' but, why are those people poor in the first place? Have you read any history? Have you studied colonialism?"

Maybe Sam Bankman-Fried was a devoted effective altruist and felt supporting candidates who made pandemic prevention a top priority was the best possible use of his money. Maybe he was propping up candidates he could count on to be "fair"—at least to his bank account—when the issue of cryptocurrency regulation came up. Leah didn't know. What she did know was that the effective altruists kept spending against her primary candidates, and it was threatening to make her own altruism less effective.

Leah was skeptical of crypto—a digital form of money that operated outside the bounds of traditional banks and regulation. It seemed like a scam, or at least prone to scams. Because some of the currency were pretend coins that needed to be "mined" using a seemingly endless amount of computers sucking up incredible amounts of energy, it was terrible for the environment. Still, Leah wanted to understand the crypto bros. And so a friend, the progressive politician David Segal, introduced her to somebody who knew a lot about it.

Marvin Ammori was a lawyer who served as the chief legal officer of a different crypto exchange called Uniswap. Marvin had gotten into the tech business by way of the free speech movement involved in the battle over net neutrality—the principle that all internet communications should be treated equally, instead of better access being given to companies willing to shell out more money. Politically, he spoke Leah's language. Marvin had mixed feelings about the industry, and agreed with Leah that it could use some cleaning up, but he also thought cryptocurrency could be used to break up the big banks (or "democratize finance," as he put it). Occupy's Heiress found Marvin convincing. They decided to work on a "progressive agenda" for cryptocurrency— to see if they could find a way to work with the Bankman-Frieds, or at least spend less time working against one another.

Leah and Marvin also started dating.

Like a lot of young people in Washington, Leah's love life tended to overlap with her work life. She'd dated a couple of politicians, including Ben Jealous, the former president of the NAACP and (unsuccessful) Maryland gubernatorial candidate, and Lucas Kunce, a Missouri populist currently on an (unsuccessful) quest to turn one of his state's Senate seats blue. She had toyed with the idea of writing a book about her romantic life, with different chapters dedicated to different archetypes: the politician, the economist, the journalist, the Silicon Valley CEO, the spy.

Leah's quest for the love she wanted had not led her to marriage, but at thirty-eight, she was thinking more about family. Earlier in the year she had taken a multi-month course to qualify her to be a foster parent. Maybe she would take in a teenage mother and her child.

We were sitting on a couch in Leah's living room, the midterms were in full swing, and Leah was still figuring out how she was faring, both politically and personally. She and Marvin had recently gone out to eat at a Mediterranean and Latin American restaurant called Imperfecto, one of four new restaurants to earn a coveted Michelin star.

"It was a date with intention," she said. "He was like: Could you be my wife and have my babies kind of thing."

Leah wasn't necessarily opposed. She had a big house and a big heart, and her causes and candidates and parties and salons could only fill so much of the space.

Chapter 14

Save the Swamp!

You can spend a lot of time living in and around Washington and still not know what people do all day. Does a fundraiser spend all day on the phone raising funds? How does a pollster poll? After nearly a decade of living in Washington, there was one job in particular that I never fully understood: What exactly did a lobbyist do?

I knew there were a lot of them—more than 12,000 in D.C. I knew they could make a good amount of money. And I knew that people hated them—which, I guess I could relate to, considering the public opinion of journalists. Most of what I knew about the lobbyist persona came from *Thank You for Smoking*, the Christopher Buckley book (and later movie) about the unscrupulous gun-for-hire tobacco lobbyist Nick Naylor.

"Few people on this planet know what it is to be truly despised," Naylor narrates in the movie version, in which he's played by Aaron Eckhart. "Can you blame them? I earn a living fronting an organization that kills twelve hundred human beings a day. Twelve hundred people. We're talking two jumbo jet plane loads of men, women and children. I mean, there's Attila, Genghis...and me, Nick Naylor."

To get a better understanding about the job, I went out to lunch with Tommy Quinn, a longtime operator who once went out to lunch with Buckley to show him what an actual lobbyist was like. ("He's the real-deal," Buckley said to me in an email. "And I like him.") We met at Joe's Seafood, Prime Steak and Stone Crab, a downtown D.C. haunt filled from lunch through dinner with poobahs who spent half their meal looking around to see who had a "better" booth than they did. Tommy had a good booth.

He also had curly hair and droopy eyelids that appeared nearly translucent and which he used to wink at me more than twelve times during our meal (eventually I stopped counting).

Lobbying, he told me while eating $27 fish and chips, is "the only job that allows the little man to petition the government." *Wink.*

Quinn got his start lobbying after a stint in the Treasury Department, and was hired to help fight the very legislation he had been helping craft while a member of the U.S. government.

"Like the FBI hiring a bank robber to help catch other bank robbers?" I asked.

"Exactly," he said. "I spent the next thirty-four years getting paid to fight that bill." *Wink.*

Quinn said that lobbyists provided many vital services to their clients. They helped set up meetings with important legislators and their staff. They provided "political intelligence" about which way a bill was likely to go. And they used their "influence" to get members of Congress to move a certain way on bills.

Money was a big part of all this. If you raised enough for a politician, that particular officeholder would be much more likely to provide good info, and might even be convinced to vote a certain way. For most bills, he said, politicians "don't really give a fuck" if it goes one way or the other. On these issues, they could often be convinced by a "friend."

It was the best job in the world, Quinn said. But it used to be better. Now there were more limitations on how much money lobbyists could spend and on what. There were fewer boozy lunches with politicians and even fewer private airplane rides. Plus, there was so much *other* money out there these days, money from the grass roots, that raising a few hundred thousand dollars for someone didn't go nearly as far as it used to.

"John Kerry is my pal," Quinn said with a *wink*, "and he says, 'Jesus Christ, Joe Biden raised one billion dollars from his fucking basement. I had to scrape and beg and pray for every dollar at every fundraiser.'"

Still, Quinn—who at the time we spoke was currently registered to lobby for groups like the American Mask Manufacturers Association, Lockheed Martin, and Aristotle International (the PredictIt guys)—wouldn't trade this job for any other. As if to prove it, he would often wear a pin that said "Save the Swamp."

*　*　*

The truth was, of course, that despite Trump's promises, the Swamp was never really in danger of being drained. It just filled up with new creatures.

"It was a crazy time," Barry Bennett, a Trump-aligned operator who had managed Ben Carson's presidential campaign before hanging a shingle—his first as a registered lobbyist—with Corey Lewandowski, Trump's former campaign manager. "I remember on the first two days we were open, we had calls from fifty-four potential clients."

Bennett turned those fifty-four calls into plenty of work. He told me that it was relatively easy to advise people like the CEO of Samsung, who had come to him worried about how he had not been invited to any White House business roundtables.

"I told him that we were talking about a guy who owns his own 757, and the thing he's most proud of is the fact that there's a flatscreen on the plane, that the TV is made by Samsung," Bennett told me, referring to President Trump. "I told him we haven't made TVs in the U.S. in thirty years. Make one. It was just that simple."

Samsung didn't start manufacturing televisions in the United States, but they happily allowed Trump to take credit for a new appliance manufacturing plant that had been in the works since before the 2016 election. Bennett became known as one of a handful of lobbyists who "had the president's ear." The international arm of Avenue Strategies, the shop he'd started with Lewandowski, picked up big contracts with clients the governments of Qatar and Zimbabwe. But making it last proved to be more complicated. Bennett and Lewandowski split up shortly after they started, and once Trump went away, so did Bennett's clients. In February 2021, Bennett shut down his own shop, Bennett Strategies. He was at the time being investigated by federal prosecutors for possible violations for failing to disclose work he did for the country of Qatar.

Brian Ballard was another lobbyist featured alongside Robert Stryk in the 2017 *New York Times Magazine* story about getting rich in Trump's Washington. He arrived with years of lobbying work down in Tallahassee and a few friends, mostly from Florida, in Congress. He soon realized he didn't "know anything" about the city, but he did know Trump, and everyone in Washington knew that, which turned out to be enough. In 2017, his firm, Ballard Partners, pulled in close to $10 million, representing companies like Amazon and British American Tobacco. By 2020, that number was more than $24 million.

"The affiliation has been wonderful for me and the firm," Ballard told me when I met him at his slick downtown office.

But what Ballard had learned was that as great as it was to be a Trump Guy during the Trump years, surviving in Washington would mean doing things the Washington Way. Like the successful firms before him, he built out a team that could work regardless of who was president and which party was in power. He hired Democrats (something he told me he had little trouble doing, despite being a Trump Guy). When I met with him in the summer of 2022, he said business was down 25 percent, but that they were still making plenty of money to stick around. He had, he said, signed an eleven-year lease on their new office.

"We have morphed into pretty much your standard K Street operation," he said.

It had taken a bit of time to get there, he admitted. At first there had been so much interest in his services that the screening of potential clients was "not always perfect."

"We made some mistakes." He wasn't interested in naming names, but clearly one of those mistakes was taking on Lev Parnas, the Giuliani associate, who ended up in jail for campaign finance, wire fraud, and false statement offenses. But Ballard said he had worked hard on professionalizing his operation, blending in with the establishment crowd, and turning down the kinds of clients that could hurt his reputation.

"I was approached by people working for Joseph Kabila, the leader of the Democratic Republic of the Congo," he said. "I was like, no thanks."

Ballard worried about what having a client like Kabila might do to his reputation. But fortunately for Kabila, there was Robert Stryk.

Chapter 15

What Stinks in Building B?

Late winter 2022

Middleburg is a town full of rich people who love horses and privacy. The area has long served as a refuge for the capital aristocracy. President Kennedy and Jackie had a retreat in the area. Elizabeth Taylor and her husband, Virginia Senator John Warner, had a farm here. Jack Kent Cooke, who owned Washington's football team, raised Thoroughbreds. So did Paul Mellon, the only son of former U.S. Treasury Secretary and extremely rich guy Andrew W. Mellon, who owned a farm with his wife, Bunny, a few miles away. On the way to Robert Stryk's, you may pass the home of Erik Prince, the billionaire who founded the private military company Blackwater.

The downtown has leafy streets and expensive knickknack stores, one of which was shut down by federal agents in 2018 for smuggling products made from endangered species. There's an inn whose tavern bar served as a surgeon's table during the Civil War, and a year-round Christmas shoppe that used to be haunted by a ghost of news cycles past. Years after disappearing from the public eye, Linda Tripp used to quietly run this winter wonderland of a store, unrecognizable to tourists because she dyed her hair black, changed her face, and spoke

German while stocking the shelves with nutcrackers and music boxes alongside her husband.

And then, just off the town's main drag, was a house marked only as "Building B."

"Who would think that this nondescript office with no numbers on it and no name on it is doing massive private diplomacy," Stryk told me on the porch of Building B on a day in February 2022. "No sign, no nothing, just plenty of security cameras."

This was my second visit with Stryk, about a month after he'd told me the story of his improbable success as a Trump-era lobbyist while drinking whiskey around a series of fires on his property. This time, he'd taken me to his place of business. Now he was telling me about "private diplomacy." These were the diplomatic services he offered, at a price, to geopolitical actors with lots of money who need a Washington fixer. The Sonoran Policy Group had been renamed Stryk Global Diplomacy, and Stryk said the ultimate goal was to "privatize the State Department."

Building B in downtown Middleburg was a little more understated than the State Department headquarters, in Foggy Bottom. In Building B, visitors entered into a small waiting room, with a cigar humidor along the back wall. Stryk loved a fine cigar, a taste he shared with his close friend Rudy Giuliani. Stryk's personal office, down the hall, was nothing fancy, just a desk and a giant television tuned to Fox News. The best part, Stryk said, was downstairs. He led me down the basement steps to a speakeasy-style bar. The back wall was loaded with booze. Stryk's own name was scrawled in LED lights across the mirror.

"Foreign leaders go crazy for this," he told me.

This bar was basically the centerpiece for Stryk's brand of diplomacy. He thought the U.S. diplomatic corps was too bound by protocol and bureaucracy to really get things done. Every meeting with the U.S. government was set up with preconditions, and there was only so much an ambassador was even allowed to say when representing his entire country overseas. Stryk might not have the pedigree, he said, or the education or even the expertise of America's best and brightest. But he also didn't operate under the same limitations.

"Let's say you're the under secretary for East African affairs and you've got a meeting in Kenya," he said. "You go in, you have this whole entourage, all your degrees, all these protocols, you can only say certain things. And then that meeting ends."

In this scenario, Stryk then swoops in with his freewheeling swagger and cowboy hat. "I come in, looking like this. I give him a bro-shake. He's got a scotch for me. He says, 'Okay, that was a wasted meeting, let's get down to business.' We fucking talk, we cuss, this and that. I get on the horn and I say, 'Okay, let me tell you what's really going on.' And then I'm the conduit bridge between the U.S. government and a foreign power."

Stryk imagined the State Department bureaucrats being jealous of him. They were making government salaries while he was making a fortune and, as he put it, "I'm hanging out, smoking cigars, drinking, and having intellectual and important conversations that they have spent their whole careers trying to get to."

There was a catch. When Stryk got these contracts from foreign governments, he had to register himself as a foreign agent. In his heart of hearts he might have been an American, but according to his pay stubs he was working for someone else. And sometimes that someone was a dictator or a kleptocrat. But he didn't have any moral qualms about working for infamous world leaders. He believed all engagement could be good engagement. It was one of the reasons he loved Donald Trump—that he seemed willing to meet with anyone.

"If I were offered a contract by Kim Jong-un," Stryk said, "I would accept it in 5.6 seconds."

North Korea never came calling, but others sought out Stryk to help them stay off sanctions lists, or in search of government funding, or at the very least the chance at a better relationship with the United States.

Stryk pulled out a chair in the basement bar, as if he were going to offer me a seat. He glanced around, wrinkled his nose. There had been a problem with the office's upstairs bathroom, he said, some kind of sewer leak.

"I'm really sorry about this," he said, using his cowboy hat to move the air around and then lighting two scented candles. "We have to get out of here; it smells like absolute shit."

* * *

Stryk's goal of "privatizing" American diplomacy was lofty to the point of being quixotic. Sometimes he would lower the scale of that particular ambition, saying that what he really wanted to be was a "supplement" to the government's foreign policy apparatus, but he talked a big game.

"The thing about Robert is that he says all these crazy things, and half the time it's bullshit, but the other half the time it's not," a former employee of his told me. "And because you never know which is going to be which, you can never fully count him out. He was sort of like Donald Trump in a way."

At the start of the Trump presidency, Stryk had launched himself on the scene with his work for New Zealand, and it paid off quickly. In early 2017, now fully on the scene, he was put in touch with the Saudi Arabian government, which was interested in his services. Shortly after that, Saudi Arabia wired the Sonoran Policy Group $5.4 million.

Stryk's bank account had been mostly empty for a decade, and at first, he said, the bank wouldn't accept the transfer. Stryk had to show up in person with a pile of paperwork to prove that this was real. Once the wire had cleared, the first call he made was to his mother. He asked her to log in to his bank account for him and take a look at what was there.

"Oh my God, what are you doing?" she said. "Where did this come from?"

It came from doing nothing. The $5.4 million was paid by Muhammed bin Nayef, the nephew of Saudi Arabia's former ruler, King Salman. Nayef had been thought of as a possible heir to the kingdom, but when Trump appeared to show favor to his rival, King Salman's son, Mohammed bin Salman, Nayef sought help in Washington—from Stryk's firm. By the time the king appointed MBS as crown prince, the money had already been paid in full, and Stryk said nobody ever asked him to pay any of it back. So he kept it.

As it often goes, making money gave Stryk the opportunity to make more money.

"All that money does is bolster my credibility that I'm a real player," he told me.

Stryk had a knack for talking his way into big contracts, according to one of his former employees. He'd show up in a black SUV, wearing designer jeans, fancy cowboy boots, and a scarf worthy of Aerosmith's Steven Tyler, and convince foreign leaders he could get things done for them.

At first, the employee recalled, a lot of their jobs consisted of trying to get photo opportunities for their clients with the newly elected president.

"Which was easy to do if you had an impressive enough client," the former employee said. "They probably could have gotten themselves the photos, but it basically cost them nothing to pay us to do it." But Stryk wasn't content just being a glorified scheduler. Stryk told me he helped broker a multibillion-dollar infrastructure deal between Kenya and the American engineering company Bechtel, despite the fact that Bechtel higher-ups didn't take him seriously at first. "They called me Billy Bob Thornton," he said.

In July 2018, Stryk organized a reception at the Hay-Adams hotel near the White House as part of a lobbying and PR campaign on behalf of the Democratic Republic of the Congo, led by Joseph Kabila, whose government was facing the possibility of additional sanctions for human rights abuses and corruption. News of this event would eventually appear on the front page of the *New York Times*, courtesy of the reporter Ken Vogel, who noted that Rudy Giuliani, then Trump's personal lawyer, was in attendance. When Vogel asked Giuliani if he had been there to serve as an intermediary between the DRC and the Trump administration, the former New York mayor said no, he was just there to "say hello to people" and impress a woman he had been dining with by taking her "to the top of the Hay-Adams to see a Washington party" with a "great view."

Later, he admitted that there could be some business opportunities worth exploring.

"We've always wanted to see what Africa's all about," he told Vogel.

Vogel also reported that in August of the same year, Stryk signed a $100,000-a-month contract with Somalia, which was trying to get the Trump administration to send it more military assistance, and that he ended the year with a $500,000-a-year contract to help the country of Bahrain to "facilitate meetings and interactions with U.S. administration officials." Stryk arranged one of those meetings with the country's ambassador and Giuliani, who by then had become a friend and unofficial business partner.

Giuliani's own dalliance with private diplomacy would, of course, end up becoming an international event, when his pressure campaign to get Ukraine to investigate Hunter Biden ended with President Trump's first impeachment. Stryk was largely spared from that ordeal, his name only getting mentioned tangentially after it was found on a piece of Ritz-Carlton stationery on which Giuliani associate Lev Parnas had written to himself, "Hire Robert Stryk lobbiest [*sic*]."

Why, and what for? Parnas never said. One of Giuliani's then-clients was Alejandro Betancourt López, a Venezuelan businessman, who had hosted Parnas and Giuliani at his castle outside of Madrid the previous summer. In 2020, the AP reported that Stryk had signed a $2 million contract with a top ally of Venezuelan President Nicolas Maduro.

"Why not engage?" Stryk said to me about Maduro. "Does he openly espouse the killing of Americans? No. Is he a terrorist? No. Is he a drug dealer? Possibly. Is he a socialist? One hundred percent. Is he a migrant, former baseball player who met Chávez and became president? Yes. Did I ever feel uneasy in his presence? No. If you ask our government, he is a murderous fucking dictator who slaughters his people, doesn't feed his people, and whatever...Is he a great guy? I don't know how to value what a good guy is. But is he better off as a friend or an enemy to us?"

Stryk thought he could help make Maduro a friend. And unlike much of Washington's diplomatic corps, he was willing to try.

"Most people, I believe, would die for the opportunity for the access I have," Stryk said. "The problem is, because there are so many strings attached in Washington, it will hurt your ability to get clients or social status...I can become a real valuable tool for my country. My value is I don't care what people think of me."

* * *

I left Middleburg, driving slowly on icy back roads, still unsure what to think about Stryk. Could this guy be a for-real diplomat?

It wasn't hard to imagine Stryk winning people over. I had enjoyed my time with him, and not just because he kept pouring me larger and larger glasses of whiskey at his farm. He was fun to be around. Self-deprecating. Off-the-cuff. Willing to chat for hours without going off the record. But I also remembered a conversation I'd recently had with an actual member of the Washington diplomatic corps, a man named Kurt Campbell. Campbell was an old Washington hand, having served as the assistant secretary of state for East Asian and Pacific affairs in the Obama administration, who had returned to duty to serve as Biden's so-called China Czar in the State Department. I had met with Campbell for breakfast a few months back, and he told me a story about a multibillion-dollar deal with the Japanese government nearly going kaput when the U.S. hosts had initially said they would not be offering food at an upcoming summit due to Covid-19 protocols.

"The Japanese found that very rude," Campbell said. Worried that the lack of hospitality could scuttle their talks, Campbell scrambled behind the scenes to find an acceptable meal to offer. He suggested sandwiches, but the Japanese asked for pancakes. Eventually they settled, Campbell said, "on the biggest fucking hamburgers known to man," which no one touched, but which were appreciated by their guests.

"People think diplomacy is just about the big things," Campbell told me, "but sometimes it's about the little things."

And as for Stryk, I did get the impression that attention to the little things wasn't necessarily his strong suit.

One evening not long after my visit to Building B, Stryk texted me. He asked how my book was coming along. I knew that he was getting a bit nervous about telling me his story. He had been misunderstood for so long, he had told me—disrespected for not being educated enough, looked down upon by the elite press and career government employees as just some sort of Trump hanger-on who lucked into a fortune. But he wasn't just checking in because he was curious about how my writing was going. He also wanted to let me know that if I didn't hear from him for a while, it wasn't because he was getting cold feet, but rather because he was just about to fly out of the country, having been called into a "hot spot" by a potential client. I texted him back that I was excited to hear how that all went.

"Dude you are a natural for this," he wrote back. "Unless you are Patrick Bateman you have a nice and genuine way about you that wants to learn and not judge people. And bc of that people want to speak with you and I think what you are writing about is something that someone without a bent should try and chronicle. So you will crush it and you might ruffle a few feathers along the way but it seems your heart and mind are in the right place which in this town puts you in the minority."

I admit, I was flattered. A little confused. Then Stryk called.

"Fuck, I'm a retard," he said. "I read your text wrong. You said I hope it goes well, and I thought you were talking about your stuff. So I was giving you my bullshit opinion. I apologize. I like meeting people, I like having friends, and sometimes I just vomit out of the mouth even though I shouldn't."

He had every right to be frazzled, it turned out. Russia was on the brink of invading Ukraine, possibly with the help of Belarus. The night before we texted, he had been contacted by the Belarusian government about the possibility of hiring his firm. Stryk didn't think an invasion would happen, but even if it did, he thought his brand of diplomacy could help avert disaster. Now he was on his way to Minsk to see if he "could help with whatever."

*   *   *

Vladimir Putin announced the commencement of a large-scale military operation. Tanks and troops entered Ukraine, bombings began, and thousands of Ukrainians fled for their lives. Stryk was in Belarus. I texted him for updates. (The exchange below has been condensed.)

Me: you alright?

Stryk: Hairy right now

Me: You safe though?

Stryk: Yes. Airspace closed trying to get a land route out of here

Stryk: Thanks again for checking in on me!!!! We have arrived the border after much intrigue and are highly confident they will open the border and let us in.

Stryk: Lithuania

Stryk: It's crazy I have to pinch myself I mean it's just nuts dude.

Me: I can't imagine. Does it feel like a war zone?

Stryk: It's surreal. I don't know what a war zone feels like.. but is a weird thing and most people had worried he would take Lithuania bc it would be an easy one for him and put him in a strategic place against the Poles. Our goal is to get to Warsaw but we are also talking about going into Kiev bc the opportunity is so great.

Me: Kiev?? Opportunity for what??

Stryk: There is nobody in what I do anywhere close to this chaos and shit show and I believe that a private solution can and will be achieved and will be the answer outside of WWIII

Me: Well, just be safe, dude. I'm on a plane now literally watching a CNN chyron about the thousands of people fleeing FROM Kiev.

Stryk: Where you headed?

Me: Florida for cpac.

Stryk: Oh wow they gave you credentials.

Me: You been in touch with your fam? They handling this ok?

Stryk: They are good my wife knows it's my passion, but I would rather be here than CPAC.

Stryk: Thanks buddy be safe yourself. Orlando at CPAC as a reporter can be rough. I wish these people actually cared about more than just destruction. I will be excited to hear what they think we should do over here. BC this crowd doesn't like alliances.

Stryk: The CPAC Crowd I meant.

Chapter 16

This Is a Great Intentional Smokescreen (Papa Bless)

Late winter 2022

Go suck the dick of the Queen!"

It was past midnight a few days after Russian troops had begun their invasion of Ukraine, and a skirmish was brewing by the pool of the Rosen Shingle Creek Resort in Orlando, Florida.

"I would defend Russia to the fucking end," shouted a college student from North Dakota. "Fuck you, you fucking NATO shill!"

Flecks of spittle flew out of his mouth. His hair was matted down with sweat and gel, and he kept clutching at the mostly empty wine bottle in front of him. The people sitting with him at the table threw up their arms and pushed away from the table.

The guy he was yelling at was British, and a lot more composed. He was standing, but still seemed committed to defusing the situation by continuing to talk as one might during a sit-down discussion. "So," he said, firmly but calmly, "you're going to defend the country that has blown up hospitals, schools, orphanages—"

The student interrupted.

"Yeah, you're going to defend the country that indiscriminately bombed the Donbas?"

He was standing now, too, and pointing a finger in the Brit's face. "Go suck off NATO, dude!"

I was at CPAC 2022, which happened to be starting just as war was breaking out in Eastern Europe. I'd come here because this conference had become the center of the Republican universe—home to the id and all the egos of the GOP. If Republicans had gone through a big break over the past decade, CPAC not only had done some of the breaking, but had come to reflect what the party had become in the aftermath. This year, Donald Trump was giving the keynote address, and the line of people who might run for president if he didn't were here to speak too: Ron DeSantis, Ted Cruz, Mike Pompeo, and Josh Hawley. The place was crawling with conservative entertainment stars—provocateurs like Candace Owens and Marjorie Taylor Greene—and the paying faithful, here for the show.

Not every exchange here had been quite as animated as this drunken kerfuffle, but this was also not completely out of character. With the war between Russia and Ukraine so new, the Republican Party seemed a bit unsure of how to respond, and so—as has been the case ever since Trump first appeared as the standard-bearer on a debate stage—there was a lot of yelling.

A crowd had started to gather around. And because CPAC was lousy with journalists, influencers, and aspiring media personalities, everyone was filming on their phones. The conference program ran from morning to early evening, but really, a video-worthy event could happen anywhere and at any time.

"You want war in Eastern Europe?" the student from North Dakota shouted. "Fuck you!"

"The only people who want war in Eastern Europe are the Russians," the Brit responded.

"Why don't you go back to Britain," North Dakota shouted. "This is my country, not yours."

Marc Caputo, a mop-topped reporter with NBC, crept through the bushes for some close-ups.

The argument had turned heads all around the outdoor bar, and had gotten the attention of James Linen, a white-haired former vice chairman of the American Conservative Union—the organization Matt Schlapp now ran—who was sitting a table over.

In the 1980s, Linen shared a CPAC stage with Ronald Reagan. Now he drew on whatever diplomatic authority he might have here, poolside at the Rosen Shingle Creek Resort, in 2022, to calm the tempers.

"Listen to me," Linen said. "Late-night drinking and seriousness are fucking alien to each other. Don't do it."

North Dakota wasn't having it.

"This guy is a UK citizen and you're going to have his back?" he shouted. "Redcoats out!"

The bespectacled Brit, perhaps seeing an opportunity to gain the upper hand by way of reason, reached into the front pocket of his blazer and pulled out two passports as proof of his dual citizenship. He held them up to Caputo's camera and smirked.

Linen turned his attention to all the rubbernecking cell phone videographers.

"Don't take videos of people arguing," he said. "It's not polite." Switching into a more contemporary vernacular, he added, "Take those videos and delete them; it's fucking loser bullshit."

Around this moment, as the student was telling the Brit to perform sex acts on Her Majesty, Linen noticed Caputo, who had moved out of the shrubbery into the thick of the argument. He tried to grab the journalist's phone. Caputo was having none of it. Before anyone could realize what was happening, Caputo smacked him with an open-handed jab. Linen's head snapped back.

"Did you fucking hit me in the face?" Linen asked.

"I was defending myself," Caputo said.

"Redcoats out! Redcoats out!" North Dakota shouted.

I'd been watching this all unfold from about twenty feet away, standing beside Jon Allen, a bestselling author of campaign books. And now, suddenly, Allen wasn't beside me anymore, and had maneuvered his way in between Linen and Caputo. Standing a head taller than anyone else, Allen didn't lay a hand on anyone, instead relying on his big body to keep the peace. Marc kept filming. The student had retreated to another table, away from the action, and was pointing at the hotel and shouting, "There were rats in there! NATO rats have infested the conference."

This year's version of the conference, which typically serves as a pep rally for the culture war, had been disrupted by the specter of an actual war. It was obvious who the good guys and the bad guys were. Russia's attack on Ukraine was unprovoked and horrifying. The problem for Republicans was that for the past five years, being on the team meant agreeing with everything President Donald Trump said. And Donald Trump had mostly positive things to say about Russian President Vladimir Putin.

In 2007 he said Putin was doing a "great job" in Russia, in 2013 he wondered in a tweet whether the Russian leader would someday be his "new best friend," and more recently he'd called him "smart" and "savvy." He once bragged about his relationship with Putin while onstage at CPAC.

"You know, I was in Moscow a couple of months ago, I own the Miss Universe Pageant, and they treated me so great," Trump said in 2014. "Putin even sent me a present, a beautiful present."

Republicans had seemed willing to go along with all this for a time, especially when they were beating back claims that a covert Russian propaganda campaign had helped manipulate American voters during the 2016 election. But this was an actual war. This was a nuclear power invading a sovereign country at the edge of Europe, and threatening to end seven decades of relative peace and prosperity in the Western world since World War II.

On the other hand, Trump had said what Putin had done was

"genius," probably because the invasion might make the guy who beat Trump look weak.

And so, in the foggiest early days of the war, conservatives seemed at a loss for what to say.

Mike Pompeo, a former Trump secretary of state who wanted to be president one day, had echoed Trump's "genius" line, which was then echoed by Russian state media. A memo from the Kremlin—which was obtained by the liberal magazine *Mother Jones*—showed that the Russian government was also urging the propaganda networks to showcase segments from Tucker Carlson, the Fox News host, who in 2019 said this on air: "Why do I care what is going on in the conflict between Ukraine and Russia?"

"And I'm serious," he added later. "Why shouldn't I root for Russia? Which I am."

Here at CPAC, Ohio Senate candidate J. D. Vance, who had already done an interview saying he didn't really care about Ukraine, took the stage and complained about the media and the left being more preoccupied with a Russian border than they were the American border with Mexico.

"Why should we care about Ukraine?" Florida Representative Matt Gaetz asked onstage.

"This is a great intentional smokescreen on the part of the Biden administration to take the focus off our problems at home," the pizza tycoon John "Papa John" Schnatter told me when I bumped into him wandering around the various CPAC booths.

Yes, Papa John had a speaking slot. A few years earlier, Schnatter, a Trump donor and Republican fundraiser, had resigned as chairman of the chain of pizza restaurants he founded after it came out that he used the n-word on a conference call with a marketing company. Schnatter had explained that he uttered the slur in service of a point he was trying to make about how the real Colonel Sanders was a racist, but he apologized no matter what the context. The marketing company on the other end of the call cut ties with him. Papa John's name came down from the stadium at the University of Louisville.

Anyway, now he was here, wearing extremely flared jeans. In addition to giving a speech, he might have been attempting to resurrect himself as a meme: Somebody reported having seen Schnatter stickers on tables around the Rosen Shingle Creek Resort. The stickers showed a smiling Schnatter draped with vestments, his head encircled by a halo that is actually a pepperoni pie, with the words "Papa Bless."

Whether or not he blessed any sticker bombing, Papa did seem to bless some kind of *Wag the Dog* theory about Russia's invasion being a sham. The idea that the Biden administration was somehow manufacturing Putin's war on Ukraine was a strange thing to suggest, but really it wasn't that much different than Trump calling Putin a "genius" for a move that might embarrass Biden. The Trump political movement was almost completely oriented to painting its *domestic* enemies in the worst possible light—even if that meant taking what it could get from foreign powers considered adversarial to the interests of America and the liberal democracies of the West.

Ultimately Republicans did settle on a message about Russia: What Putin was doing was reprehensible, and the fact that Putin was doing it at all was Biden's fault.

"I wonder, if Donald Trump were still president, would Putin be doing this?" the British politician Nigel Farage asked of Senator Ted Cruz in an interview.

"No," Cruz said. "I think there's no chance. I had dinner with Donald Trump last night. I think the chances that Putin would be invading Ukraine today are essentially zero."

On this, everyone at CPAC could agree. Everyone here believed Donald Trump was a better president than Joe Biden. But that wasn't the only question being asked.

Jordan Klepper, a correspondent for *The Daily Show* on Comedy Central, roamed the halls of the conference asking attendees whether they would rather have Joe Biden or Vladimir Putin as their president. Klepper put the question to a man who, as it turned out, was running for office in Virginia.

So Biden or Putin?

The man responded in a meek voice.

"Trump?"

Chapter 17

Welcome to the Canceled Hall of Fame

Late winter 2022

In the middle of the CPAC exhibition hall, somewhere between the booth selling books of Donald Trump's tweets and the booth trying to ban books with "adult themes" from school libraries, Matt Schlapp sat at a folding table signing copies of his own book, *The Desecrators*.

"It's the story of the radical left trying to destroy the country and how to fight back," Matt said, handing one to an attendee. "And it's also the story of our own cancellation."

By 2022, it had started to feel like everyone had a story about being canceled—and that everyone defined the term differently. In my mind, to be canceled meant suffering an extreme public shaming that ruined the trajectory of a person's life. Justine Sacco, *she* was canceled. Sacco was the young communications staffer who, before boarding a plane to Africa in 2013, tweeted, "Hope I don't get AIDS. Just kidding. I'm white." Her tweet had gone viral while she was still up in the air, trending with the hashtag #HasJustineLandedYet. By the time she'd landed, she was the most talked-about person on Twitter, mostly due to people calling for her to lose her job. She lost her job.

The term "canceled" wasn't used much back during the Sacco saga, but "Call-Out Culture" was becoming a thing. At first it seemed almost righteous, knowing that all those bad bosses, racist dog walkers, and celebrities who were rude to restaurant workers had to watch their step. But mob justice wasn't perfect. Sometimes the wrong people got blamed for things, just because they looked like some asshole in a viral video, or shared the same name. Some punishments didn't really fit the crime. Did Justine Sacco deserve to lose a job and her reputation over one dumb joke?

Soon there was a cancel culture backlash, and politicians ready to capitalize on said backlash. Conservatives especially were always complaining about cancel culture *run amok*—which mostly just meant that some portion of the population had taken offense to something offensive they had said. It wasn't a new tactic, exactly. Republicans had been yelling about "political correctness" for years and had essentially made defund the "PC Police" a party platform.

"The wave of cancel culture spreading the nation is a serious threat to fundamental free speech," the congressman Jim Jordan wrote in a 2021 letter to the House Committee on the Judiciary calling for a committee hearing on the subject. He had certain examples in mind: a *New York Times* editor who resigned after publishing a controversial column from a Republican senator; Trump being "de-platformed" from Twitter; guests being disinvited from college speaking engagements. The Michigan Republican Party included different examples in the "Cancel Culture Hall of Fame" section of their website: Abraham Lincoln (some students at some college wanted to take down a statue, but failed), Mr. Potato Head (Hasbro decided to drop the "Mr." from the brand name), and Tucker Carlson (whose show, as of this writing, had not been canceled).

Democrats would sometimes try to turn the tables on Republicans, pointing out (rightfully!) that it was conservatives who were out there banning books from libraries, threatening teachers who taught about America's racist past, and passing "Don't Say Gay" bills in Florida. Other than that, though, liberals tended to try and avoid talking about cancel culture, and certainly tried to avoid being canceled themselves as there were fewer business opportunities on the left for that kind of thing.

Former Senator Al Franken got to host a podcast after allegations of groping, but that wasn't better than being *current* Senator Al Franken. And after TJ Ducklo was "canceled" from his job as the White House deputy press secretary after threatening a reporter, he found work as a crisis communications expert in New York. He got a job working for Risa Heller, the former Chuck Schumer aide who picked up controversial clients like former Representative Anthony Weiner and Jared Kushner. Heller loved telling newly canceled clients that TJ had been canceled too, as a way to put them at ease. But part of what made TJ a Democrat was that he would rather never talk about any of this ever again. And part of what made Matt Schlapp a Republican was that he did.

In 2020, the so-called mob came for Matt. It began with an article written by a liberal muckraker named Judd Legum, which he had headlined A SCHLAPP IN THE FACE.

Legum—a reporter who once edited the lefty website Think Progress and now penned his own investigative newsletter—had reported that in the wake of George Floyd's murder, companies like Verizon, Comcast, and Walmart had claimed to be advocates of the Black Lives Matter movement, and yet were still paying for Matt's lobbying services. This was a problem, Legum wrote, considering that Matt had recently said BLM was "hostile to families, capitalism, cops, unborn life and gender" and had used the expression "All lives matter"—a phrase often uttered by anti-BLM activists—in a tweet.

Legum's first post pointed out Verizon's supposed hypocrisy, and when reached for comment, the communications giant severed ties with Cove Strategies, Matt's lobby shop. One by one, after a series of follow-up posts, each company ended their business relationships with Schlapp, and by 2021 his contract money went from $2.4 million to just $390,000.

Still, the ordeal had an upside. The Schlapps were obvious creatures of the Swamp and had often been looked at skeptically by the MAGA masses. Perhaps the cancellation could give Mansion Drive homeowners a sheen of relatability.

It had become quite clear, looking around CPAC Orlando, that the biggest draws were people who had been kicked off various media platforms: CPAC panelist Alex Berenson, banned by Twitter for violating its rules on Covid misinformation (Berenson sued); CPAC speaker Representative Matt Gaetz, who was having a hell of a time getting on television lately with the investigation into alleged sex trafficking hanging over him (While Gaetz would ultimately not face any charges, at the time his friend Representative Ken Buck of Colorado said, "It's been hard on him. Fox News has really kept their distance from him."); and of course, keynote speaker Donald Trump, banned from Twitter and indefinitely suspended from Facebook after January 6th, when his lies about the election culminated in a violent siege on the Capitol.

The canceled were everywhere I looked at CPAC.

They were on the fourteenth floor of the hotel, in Matt's "presidential suite" after-party: Caroline Wren, a Republican fundraiser, standing by the billiards table, cursing the name of a *Washington Post* reporter who detailed Wren's role in organizing the January 6th Stop the Steal rally.

"That bitch!" Wren said, wearing a hat that simply said "Subpoenaed."

Matt was trying his best to get canceled, sitting on a plush leather chair, responding to the suggestion that Senator Tim Scott might make a good vice presidential pick for Trump.

"You think he picks a gay vice president?" Matt said. "You think that's going to work out great? I'm okay with it, if you're okay with it?"

There had never been reports of Scott being gay—take it from me, a reporter who once asked the senator about his virginity. The joke said much more about Matt and his complicated feelings about homosexuality. Publicly, he had been more accepting of gay people than much of the CPAC universe, announcing from the start of his tenure at the ACU that gay conservatives were all "welcome" and taking meetings with groups like the Log Cabin Republicans, an advocacy group of gay conservatives.

But privately things were more complicated. Ross Hemminger, a former CPAC spokesman, once told me that in 2015 he had asked Matt if he would ever attend a gay wedding. This was a question being asked of Republican candidates for president at the time, and Hemminger thought Matt should have a good answer prepared for himself. But Hemminger was also curious because he was himself a gay conservative—something he was open about with Matt—and he and Matt had become close work associates.

"He said he would never attend a gay wedding," Hemminger said. "And then I asked, 'Well, you'd come to mine, though, right?'"

Hemminger was surprised and hurt when Matt still said no.

"I don't think he's a bigot or a homophobe," Hemminger told me. "I think he's conflicted."

Once, after Matt angered certain right-wingers by referring to a trans swimmer by her preferred pronoun and saying "her story deserves compassion" on Twitter, I called him to ask about it.

"I'm not a big trans advocate," he told me. He said he had been moved by the swimmer's father's love for his child.

"I don't know what his politics are," he said about the father, "but I think that's how I would be. I don't want my kids to be gay. People might call me a bigot for saying that but I really don't want them to be. But if they are, what am I going to do? Fight with them every Thanksgiving? Make it so they don't come over to my house?"

Now, at the CPAC after-party, Matt laughed at his own joke, drink in hand. Last year at one of these parties, Matt had had so many martinis ("Hold the vermouth!") that he announced his intention to bust into Disney World and "raid the Magic Kingdom." That was when his daughter cut him off.

Drinking: *canceled*.

Outside the CPAC resort, among the ticket-paying attendees, Libby Hilsenrath smoked a cigarette. She had come from New Jersey and was currently in the midst of a five-year lawsuit against her son's public school, which she accused of showing a video that promoted Islam. Now she felt canceled by her hometown and family— her neighbors didn't want anything to do with her; even her own son couldn't stand her. Hilsenrath was standing beside another woman, Robin Patch, who nearly got canceled on the flight over when she had accidentally set off the smoke alarm after going to the bathroom to hit her THC vape. When the plane landed, the cops arrived and threatened to cancel her right to jail.

"I had to play the vagina card to get here," said Patch, who was wearing a bright pink dress and bold red lipstick. "I started yelling, 'I'm on my period! I'm on my period! None of you have a vagina! I'm the only one here with a vagina and it's bleeding!'"

"So what happened?" Hilsenrath asked.

"It wasn't true," said Patch, a candidate for city council in Southern California. "I mean, it's true that I have a vagina—I don't just *identify* as a woman—it just wasn't bleeding."

"But what happened?" Hilsenrath asked.

"It worked!" Patch said. "Nothing was going to keep me from getting here today!"

Patch: uncanceled.

Marjorie Taylor Greene: uncancelable.

Here she came now, power-walking through the hotel on the second full day of the conference, followed by a throng of reporters.

"Congresswoman, how do you justify going to a White nationalist, Hitler-sympathizing, pro-Putin event last night?"

Greene had just finished her panel called "They Can't Shut Us Up." Her security detail, made up of local police and various members of her staff, formed a human shield. Onlookers turning toward the entourage might spot flashes of blond hair zipping past the media booths, where television, radio, and right-wing podcast programs had set up to broadcast the many insights of people like Seb Gorka, the former Trump official and current fish oil supplement salesman; and John Fredericks, a former newspaperman and cochair of Trump's Virginia campaign, who called himself "the Godzilla of Truth."

Greene, a freshman representing a Georgia district northwest of Atlanta, was her own kind of rampaging presence in the political metropolis. She came to Washington after openly trafficking in QAnon conspiracies, a mosaic of right-wing fringe theories that was loosely organized around the idea that Democrats are devil worshippers and child molesters and that Donald Trump was the savior who was going to protect the world from perdition. (The FBI has called the movement a domestic terrorism threat.) Since getting to the Hill, she had shown a penchant for trolling her colleagues, pulling stunts like yelling through the mail slot on the office door of Democrat Representative Alexandria Ocasio-Cortez, and recording herself saying "Joe Biden isn't a president; he's a piece of shit."

Greene presented a theoretical dilemma at a place like this, which was nominally against "canceling" people (unless they criticized Trump, or Trump criticized them. See: Romney, Mitt). If you think of the House GOP as less a legislative caucus than a right-wing website, she was the comments section come to life. If Republican leaders were expected to be the moderators, they had mostly left their stations.

And anyway, past attempts to check MTG's behavior hadn't done much to bring her in line. When the Democrat-led House of Representatives stripped her of her committee assignments—a meaningful punishment for any congressperson trying to get things done—the move only raised her profile. She gleefully accepted the punishment, like a school-skipping student might welcome an at-home suspension. Plus, it gave her a fresh example of how Washington simply can't stand her, which is true and also a reliable message with Republican donors, who showered Greene with money. Only a year into her first term in Congress, Greene was a celebrity. Trump loved her. Today there were even more press around her than usual. And she wasn't stopping to give any of us the time of day.

"Congresswoman, this is serious," NBC's Vaughn Hillyard said, walking backward and somehow avoiding tripping over anyone.

Greene's latest offense: The night before appearing here at CPAC, she spoke at a nearby event organized by Nick Fuentes, a self-described White nationalist whose views are so extreme that Schlapp and the other CPAC organizers have banned him from their conference. He's the leader of a group that calls themselves Groypers—whose aim, according to the Southern Poverty Law Center, is to attack Republicans from the right until they become a "truly reactionary" party and recognize that America's "White demographic core" is central to its identity. Fuentes was currently trying to apply pressure to Republicans by hosting his own event, the America First Political Action Conference, at the same time as CPAC, just a few miles down the road.

The Russian invasion of Ukraine had been a topic of discussion at that conference too, but there was no confusion about whose side Fuentes was on. The previous night, he had taken the stage at the America First conference with a Cheshire Cat grin and said that the media is "saying, 'Vladimir Putin is Adolf Hitler. They say that's not a good thing.'"

The crowd, made up largely of a few hundred young men, had chanted Putin's name.

After that, Greene had spoken to the same crowd, remarking on how important it was that they be included in America's political discourse.

"You know what it's like to be canceled," the Georgia congresswoman had told them. "That's why I'm here to talk to you tonight. I don't believe anyone should be canceled."

Now, at CPAC, Greene in an act of self-cancellation refused to answer any questions. She kept walking through the massive resort, past the mingling attendees, past the long line at the coffee shop, and past the Mexican restaurant with tables full of people drinking margaritas the size of their heads. She ducked behind a curtain, into a VIP area.

"You attended knowingly," Hillyard tried again. "Are you a White nationalist?"

But it was no use. Greene was hiding out in the enclosure, huddling with her entourage—safe in the warm embrace of CPAC.

Here, too, was Mike Lindell, the former cocaine addict who founded the company MyPillow, holding forth in the hotel lobby and signing autographs for days on end. Lindell had shown more commitment to Trump's "stolen election" narrative than pretty much anyone outside Trump himself. The upside: The Republican base loved him for it. The downside: He was currently on the receiving end of a $1.3 billion defamation lawsuit filed by Dominion Voting Systems for making allegedly defamatory claims about the election technology company amid his crusade to get Trump reinstalled in the White House. As a result, he no longer got to speak on Fox News, nor did he have access to traditional social media accounts. But he had Lindell TV. And he had CPAC, where he was swarmed by fans wherever he went.

"Being canceled, I've used that to get the message out," I overheard the motor-mouthed pillow magnate telling an attendee.

Matt and Mercy were getting the message out too.

"I learned something about Matt and Mercy Schlapp that I didn't really know," Deal W. Hudson, who coauthored the *Desecrators* book, said onstage with Matt and Mercy. "What they have sacrificed to run this organization. How they have been threatened. How they have lost money."

"My question for you is this," he continued, shouting from the stage, channeling his inner fire-and-brimstone preacher. "Do you have their back?"

His voice grew solemn.

"Here's what you do," he said. "You pray for them. You buy the book, which, by the way, is on discount here."

Chapter 18

Trying to Transcend the Morass of Shit

Early spring 2022

Shortly after CPAC Orlando, I headed back to the home of Ian and Carin Walters in rural Maryland to hear about how Ian's own story of being canceled started him on a path that eventually led to self-imposed exile.

"The first damn thing that really changed everything was the Michael Steele event," Ian said. We were in his kitchen, and Ian was leaning on the counter, thinking back to 2018. It was then that Matt asked Ian to speak at CPAC's signature event, the Ronald Reagan Dinner. Ian had been working on and off for the ACU for two decades, and Matt wanted to recognize his loyalty and longevity. It was supposed to be a capstone moment in the early phase of Ian's career. Instead, it was a disaster.

In his speech, Ian looked back to the year 2008. It was a difficult time to be a Republican back then, Ian said. His party was lost in the wilderness, and Obama had just been elected president. In the speech, Ian said that electing a Black person to the White House was both a "big deal" and "something we were all proud of." But the way Republicans responded, Ian said, had been embarrassing.

"We weren't sure what to do," he said. "And in a little bit of cynicism, what did we do? This is a terrible thing: We elected Michael Steele to be the RNC chair because he's a Black guy, and that was the wrong thing to do."

After the speech, he headed to the back of the room, where the bass player of the house band complimented his performance. Ian had felt good about it too. Then, a colleague told him he was trending on Twitter. A liberal website had picked up the remarks and said that there had been an "audible gasp" in the room when Ian had delivered the line about Steele.

Ian quickly reached Steele on his cell phone and tried to apologize. Steele did not accept his apology, instead accusing Ian of being "part of Jim Crow" before hanging up the phone. Ian crumpled onto the floor and cried.

NPR covered the flap under the headline THE REPUBLICAN PARTY'S "RACISM PROBLEM."

FORMER REPUBLICAN CHAIRMAN IS DONE WITH RACIST INSULTS, the magazine *Mother Jones* reported.

On MSNBC, Steele talked about not accepting Ian's attempted apology, calling it "just not acceptable enough."

Ian couldn't quite believe what was happening. Maybe it was naive to have thought that, as a person of color, he could speak about race without being called a racist. Maybe he thought that people would understand that he wasn't criticizing Steele per se, but what he saw as a cynical selection process by Republicans. Steele *had* had a rocky tenure leading the Republican National Committee. He had been run out of the job in part because he had allowed RNC staff members to expense trips to strip clubs. But that wasn't the point. "My beef was never with Steele," Ian wrote in a damage-control essay for *The Hill* newspaper titled "Talking About Race Isn't Racist." Rather, he wrote,

"It is with those Republican leaders who cheaply believed that elevating him meant that there was no need to talk any further about our failures on race, as a party and as a nation."

But Ian wasn't able to spin out of the skid, not even with his two decades of political-comms experience. Liberals were disposed to see him as another racist Republican who couldn't be bothered with bringing Black people into the party, and establishment Republicans were disposed to see him as another example of how Donald Trump's influence had made more and more Republicans talk like assholes. The damage was not confined to Ian's professional spheres.

Ian was a spokesman by day and a musician by night. The side hustle didn't pay for shit, but it was a way to keep sane. He loved music, and as a whiz on the keys, he could always find bands in need of a piano player. Sometimes the gigs would be playing jazz standards at holiday markets or upscale restaurants in Old Town Alexandria. Occasionally he'd play rock covers down at an outdoor venue next to the Washington Nationals ballpark that would fill up with day drinkers before weekend games. But Ian's favorite spot to play music was the Wonderland Ballroom, a dive bar in Columbia Heights—a residential neighborhood with two main drags of bars and restaurants. Wonderland, like many of the spots running up and down 11th and 14th Streets, served an eclectic clientele of regulars but was mostly known for the type of young professionals who change into flannel shirts to grab beer and shot specials after work. It served greasy eggplant fries on its large outdoor patio, and the upstairs of the bar hosted hipster dance parties, live podcast tapings, and concerts.

It was generally a left-leaning crowd. Some people knew Ian was a conservative (the NRA bumper sticker on his car was a bit of an outlier). But Ian was welcome anyway. When the bar celebrated its thirteenth birthday in the summer of 2017, Ian was on the Facebook invite: "Our house musician, Ian Walters, will drunkenly be playing music, INCLUDING his very own song 'Nick's Mom,' an ode to his least favorite Wonderland bartender's mother set to the tune of 'Piano Man.'"

But when the news broke about his Steele comments a year later, Ian was no longer welcome.

"They put out a public statement about me," Ian said about the bar.

He fell into a depression that lasted well into 2019. Carin was patient, as always, but all the moping around took a toll on her too. For the first time in his adult life, Ian started to wonder whether this life in politics was really worth it anymore. The playing field was dark—darker than he had noticed before. "This was not the fun endeavor I had begun in high school working at talk radio stations and stuff like that," he said. "I know it's not supposed to be a carnival and fun all the time. This is a serious business. But to ruin someone's life and reputation and career prospects—to be on the receiving end of that was devastating."

Did Ian really not know what politics had become before it came for him? It wasn't a recent phenomenon. Ian's very own early heroes included Patrick Buchanan—who wrote a book about "immigrant invasions" imperiling Western civilization—and Rush Limbaugh, a conservative bully who called feminists "feminazis" and ridiculed his own fans as "dittoheads." Ian had also spent two decades working for CPAC—a sort of birther place for Trump's political journey. In 2011, Trump teased a presidential run that never materialized, but which started his eventual path to the White House. In 2013, on the heels of his hunt for Obama's birth certificate—a racist play to make the then-president seem less American—Trump returned to tell the audience that America had become a "laughingstock."

What had happened to Ian was minor in the scheme of things. He didn't actually lose his job. Matt Schlapp stood with him, and Ian continued to speak at CPAC events and lead a growing team of press aides there. The MAGA crowd was in his corner. Still, being canceled had felt personal to Ian, and it was changing the way he saw the world and he didn't know how to handle it.

"Maybe other people would have parlayed that into a 'free-speech tour' on college campuses," he said about his so-called cancellation.

"Maybe they could have parlayed that into an 'I've been canceled' tour. But not me."

He certainly could have gotten himself a choice speaking slot at the previous CPAC with a story like that.

"I could have," he said. "But I'm trying to transcend the morass of shit."

Chapter 19

The Billionaire's Brother

I spent a lot of the last year staring into the eyes of politicians," Gabe Bankman-Fried said. "And I don't think it's a hopeless endeavor. I mean, you get a sense for who is legit."

Gabe sat in a swivel chair in a sparsely furnished office, in a mostly empty $3 million Capitol Hill row house that served as the new headquarters for Guarding Against Pandemics. A floor below, three young women were perched on a built-in window seat in the kitchen, ordering "plant-based" food for themselves and Gabe. The weather was nice, so they talked about eating it outside, on the 1,000-square-foot terrace that the organization planned to use for fundraisers and meet-and-greets with Hill staffers and their bosses. Gabe—much like his billionaire brother—lived with roommates. He basically lived in a closet, he liked to say. But this house had a bedroom ("for zoning purposes"), and Gabe had been staying there more and more often. Gabe looked a bit like his brother, but shorter, with a bit more stubble, and closer-cropped hair. He was smirking now as he told me about his methods for figuring out whether a politician was full of shit.

Politicians had been seeking meetings with him for months now, trying to get the GAP endorsement and presumably some of the money that would flow toward them afterward. Gabe's job was to figure out which of these candidates actually cared about preventing pandemics, and which of them just pretended to.

Being a gatekeeper to his brother's fortune was a relatively new experience for Gabe. He had graduated from Brown University in 2017, and quickly got a job on Wall Street as a trader. He'd started in finance, he said, as part of an "earn-to-give" philosophy—a tenet of effective altruism that encourages people to make as much money as they can so that they can give it away. But Gabe left after eight months, determining that he could do more for the causes he cared about by actually working on them.

He moved to Washington, D.C., took a data consulting job at Civis Analytics—where he worked under David Shor—and then moved into a legislative correspondent job in the House of Representatives. The Bankman-Frieds had come from a political family: Their mother was a law professor at Stanford, who started the Mind the Gap organization, which helped move millions of dollars into Democratic causes, and their father, also a law professor at Stanford, had achieved a small amount of fame for his personal crusade against companies like Intuit and H&R Block to make filing taxes easier—and free. At the start of his job on the Hill, in 2019, Gabe was making $40,000 a year. He wrote a lot of letters. He saw, from a distance, how things got done in Congress. For the most part, members really only cared about a couple of issues and the rest of their decisions were farmed out. Often they would vote certain ways on legislation because the Speaker of the House told them to and they didn't have any reason not to go with what the boss said. Other times, members and their chiefs could be swayed by a convincing or well-heeled lobbying operation. There were a lot of meetings among top staff in the office for this reason. But no one wanted a meeting with him.

Now that he and his brother were well on their way to spending $70 million over the past year on campaign donations and other initiatives, Gabe's days were all meetings: with candidates, with Chuck Schumer, with top White House officials. He knew they only really wanted to talk to him because of the money—to "kiss the ring, or whatever"— but he didn't care. He was happy to watch them "debase" themselves for a possible payday, as long as he got a chance to speak. They were the hottest new thing in Democratic politics—donors on the scale of a George Soros, and open for business.

There was obviously a serious issue at the heart of this, but listening to Gabe talk reminded me of the way people talked about their fantasy football teams. He and his brother had so much money to play with— to stock their rosters—it basically was just that to them: play money. They didn't seem to have a definitive rubric for what kind of candidate they were willing to support—all a politician needed to do for a chance at an endorsement was convince Gabe that they had pandemic preparedness as a top-five issue, and that they'd given some thought to the matter.

Sometimes politicians came in completely unprepared, which surprised Gabe. There was the time that Nikki Fried, Florida's agriculture commissioner running against Charlie Crist in the primary for governor, took a meeting with Gabe and, in his telling, prattled on with her stump speech without talking about pandemics at all.

"One thing she did mention many times on the call was how Jewish she was," Gabe said. "She saw my name—no relation, by the way— and thought I'd find that compelling. It was the only way she customized her pitch."

She asked for $3 million. Gabe had been laughing about this ever since.

Still, Gabe would rather have people asking him for unholy sums of money than not want to talk to him at all. Because for whatever reason, people in Washington had a hard time listening when the conversation went to pandemics. It wasn't clear that politicians were willing to spend money getting the country out of the current pandemic, let alone allocate funds for the next one.

In 2021, as part of a proposed infrastructure bill, Biden had allocated a $30 billion investment to mitigate the risks of future outbreaks.

The money would have gone to face mask and respirator production, replenishing medical stockpiles that had been decimated by Covid, and to proactive development of vaccines. Considering we were still in the midst of an ongoing pandemic—one that had killed hundreds of thousands of Americans already—Gabe thought that maybe there could be bipartisan agreement that such spending was necessary. He believed there was a chance that in our lifetime there would be a pandemic that would make Covid look like the chickenpox by comparison. He worried that he may be alive to see a virus wipe out 10 percent of the population. Other people in Washington? Not so worried. The money was some of the first to be slashed during negotiations.

Gabe made it his mission to make sure that money didn't end up on the negotiating room floor. Gabe was three years younger than his brother, Sam, and the two weren't particularly close growing up. But they had become closer as adults, and perhaps more important, they were inextricably linked in the public eye. There could be problems with this—GAP could get defined in the shadows of Gabe's famous brother. People would believe that it was just a front for Sam to buy crypto-friendly members of Congress. Gabe had wanted GAP to be a nonpartisan organization, but would anyone see it that way if Sam gave away hundreds of millions of dollars to Democrats?

"So, um, yeah," Gabe said, swiveling around in his office chair and scratching at his stubble. "There are some downsides to being associated with a billionaire. People write about the other stuff that he's doing."

But Gabe was willing to bet that the upsides far outweighed the downsides.

"I think it's a net positive," he said.

And at first, they seemed to be. When, for example, Gabe called every person in politics he knew to plead the case for $30 billion in pandemic prevention money, people took the calls. He was mostly a "one-man advocacy group," but Gabe did bring in some help, including Sean McElwee, who had his own network to "socialize" the importance of the legislation. Sean might not have known a ton about pandemic prevention, but he had a real knack for political marketing. Once, on a conference call, Gabe's team was trying to put into words why it was so tough to convince legislators to allocate money to prevent a future pandemic.

"The problem is," Sean said, "you can't hold a press conference in front of a pandemic that never happened."

Gabe liked Sean's style. He liked that Sean seemed to know lots of people and was shameless about promotion—of the self-varietal and otherwise. Gabe would sometimes show up to Sean's poker nights. Once, he brought his dad, who was visiting from California. Another time, Gabe polled the table on whether or not his brother's crypto exchange, FTX, should take money from Saudi Arabia (the two people who told me about this said they'd found it odd that Gabe, a guy who claimed not to be involved with crypto, felt comfortable seeking advice on the subject from a group of Washington insiders he hardly knew).

Gabe even liked Sean's political gambling habit. Sure, there might be ethical concerns, or at the very least the *perception* of ethical concerns, but assigning probability to outcomes was actually kind of a tenet of effective altruism—a way to keep yourself honest about the outcomes of your actions.

"I think it's really good practice," he said. "I was a trader on Wall Street and it's a big part of the culture. You have to be able to defend your claims."

In fact, Gabe said, if he had the choice between hiring a pollster who made bets on PredictIt and one who did not, he would be inclined to choose the gambler.

"But I think I'm abnormal in that way," he said.

Gabe never bothered trading on PredictIt, he said. There just wasn't enough money to make it worth his time, what with the $850 cap on markets. Such limits didn't exist if he were to gamble on the crypto exchanges, but Gabe said he couldn't do that since technically it wasn't legal for U.S. customers. Plus he got an adrenaline rush on what felt like an existential wager on whether the country would safeguard itself or not.

Gabe lost that bet. He'd hoped for $30 billion. He got zero.

Gabe realized he could get people to listen to him, but getting them to act would require more than a persuasive argument. And so going forward, he took a different approach. He knew that Democrats scrunched up their noses at money in politics, but he was of the opinion that there wasn't nearly enough of it. There was an article he read somewhere, he said, about how Americans spent more money on almonds each year than they did on candidates. He thought politics was more important than almonds. So he was willing to do his part to help bridge the spending gap.

"I think a lot of politics is getting people to do the right thing for the wrong reasons," he said.

Now that he was a rainmaker—or at least the assistant to the rainmaker—people would hear what he had to say. Just as long as the money didn't dry out.

Chapter 20

Look at This Coalition

Spring 2022

In early May, Leah Hunt-Hendrix invited me to her home and told me that she and the Bankman-Frieds had come to a sort of detente.

The new boyfriend, Marvin, had been incredibly helpful on this, Leah explained. Marvin was a big shot in the crypto world, so when he had called folks at a crypto-aligned super PAC (one to which Sam Bankman-Fried had donated $2 million), they were willing to listen to what he had to say. They had almost seemed starstruck to hear from him, Marvin would tell me later, and asked if he would be willing to advise them. He said he would and that his first advice was not to spend against one of Leah's preferred candidates—Maxwell Alejandro Frost, a twenty-five-year-old Afro-Latino activist, musician, and former Bernie staffer from Florida who stood a good chance of becoming the first member of Gen Z elected to Congress.

"I told them that he was good on crypto and that he was going to win," Marvin told me. "And so they backed off." Meanwhile, Leah helped create a crypto advisory council for Frost that included herself and Sean McElwee (who said he had encouraged Gabe Bankman-Fried and his organization Guarding Against Pandemics to endorse Frost) and a balanced slate of other invitees—Ethereum evangelists and bitcoin buzzkills alike. But just as Leah was explaining to me about how excited she was about Frost as a candidate, the doorbell rang.

"Oh," she said. "That's got to be Greg Casar. I forgot to tell you that he was going to be staying here." This type of thing was such a common occurrence that Leah said she sometimes felt like she ran a "congressional Airbnb." (Frost, for example, had been a guest on previous trips to Washington.)

Leah, dressed in a bright red dress, opened the door and greeted Casar, a bearded guy with noise-canceling headphones around his neck and a black-and-white Led Zeppelin shirt.

"Ben," Leah said, "this is Greg Casar, the next congressman from Texas."

Casar, a thirty-three-year-old community organizer and Austin city councilman, had recently won a primary in one of the only Democratic districts in Texas and was now on a glide path to Congress. Casar had earned early support from Leah and Way to Win for his work on affordable housing, paid sick leave, and living wage increases. He associated himself with various labels: Democratic Party, the Working Families Party, progressive.

"The last reporter you introduced me to, Ryan Grim, just called me boring," Casar said, adding, "It was nice, said in a nice way. He thinks being a normie, a lefty in a Led Zeppelin shirt, is a good thing for the party."

Casar was the kind of progressive success story that was at the core of Leah's strategy: Get more progressives into Congress by running them in safe blue districts, where they only had to worry about winning primaries. The focus was mostly on open primaries, where there was no incumbent running for reelection, because those seats would be easiest for newcomers to claim. The goal wouldn't be to get *more* Democrats elected, but *better* ones—populists who embodied the legacy of Occupy whether they were stars like Alexandria Ocasio-Cortez or normies in Zeppelin tees.

The problem was that not all of Leah's candidates were having the same kind of success as Casar, especially women and in particular women of color. One of her favorites, Nida Allam—a Durham County commissioner and the first Muslim woman elected in North Carolina—looked to be in good shape in her primary until outside money from both Sam Bankman-Fried's crypto crew and a PAC associated with AIPAC flooded the airwaves with attack ads. A similar thing appeared to be happening in Oregon, where Bankman-Fried had dumped millions into a race in the 6th district, where Carrick Flynn, an effective altruist, was running against Leah's preferred candidate, a state legislator named Andrea Salinas.

"To raise that much money and then have it be washed away by people on your own side must be frustrating," I said.

"Yeah," she said, "and by a kid too. If I were Andrea Salinas, it would be so infuriating. She raised all this money, and did the work. But it's [the Bankman-Frieds'] first cycle, and sort of chaotic. I want to get them on our side."

"These two things are all people call to ask about," said Casar. "Crypto and politics of the Middle East. I keep knocking on doors and they want to know about housing and healthcare, but I have to spend all my time talking about these other issues."

"My lesson from this," said Leah, "is if you have a super PAC and you come in with enough money per district, you can make the political field care about whatever issue you want."

Leah didn't love that this was true, but it was also why she spent so much of her time trying to raise money. And she was getting more pragmatic too, whether she liked it or not. In fact, the very next day she was cohosting a fundraiser for Frost, her name appearing on the invitation alongside Gabe Bankman-Fried's and Sean McElwee's.

"Oh, I love that guy, I was just texting with him," Casar said.

"You should come to the fundraiser tomorrow!" Leah said.

Casar said he'd try if he could, but in the meantime he was running late for some event with progressive organizers happening a few blocks from Leah's home. He went downstairs to put his stuff into the guest room and to change and returned wearing a sheepish look on his face.

"Just FYI," he said. "Malcolm may have gotten a bit territorial and pooped downstairs. I threw it away, but I'm not sure if you have something you'd want to spray on the carpet or anything."

* * *

The next evening I was at Roofers Union, a rooftop bar in Washington's Adams Morgan neighborhood, for the Maxwell Frost fundraiser. It was a beautiful late spring evening, the sun hanging around through the start of happy hour. A couple hundred guests gathered on the open-air patio, perched high enough for views all the way to the Capitol for anyone who wasn't too busy navel-gazing with their fellow young operators. Frost was a star—"You're looking at a future president," Ari Rabin-Havt, a former top aide to Bernie Sanders, told me with genuine admiration—but plenty of the people here were just as interested in getting a piece of Gabe Bankman-Fried. Sam Bankman-Fried had promised to give his fortune to charity, which meant wherever Gabe went in Washington, he would be swamped by professional liberals with elevator pitches in need of funding: a candidate, a think tank, a half-baked idea to have the rich Bankman-Fried buy all the guns in America to have them melted down.

"It's so gross," said Rabin-Havt after watching a procession of young politicos greet the billionaire's brother.

"You have all these fucking Democratic operatives being like: 'Let me tickle your taint. I'll take the left ball, you take the right ball. And oh, by the way, would you consider a donation to my blabbity blah blah.' Tell me what Gabe Bankman-Fried has fuckin' accomplished? Other than being sperm ejaculated from the same fucking nuts as his brother, what has he done in life? I'm not trying to insult the guy."

It was spring in Washington, a season of hazy beers and untucked short-sleeved gingham shirts—unless you were Gabe, who wore an unseasonable black blazer with a pressed white shirt and slacks. The crowd here had manners enough not to ask for money, of course. They just wanted to exchange business cards, maybe set something up later. A tickling deferred. "It must be uncomfortable for him in a way," Rabin-Havt continued. "Say what you will about his brother, there are critiques of what he's built, but you have to have something in your head to do that at that age. In another world you're Dane Cook's brother stealing his tour merchandise. You're fucking Johnny Drama in Entourage."

The gang was all here. Leah Hunt-Hendrix, a cohost of the event, mingled through the crowd, giving hugs and seeming genuinely happy to see people. Sean McElwee, another cohost, stood nearby telling the candidate's campaign manager to make sure Frost kept his remarks short. People hadn't come to hear a speech, he advised, they'd come to schmooze.

Frost had managed to bring together some of Washington's best frenemies. "Look at this political coalition," Gabe was saying into a microphone as the crowd grabbed seats at high-top tables and settled in for a round of remarks.

Ari took a spot at the back of the bar—about as far as he could get from Gabe—where a pair of low-level congressional staffers (still wearing their badges from a day on the Hill) groused about the lack of drink specials. Rabin-Havt had done just about every kind of job in progressive politics. He had worked for Harry Reid, the former Democratic majority leader; he had worked for David Brock, the Republican apostate who now ran a web of liberal organizations (Media Matters for America, Citizens for Responsibility and Ethics in Washington, plus a bunch of super PACs) known colloquially as "The Brocktopus."

Rabin-Havt had mostly left D.C. politics and was free to talk shit and share old war stories from the Bernie campaign, which he was now doing at the back of the bar. One time, he "lost Bernie in Kentucky" after the candidate went for a walk and the campaign "couldn't find him for an hour." And then there were Bernie's traveling requirements: the wool blanket, the need for every hotel room to be put to

167

60 degrees, and his supernatural love for a very specific type of cough drop.

"He was obsessed with these lozenges for his throat, Grether's Pastilles," he said. "They're the same ones that Ariana Grande uses so everyone wanted to know if he heard about them from her."

"Well," asked Ryan Grim. "How did Bernie hear about it?"

"Um," Rabin-Havt said. "I think, Danny Glover."

Rabin-Havt now spent most of his time swimming with sharks. (That's not a metaphor; his latest hobby was photographing sharks underwater.) He hadn't really come here to network. He was here because he believed in the candidate. Rabin-Havt had worked with Frost on the Bernie campaign, and the kid was the real deal. "I've never met anyone with as much natural ability as him," Rabin-Havt said. "He's so fucking talented."

Wearing a crisp tailored blue suit and a white turtleneck, Frost told the rooftop Democrats his own story of how, and why, he got here. He hadn't exactly expected to get into a life of politics, he said. Ten years earlier he was a high school student who dreamed of being a professional jazz drummer, following in the footsteps of his musician father. One Friday, after jazz band practice, Frost had been sitting in a diner with his friends loading up on chicken tenders when a silence fell over the restaurant. The televisions were reporting that someone had walked into an elementary school in Sandy Hook, Connecticut, and opened fire.

"I couldn't stop thinking about it," Frost said. "I came to Washington for the memorial. It was there that my life was changed."

He sat in on private and public vigils, watched families cry up close, and told his mother he wanted to get active. He began working on campaigns—for the American Civil Liberties Union and for the gun control movement March for Our Lives. When Derek Chauvin murdered George Floyd, Frost took to the streets, where he was teargassed, arrested, and jailed. He considered running for Congress when Val Demings, the congresswoman from his district, decided to leave her seat and run for Senate, but he felt the idea was too far-fetched—he would only barely reach the age of constitutional eligibility by swearing-in day. But the fact that he was thinking more about who he wanted to be—how to translate his anger into power—caused him to think more about where he came from. Frost knew he had been adopted, but there were questions he'd never asked his parents.

"I don't know anything about my bio family," Frost said. "So I asked my mom. And what I learned was an incredibly sad story."

He learned that when he was born, he was "trembling for two weeks," suffering from withdrawals from crack cocaine.

The revelation that Frost had suffered due to his mother's addiction was surely jarring, but he was mature enough to understand that wealth was not the only thing that families pass on to their children.

"I wasn't mad," he said. "Just incredibly sad that she was born into a zip code where she got into this cycle of drugs, poverty, and crime." He found her number and called her up. She told him that he had seven siblings, all of whom lived nearby in Orlando.

"I had you at the most vulnerable point in my life," he recalled her saying. "Which is why I put you up for adoption."

Leah was nodding along, rapt. Sean was on his phone, checking on his PredictIt bets.

"Hearing that was almost spiritual," Frost continued. He now knew the whole truth about his inheritance, and it was time to get to work on a legacy of his own making. "I hung up the phone," he said, "and decided I was going to run for the United States Congress."

Rabin-Havt was right: The guy had talent. And he knew how to work this kind of crowd. Already Frost had blown away his opponents in fundraising. The money earned him influential endorsements, which led to more money and more endorsements. It also turned his youth from a disadvantage (younger candidates can have a hard time being taken seriously) to an advantage (once proven to be *serious*, young candidates are exciting!). Frost knew there was something ironic about a progressive only being taken seriously once he proved he could bring *more* money into politics. But he also knew that this was the only way to play the game.

"This campaign is about community," he said, wrapping up. "It's about love."

Afterward, I asked Sean what he'd thought of the performance.

"It was a speech," he said, barely looking up from his phone.

Leah, on the other hand, couldn't have been happier. It had felt like she had been on the other side of too many Democrats for much of the past year. Frost seemed to be a candidate that everyone at this bar could get behind: Someone who thought crypto was important and here to stay, but perhaps in need of some guardrails. A Bernie Sanders–supporting activist, who wasn't yet ready to commit to being labeled a potential new member of The Squad. A candidate for Gabe to introduce to the crowd, for Leah to watch intently, for Sean to take some credit for, and for Rabin-Havt to brag about to anyone who would listen at the back of the bar.

Taking it all in, Leah echoed what Gabe had said earlier in the night.

"Look at this coalition."

Part 4

The Undone

Chapter 21

The Spiritual Chief

During an ayahuasca meditation, Veronica Duron had a vision that stayed with her ever since. The hallucinogenic tea put her in a room with a large burning fire. A group of women walked in. Some she recognized, others she couldn't place. Maybe she knew their energy? The setting was beautiful, but the details were hard to grasp, like trying to capture a falling leaf in an autumn breeze. The women surrounded her. One by one they told her that they had always been by her side; that they would never leave. She felt, for the first time, unconditional love. It was the most beautiful feeling she had ever felt in her life.

Veronica told me about this vision on a park bench just outside the Capitol building. She brought it up because I was wearing a T-shirt featuring the country singer Sturgill Simpson—who happened to be a favorite of hers. She had quoted one of his lyrics: "Marijuana, LSD, psilocybin, DMT. They all change the way I see, but love's the only thing that ever saved my life." She told me she could relate.

Which caught me a little bit off guard, given that I'd only just met Veronica, and I was a reporter, and she worked for a U.S. senator.

But her fond feelings about the healing powers of "mother ayahuasca" were in tune with Veronica's Friday outfit: typical Washington work clothes with unconventional accents. Each accessory had a purpose: She wore rings of pyrite and amethyst to bring her abundance; a hamsa hand necklace and sandalwood bracelet for protection; an Egyptian cross adorned with a clear quartz stone representing everlasting life; a thumb ring with a deer head and a tattoo of a raven—two of her spirit animals.

She also wore a congressional ID badge on a lanyard.

Veronica Duron. Chief of staff.

I asked Veronica if her boss, Senator Cory Booker, ever expressed any interest in ayahuasca, or the other "plant medicines," such as psilocybin mushrooms.

"I think he is interested in it in different ways," she said. "Like, I don't know that he will ever do it himself. Maybe he will, I have no idea. But I think he sees the benefit of all this."

As surprising as it was to be having this conversation, it didn't strike me as particularly scandalous. There was a real substance abuse problem on Capitol Hill, but that had a lot more to do with overworked staffers trying to dull their overcaffeinated minds after work with beer and shot specials. Veronica was less interested in self-escapism than she was interested in self-improvement. Plus, attitudes about hallucinogenic drugs had shifted dramatically in recent years. There were studies that indicated psilocybin and ayahuasca could help veterans suffering from post-traumatic stress disorder, and headlines that indicated hallucinogenic drugs were no longer part of the counterculture, such as MOMMIES WHO MUSHROOM and ARE MUSHROOM MOMS THE NEW WINE MOMS?

"I had such a beautiful experience, I'm pretty certain it won't be my last," the NFL quarterback Aaron Rodgers told a podcast host about his own journey with ayahuasca.

"They didn't simply allow me to escape reality for a while, they let me redefine reality," Prince Harry wrote in his memoir, *Spare*, about using psychedelics after a therapist recommended them for PTSD.

The benefits of psychedelics were the subject of a bestselling book and a well-received Netflix docuseries, both called *How to Change Your Mind* and both by the journalist Michael Pollan. He even wrote about his own journey with hallucinogens. And all around Washington, there were now fancy wellness shops, with the kinds of prices that catered to high-net-worth individuals as well as the same kinds of Hill staffers that probably used to go through Pablo.

Even in the stuffy offices of Capitol Hill, a lagging indicator on cultural shifts, odd bedfellows like conservative congressman Dan Crenshaw of Texas and his liberal colleague Alexandria Ocasio-Cortez of New York had united behind a common belief that the government should spend money on studying therapeutic uses of psychedelics.

Still, the cultural shift was recent (and uneven) enough that you didn't hear a lot of congressional staffers talking openly about their own usage. Especially Hill bosses. But Veronica said she wasn't stressed about the disapproval of more buttoned-up colleagues.

"One thing that has come out of my spiritual journey is not really caring what people think about me," she said. "It's very freeing in a place that judges everything. It's just me. It's kind of like, take it or leave it."

Veronica grew up in San Antonio, in a neighborhood made up of fellow Mexican Americans. Her mom worked for the telephone company. Her dad, who moved out when she was ten, mostly did odd jobs. During college, at the University of Texas at Austin, Veronica interned in the Texas state legislature and watched as Republican lawmakers passed an amendment to the state constitution that preempted the validity of same-sex marriages. It woke her up to the importance of behind-the-scenes political maneuvering.

"At that point there were enough Democrats that if they all stuck together, it would have failed," she said of the same-sex marriage ban. "But two flipped and voted for it and it passed. It was my first realization that, 'Oh my God, politics can changes people's lives.'"

Veronica came to Washington via a fellowship with the International Hispanic Caucus Institute, and worked in the office of Solomon Ortiz, the former Democratic House member from Texas. Eventually she moved to the office of Chuck Schumer, the New York senator who was then the chair of the Senate Democratic Policy Committee, and became one of his top aides on healthcare policy. The Texan was suddenly surrounded by New Yorkers.

"They talk so loud!" Veronica told me. "I was always like, 'Why is everyone yelling at me?'"

The volume only got more intense when Trump won the White House and Schumer became the minority leader. Suddenly, the landmark healthcare law the Democrats had passed with President Obama was under legitimate attack. Veronica remembered weeks of long, stressful nights before Republicans finally took their repeal effort to the Senate floor. On that night in 2017, John McCain—the Arizona Republican and deciding vote—gave a dramatic thumbs-down. The Republicans had spent the better part of a decade raging publicly about ending "Obamacare." But in this case the Democrats had stuck together while the Republican maneuvers had failed.

At the Capitol, Veronica had sometimes felt like an outsider—not just as a Texan in a New York senator's office, but also as a Hispanic woman in what remained (despite the growing membership of the Congressional Hispanic Staff Association) a very White Senate. But she appreciated the power and importance of the inside game, and as Cory Booker's chief, she was now playing it at a very high level. Her ability to work the politics around the legislative process could change people's lives. Like, for example, making it easier for the government to legalize—or at least decriminalize—certain drugs.

After all, plant medicines had changed her life. They helped her deal with past traumas. Repair relationships with her family. Figure out her path in life. And one other thing that made it easier for her to discuss: Her boss kept hearing about it from people he knew anyway.

"Cory hears from his wealthy friends and supporters who microdose every day and have these experiences," said Veronica. "And he is like, these healing experiences shouldn't be just for rich White people. Everyone should have the opportunity to change their life."

That was the ideal. But Veronica knew, too well, that the inside game didn't always work out either.

Chapter 22

Police Unreformed

In March 2020, police officers in Louisville, Kentucky, acting on bad information, raided the home of a twenty-six-year-old Black medical worker named Breonna Taylor, breaking her door off its hinges. Taylor's boyfriend, thinking the officers were intruders, fired at them once; the police returned fire, hitting Taylor five times, killing her. About two months after Taylor's death, police officers were called to a scene outside a grocery in Minneapolis, where a Black man named George Floyd had been accused of using a counterfeit $20 bill to buy cigarettes. The officers handcuffed Floyd and later restrained him on the ground, where an officer named Derek Chauvin kneeled on his neck for more than nine minutes, during which time Floyd said he couldn't breathe, called for his dead mother, pleaded for his life, and lay motionless while a teenager recorded a video of the murder that would enrage people across the country, shocking millions out of pandemic quarantine and into the streets.

People knew what had happened to Taylor and Floyd was horrific—and many of them believed something about policing needed to change. By that summer, the protests reached a historic scale, with tens of millions marching in large cities and small towns. The protests were overwhelmingly peaceful, with violence breaking out on rare occasions.

According to a Gallup poll from that summer, 58 percent of Americans agreed that "major changes" were needed to make policing better, with an additional 36 percent saying that "minor changes" were needed. In other words, the political conditions were ripe for police reform. It would take both Democrats and Republicans working together—an increasingly rare occurrence amid the partisan hostility of the Trump years—but it seemed possible.

On Capitol Hill, Jennifer DeCasper, the chief of staff for Republican Senator Tim Scott, encouraged her boss to go have a discussion with the Majority Leader Mitch McConnell about taking point on a police reform bill. Scott had been hesitant about leading on issues like this when he and Jennifer first came to Congress, but he was ready now.

"I think I had planted and watered that seed for so long that he was comfortable enough to tackle the issue," she said.

When Scott asked McConnell what the plan was to tackle the issue, McConnell's response was simple: "You tell me."

It was an invitation for Scott's office to take point, which, Jennifer told me later, "was terrifying."

"We had never led on an issue like this before," she said.

But it made sense. Scott hadn't been in the Senate for long, but he was respected by his colleagues. There was also the obvious fact that Scott was the only Black Republican in the Senate, which could make him a better messenger when it came to specific issues having to do with race and policing.

The killing of Black people by police officers was not something most Republicans were keen to think or talk too much about. But the killings of Eric Garner in New York in 2014 and Walter Scott in South Carolina in 2015 had played a role in changing the trajectory of Tim Scott's career after he came to Capitol Hill a decade earlier. They moved him to begin doing something that his White colleagues were neither inclined nor qualified to do: speak out about the persistence of racism in American life, starting with his own experiences—like all the times he had been pulled over by police for "nothing more than driving a new car in the wrong neighborhood," or the time a Capitol police officer had looked at the special lapel pin he was wearing (the one they only give to senators) and said, "The pin, I know. You, I don't. Show me your ID."

Scott began by telling these stories in closed-door meetings with his colleagues. He continued by telling them on the Senate floor. Now, in the aftermath of the Taylor and Floyd killings, he was being given the task of addressing bad policing as a member of a lawmaking body so insulated and White that almost nobody there knew firsthand the humiliation of having been racially profiled by law enforcement.

Scott crafted a bill that would have restricted the use of choke-holds, though not ban them outright, and penalized departments that did not require body cameras. Unlike a Democratic bill that passed in the House, Scott's bill would not have ended qualified immunity, which protected officers from being held civilly liable for violating the constitutional rights of citizens.

The American Civil Liberties Union opposed what it called Scott's "rushed" legislation filled with studies and commissions instead of action. Talking about the bill, Speaker of the House Nancy Pelosi said Republicans were "trying to get away with murder."

The insider politics of this situation were tricky. Just because there was public support for police reform in general didn't mean everyone was on the same page about the particulars. Republicans had a majority in the Senate and Trump was still in the White House, so a successful reform bill would have to be acceptable to a party that wanted to be seen as pro–"law and order" and a president who had once encouraged officers to let handcuffed suspects' heads hit the edge of the doorframe when they put them into the backseat of the squad car.

Democrats had control of the House, but they weren't about to give up too much during negotiations with Scott. And then there was the matter of the 2020 election, which was only a few months away. A nominal win on police reform might give Trump a boost, but if

Democrats resisted long enough to run Trump out of office, and also managed to retake the Senate, then they could write the police reform bill they *really* wanted in the next Congress.

Scott's Senate bill was dead on arrival. Afterward Scott cried foul on the Senate floor. He said his bill had most of what Democrats wanted in it, and they were letting "presidential politics get in the way of change."

By 2021, the situation had changed enough for another try. Biden was in the White House, and Democrats had control of Congress. They'd need a 60-vote majority to get anything through the Senate, but Veronica Duron, newly installed as Booker's top aide, thought the atmosphere was finally right to get something done.

"I don't know how close or serious we got in the first time period because everyone was in their corners," said Veronica. "But 2021 was different."

For months Booker and Scott would meet, figure out the things they agreed on, and table the more controversial aspects of any possible bill until later. The two senators had a good rapport with one another—a rare bipartisan friendship that both of their staffs insisted was genuine. They met for dinner. They talked about their faith. Booker hung a photo in his Senate office of him and Scott sharing a fist bump. And they did have a history of getting things done—namely getting a program in the 2017 tax cut bill that helped encourage investment in lower-income areas known as "Opportunity Zones." (This particular program, loved by developers, has been derided as a windfall for the rich—but they got it done nonetheless.)

"I have had moments in this negotiation that have given me solace and strength as I watch Tim Scott share stories about his own encounters with police, even as a United States senator," Booker told the press as they worked through police reform. "He is not caving to the politics of this. He is sincere. We may have disagreements on a lot of the parts of the bill, but I'm telling you, as a Black man, Tim Scott is sincere in wanting to see us address these problems."

That may have been true, and both Veronica and Jennifer, who served as chief negotiators under their bosses, believed it. They worked well with one another too—not always agreeing on the policy, but never doubting the other's intentions. By the summer of 2021, Veronica thought for sure they were about to have a deal. Scott's office had told them that if they were able to get police organizations on board with their legislation, they would be able to get enough Republicans to pass the thing. They slimmed down the legislation to remove many of the trickiest components—like qualified immunity and the criminalization of excessive use of force. Instead, their proposal included language about only awarding federal grants to law enforcement agencies once they met certain use of force standards. And Veronica got word from the Fraternal Order of Police and the International Association of Chiefs of Police that if Republicans could agree to the text they'd seen, they would endorse the package themselves.

"It was on Booker and Scott at that point to say this is the package, and if it came back to us and nothing had materially changed, we would have said, 'Yeah, that's great,'" Jim Pasco, the head of the FOP, told me.

"This was huge," Veronica said. "People thought it would be impossible, and we did it."

With the two police organizations potentially on board, Booker's team took the deal to Scott's office. Veronica thought they might actually have an agreement. Her hope, however, was short-lived. Not long after Scott's office got the proposed legislation, someone leaked it to the National Sheriffs' Association, one of the largest sheriffs' groups in the country and a very conservative and powerful presence in South Carolina.

"I don't know that Scott did it," said Pasco. "But whoever did it had to know the sheriffs were going to break bad. Because that is what they do."

With the Sheriffs' Association as a shield, Scott rejected the offer. Even though the bill would have added millions of dollars to police department budgets, he accused Democrats of wanting to "defund the police," something that almost no one in Congress had been saying for months. It made Booker's team, and other Democrats, pretty sure that Scott hadn't been serious about passing legislation for quite some time. Even if he had been serious at first, he just didn't seem to have the buy-in from his fellow Republicans to take any kind of action that could be construed as not backing the Blue.

"But if that was bad for police, then why would we have been involved?" Pasco said.

A lot had changed since 2020, but also things were still the same in plenty of ways that mattered. Sure, it was no longer a presidential election year, but Washington is never far from another contest. In fact, there were some on Booker's team who had come to believe that Scott didn't want to have a police reform bill weighing him down if he ever decided to run for president.

"It was clearly about politics," said Pasco. "That was the calculus there."

Chapter 23

Your Allies on the Other Side Are Allies Second and Opponents First

There's a cliché about Washington that nothing ever gets done here because nobody cares about anything other than scaling the greasy pole of political influence. In fact, Washington is full of people who *do* actually care about changing people's lives for the better. But caring isn't enough; the people working against you care too.

When Jennifer DeCasper got word that police reform was dead, she broke down crying. Veronica felt beat up by it too, and she told me the failure "broke" her boss's heart. Cory Booker was having a run of bad breaks by that fall. His brother had suffered a stroke and Booker had to split his time between being a senator and being a caretaker. And on top of that, Booker had just broken up with his girlfriend, the actress Rosario Dawson.

"He was the one who broke it off," Veronica told me. "She actually just introduced him to her new boyfriend, which I was not happy about, but he takes all that better than I do."

(Booker had a way of keeping things civil with his exes—which was fortunate, because a woman he briefly dated years ago, Gisele Barreto Almeida, had ended up marrying a guy whom Booker was now trying to help win an open Senate seat in his neighboring state of Pennsylvania: John Fetterman.)

Booker kept having meals with Scott. He considered the Republican a real friend, and still nurtured a belief that at some point a version of the bill could be brought back to life.

Jennifer came away from the police reform failure with a slightly more gimlet-eyed view.

"You have to have a certain awareness that your allies on the other side of the aisle are allies second and opponents first," she said.

Jennifer trusted Veronica as a negotiating partner, and liked her as a person. She had just come to believe there were enough people on the Democratic side of the aisle who were too ideologically rigid to accept a compromise, and who also didn't want to pass a bill that her Republican boss could claim credit for. Jennifer dismissed the idea that Scott's own political ambitions got in the way of a deal. But there was one small detail that made that argument a little harder to believe. Jennifer no longer worked as Scott's chief of staff; she had recently left Congress to help run Scott's outside spending operation and prepare for the possibility of a presidential run.

Jennifer left her job on the Hill feeling a little ambivalent. She still believed it was possible to get things done there. And she also believed that the culture of the place was beginning to change. Police reform never passed, but the conversations around it had people—especially people in her own party—talking about and thinking about the Black experience in America. The congressional staff was still overwhelmingly White, but the demographics were moving in the right direction every year, and young staffers of color were starting to find their voice.

"I've never seen so many White people care about Black people before," she said.

As we wrapped up the interview, Jennifer asked me whether I had been in touch with Jamarcus. She had been wondering about him ever since she sent me Pablo's article, and knew that I had reached out to him.

"Is he still in town?" she asked.

Chapter 24

Nobody Saw What I Was Seeing

Jamarcus Purley was still in Washington, but not for long. He was moving back home to Pine Bluff. Three days before his departure, I met him on the roof of his D.C. apartment building. It was a bright, cool morning. Jamarcus wore a silver chain and a gray peacoat, which he removed, revealing the crimson Harvard sweatshirt underneath.

Jamarcus once told me he had been playing roles his entire life: In elementary school he pretended to care about church, in high school he pretended to care about academics, in college he pretended to care about whatever his White friends cared about so he could fit in. In Feinstein's office he had pretended not to care—to keep to himself his feelings about the senator, about what he considered a lack of support for his community. But now, for the first time, he said, he could be truly himself.

He had come out as queer. This was something he had kept hidden for years. He told me he'd always wanted to run for office someday and had convinced himself that the only way he could be accepted as a politician was if he acted like a "stereotypical heterosexual Black man." But when things started to go south in Feinstein's office, he got to reading James Baldwin's *The Fire Next Time* and had a realization.

"I was like, 'You're never going to do anything radical in your whole life if you can't even come out as queer,'" he said.

He was reading more than ever—George Orwell's *Animal Farm*, Sun Tzu's *The Art of War*, Machiavelli's *The Prince*. He had stopped using mushrooms and smoking weed. And he was ready to move back home, to split time living with his mother and his sister. It would be good for him to be around people again, he'd decided. He'd spent too many months "self-isolating," and he knew that could be a dangerous path.

Jamarcus exuded calm, at least by Jamarcus standards. He had an easy smile as he talked. He grabbed a seat on a patio sofa and kicked his feet up to recline.

"I just feel in control," he said. "I don't know what's going to happen, but I have confidence and positive energy."

He still had big plans: to take the GRE, get into business school, and maybe figure out a way to start that video production company he'd been thinking about—the one that could help distribute works by Black artists. But he had some smaller plans too. He wanted to do some teaching at his old high school, the one that was going to be torn down sometime in the next year. He was going to get in touch with the mayor's office and see if there were opportunities for him there. Who knows, he said, maybe one day he could run for mayor himself. It was, of course, possible that Jamarcus was just playing another role here, with me as his audience—that of the man who had to lose everything to finally regain perspective. It was also possible that Jamarcus wasn't even trying to convince me, but to convince himself that it had all been worth something.

From the perspective of an outside observer, it seemed as if Washington had failed Jamarcus, and that in a sense he had failed here too. Ultimately, the point of his protest was largely lost to the public. He had done something so out-there by Washington standards that people had to squint to see what they were looking at. The small amount of press attention dried up quickly, and he was headed home with no future prospects in a city where he had tried to make it. There were plenty of Hill staffers who saw what he did as heroic, but beyond that, he was more likely to be seen—if he was seen at all—as someone in crisis. I asked him if he had any regrets.

"My therapist told me, when I was in therapy a few years ago when I got depressed, that I don't have to think in these binaries like we do in Congress," Jamarcus said.

So instead he tried to look back on the year with some nuance. He didn't regret taking mushrooms, because they gave him the courage to say what he had long been feeling; but he wished that the drugs hadn't made it harder to think strategically. If he had been quicker, he said, he could have had recordings of Senator Feinstein and the office and could have used them to prove the points he was trying to make. The problem, he said, was ultimately one of collective action.

"Nobody saw what I was seeing or didn't want to speak about it," he said.

Congress could do that to people, Jamarcus realized. It could keep people quiet just so they could stick around. He knew that he wasn't the only person who struggled with this. He saw it in the way people carried themselves in the office, and he saw it with how people treated themselves after work. There *was* a drug problem on Capitol Hill, Jamarcus said. But it wasn't mushrooms or psychedelics, it was alcohol. Congressional staffers would work all day and drag themselves to the bars afterward just to dull their fried brains.

"It's just baked in," he said. "It's what happens when you destabilize a workforce."

Before we said goodbye, I asked him whether he had been paying attention to the work being done by Dear White Staffers and the Congressional Progressive Staff Association. These were the staffers who had banded together to get their voices heard on the Hill—through a combination of inside-game organizing acceptable within the Capitol Hill complex, traditional activist protesting, and the anonymous new media tactics. I told him that a number of offices had recently unionized, and were fighting for higher wages and better working conditions. Jamarcus, who often talked a mile a minute, sat quietly. Tears welled in his eyes and he began to sob.

"Sometimes it feels like you are doing shit alone, like you don't have anybody," he said, trying to compose himself.

It was the first time in a long time that Jamarcus thought that maybe things could change, even if he wouldn't be around to see it.

Part 5

The Game

Chapter 25

The Original Big Boy

That's the original Big Boy," Frank Luntz said.

We were standing in the backyard of Frank's home—a property he had long ago decorated with the zeal of a child who'd lucked into a large sum of money. He'd filled his kitchen cabinets with shoeboxes full of baseball cards. He'd installed a Riverboat Gambler pinball machine in the basement. He'd placed a life-size mannequin of the Terminator by his back door. And there, by the deep end of a peanut-shaped swimming pool, by way of Big Boy Restaurant: the iconic mascot of a portly child, triumphantly hoisting a hamburger above his head.

"There was a Ronald McDonald too," Frank said, sighing. "But it's gone."

Back when Frank was a hotshot Republican pollster, this Virginia home had been the center of his social life. Senators, congressmen, lobbyists, Democrats, Republicans—they'd all come down from Washington to see him. He was known especially for his annual All-Star Game party. Former Senate Majority Leader Harry Reid, a serious baseball fan, showed up to that once. Another time the Republican crew from the 2000 presidential recount came by to watch the game on the big screen and then tell war stories about hanging chads and Brooks Brothers rioters until the wee hours. But now...

Now the pool had been dry for months. Now vines had begun to grow up the side of Frank's house. Now the Terminator had been partially crushed by a felled tree. Now a layer of green slime grew on the cherubic, totemic mascot of a fading fast-food chain. Now the guests—like Ronald McDonald—were gone.

"Now they don't drop by," Frank said, resting a hand on a rusty patio chair.

Frank wasn't dropping by much either. It had been more than a year since he had spent the night in this house, opting instead for time at his properties in Los Angeles or the United Kingdom. He had returned to move out.

"Nobody was coming to visit me here," he said. "I didn't have a choice."

I'd come to visit Frank because he was a Washington archetype, a master of what people in politics love to refer to as "the game." All that shape-shifting, money raising, spinning, and calling opponents the greatest threat to American democracy since the redcoats—it's not so bad if it's just part of a game, especially if the victor gets to be in charge, or pass some legislation in real life.

A lot of things in Washington can be gamified. Bill Clinton used to game out where to go on his family vacations with the help of a pollster. Campaign managers will spend an entire election figuring out the best ways to demonize their opponents, and then host the equivalent of a postgame press conference at the Harvard Institute of Politics to open up their playbooks and explain to the audience how they won (or lost) a presidential election. There are always different players, but the rules of the game don't change much: Raise money, hew to popular messaging, inflame voters. In this way, people like Matt Schlapp or Sean McElwee weren't new types, but updated versions of an older model. An older model like Frank, an original big boy.

Frank blamed the lack of guests on the house being too far away from Washington, D.C. But it wasn't the location of the house that had changed; it was Frank's place in the Republican Party that had shifted. It had a lot to do with Donald Trump.

Frank hated Trump. He thought he was a bully who promoted a politics of revenge. He thought the election deniers who followed Trump's lead were a threat to democracy. He hated him so much he said it nearly killed him.

"Donald Trump made my head explode," he said.

* * *

In early 2020 Frank checked himself into a hospital after a tingling in his arm had crept up his shoulder and began to spread across his face. Doctors told him his blood pressure was an alarming 197 over 122 and that he had suffered a stroke. There were a lot of reasons Frank was having this medical emergency. Genetics were a part of it. His lack of exercise and unhealthy eating habits didn't help. But a lot of it had to do with stress, and the fact that when Frank got upset about the state of the world he was less likely to take his blood pressure medicine. He was at that time constantly upset about the state of the world. He blamed Trump.

"I had a stroke because of Trump," Luntz said. "I didn't have the guts to speak out enough about him and it drove me crazy. Every time I spoke out, I felt the backlash, I felt it on social media, I felt it a little bit with my clients, I felt it with my friends here."

Frank opened the back door to his house and walked inside over a welcome mat with a faded cartoon of Bill Clinton and the words "I feel your pain."

That morning a crew, to protect the floors, had unfurled a roll of red plastic that looked just like a red carpet and had begun hauling Frank's belongings to a truck parked out front—using a dolly with the word "Liberator" printed on the back. All that was left on the first floor now was an old-timey British phone booth and a box of trinkets by the front door.

"I'm finding all this shit from ages ago," Frank said, picking up an ashtray from the Hollywood Brown Derby, a long-lost Tinseltown haunt.

"One of the greatest restaurants from all time," he said.

Frank hurried down to the basement. He kept a lot of stuff down there, and he supposed he should figure out what was worth keeping. He scanned the room. There was a Margaret Thatcher poster on the wall: Gotta keep that. There was a dummy wearing a Bill Clinton mask crumpled up in a wooden electric chair, a prop from the original Addams Family movie: Keep. But what about the *New York Post* newspaper box in the corner? The one with the front page prominently displaying the headline RUDY WOULD WIN TODAY. That was Frank's work. He had conducted that poll, and Rudy Giuliani—a U.S. attorney with designs on running for mayor of New York—had liked it so much that he had hired Frank to work for him. Given what Giuliani had become—a Trump lackey, embarrassingly parroting the former president's biggest lies—maybe Frank would want to dispose of this particular artifact? Nope. Keep it.

"No regrets at all," Frank said. "He was the most amazing mayor. It's a shame what happened to him."

* * *

Frank may be a victim of a Republican Party gone awry, but he is not without blame. He had, after all, helped create the modern GOP; a Dr. Frank (PhD), nearly killed by a monster of his own making.

He was, after all, once one of the most prominent messaging gurus in the Republican Party. In 1992, he served as the pollster for Pat Buchanan, a proto-Trump nativist who made building a fence along the border with Mexico a signature issue in his "America First" presidential campaign. He helped Giuliani become mayor, and his fingerprints were all over the Contract with America, a document he cowrote with Congressmen Newt Gingrich and Dick Armey that listed the party's legislative agenda and helped gain 54 House seats and 9 Senate seats in the 1994 elections.

"He was one of six or seven key people that worked through the language and tone," Gingrich told me in an interview. "He was a very good reflector of what was going on in the country. He observed it, codified it, and put language to it."

Frank was a language guy, through and through, and helped Republicans win debates and elections with their word choices. He told them to call the "estate tax" the "death tax" so it sounded bad, and to call global warming "climate change" because it sounded not so bad. But in recent years, especially with Trump coming to power, Frank started to break from his party. The first time I met him was at an event in 2015, an early gathering of potential Republican candidates for president (attendees refer to these as "Cattle Calls," which Frank the linguist might point out is a telling reflection of the low regard in which Americans hold their politicians).

"There are some very serious people here," he told me after I'd mentioned that I had just come from a Trump speech. "And some very not-serious people here."

Frank, Gingrich told me, seemed to underestimate Trump's resonance, and when he won, "Frank found that very hard to accept."

But like most Republicans, the skeptic had a moment where he thought maybe he could work with this president after all. Instead of being shut out of the White House entirely, Frank used his connection to his friend and White House Chief of Staff Mick Mulvaney to advise the administration. His big idea? If Trump wanted to get his border wall with Mexico built, he should use less-politicized words. Instead of calling it a wall, he should consider calling it a "barrier."

"What do you want me to chant, 'Build the Barrier'?" Trump had said, laughing, in a conversation aboard *Air Force One*. The ridicule was too much for Frank to bear.

"Everyone who goes to work for Trump thinks that they're special and that they won't end up the punch line to one of Trump's jokes," Frank said. "It's like going up to the firing squad and being sure that this time the guns are going to jam."

A member of the moving crew popped into the basement to let Frank know they were having trouble moving a large lamp from his bedroom. Frank walked upstairs to watch the crew struggle for a minute before he continued the tour. He showed me a Red Sox jersey signed by the 2004 World Series team, a room full of dolls, and hats, and mini statues that all looked like they had something to do with World War II, and a glass encasement that held a Confederate soldier costume from the movie *Gone with the Wind*.

We walked into the empty TV room, the place where his politics pals used to gather and watch baseball. He showed me his Sandy Koufax autograph and told me about the breakfast he once had with the great Dodger pitcher, the legendary Yankees manager Joe Torre, and the Cardinals all-time ace Bob Gibson at the Hall of Fame. He opened his kitchen cabinets to reveal his card collection and told me that he kept the really "special" ones at his Los Angeles home, a mansion that features a scaled-down replica of the White House's Oval Office and Lincoln Bedroom. He leafed through various letters that had been sent to him, including a gracious note from the Republican Congressman Joe Wilson, who was famous for shouting "You lie!" at President Barack Obama during a speech to a joint session of Congress.

"I'm trying to decide what to take with me," he said. "I left this place emotionally a year ago."

Frank told me he was finished being deeply involved with politics. He was a professor now, currently teaching a class of international students enrolled in New York University's Abu Dhabi program. He was "done with D.C."

Except he wasn't.

In addition to the Virginia home, Frank had a condo, located in the Penn Quarter—a neighborhood of high-end clothing stores and expensive restaurants located near the National Portrait Gallery. He had bought four separate penthouse apartments and smashed down a bunch of walls to turn them into one enormous apartment. The construction had taken much longer than he expected; cost a bunch more too. And worst of all, Frank said, it had been so loud that "everyone in that place hated me." He said he would love to offload the condo, but he had put in too much to consider it.

Frank had shared that apartment with one of his closest friends, the Republican Congressman Kevin McCarthy. The future Speaker of the House had a different kind of relationship with Trump. After briefly saying Trump had borne some responsibility for the January 6th attack on the Capitol, McCarthy had flown to Mar-a-Lago and kissed the ring, signaling that the former president was still the leader of the party. This was the kind of behavior that had inspired Trump to call him "My Kevin."

Why would Frank want to share a Kevin with the man who nearly made his brain explode?

"Because he is in person an even better person than he is in public," Frank said. "And I try to be eighty percent as good as he is."

Frank said that he and McCarthy had been friends since the early 1990s, since even before the Contract with America, dating to McCarthy's days as a staffer for California Republican Congressman Bill Thomas. Frank and McCarthy had worked closely over the years, mostly on messaging. Even after a lot of the party had turned on Frank, McCarthy would invite him to speak at the Republican House retreat to share information on polls and focus groups. After Frank's health scare, McCarthy was one of the only people to check on him daily, making sure his friend was taking the prediabetic medicine he needed to keep his blood sugar count in check.

"I can't jab myself," Frank said. "People laugh at me; I know this will be the source of ridicule. But I cannot cause myself visceral pain."

And so when McCarthy and Frank were together, there would be times when McCarthy would do more than just remind his friend to take his medicine; sometimes he would grab the syringe and jab Frank himself.

Washington had given Frank more riches and mementos than most people would accumulate in many lifetimes. He helped change Washington, and then a Washington changed by Trump nearly killed him. But he still couldn't leave, not entirely. He was too invested.

As movers carted away belongings out of his Virginia home, Frank told me he had to get into town for meetings on the Hill with seven senators (he wouldn't say who). In the coming weeks and months he'd continue to show up on television to talk about polling and political focus groups he had run. He'd never stop giving his friend McCarthy strategic advice. It seemed unlikely Frank would ever fully leave. Washington may have almost ended his life, but it also has helped keep him alive.

Before I left, one of Frank's neighbors walked in through the open front door. He walked up to Frank and said he would like to buy the house.

"What's your number?" Frank asked.

"I don't know," the neighbor replied. "I guess a lot like this will go for one and a half million?"

"I've already been offered one point eight five," said Frank.

"Okay, okay, so we have a number to beat," said the neighbor.

"I'm not going to sell it immediately yet," said Frank. "I'm going to try and rent it first because I can't get everything out. My guess is you'll want to knock it down. Everything else around here is so big."

It was true. Frank's home no longer fit in with a neighborhood that was otherwise mostly mansions. But the neighbor shook his head. He didn't imagine it would be worth tearing the whole thing down.

"No," he said. "It's an easy type to remodel."

Chapter 26

Chaos Is Good

Spring 2022

This was the worst experience of my life," Robert Stryk said. We were back at Alibi, sitting on Stryk's porch and sipping whiskey. It was the first time I had seen him since he'd returned from Belarus, but it wasn't the experience in a war zone that had shaken the private diplomat. It was his experience in a podcast booth. On the journey back to the states, Stryk and his partner in private diplomacy—a former Virginia congressman and Navy SEAL named Scott Taylor—had made a pit stop in England and sat for a lengthy podcast interview.

Stryk, who had invited me over to listen to the episode, said being in a recording studio for the first time had made him "incredibly anxious," but I thought the questions were easy and Stryk had come across well enough. It helped that Taylor had hyped Stryk to the host, calling him "the most successful" foreign lobbyist and fixer in Washington "than there may have ever been." They dubbed themselves "the Congressman and the Cowboy." The host, a guy named Paul Blanchard ("media consigliere for global CEOs, entrepreneur, broadcaster and author," per his website), never pressed them on the controversial aspects of their work.

"The clients I work with, most people won't work with," Stryk said on the podcast, which was called "New Thinking." "For whatever reason, they think they are bad or whatever."

"And they may be," Taylor chimed in. "But everyone deserves representation."

It took almost two hours for us to listen to the seventy-minute interview. Stryk kept pausing the tape to ask me my opinion on various moments, like whether he sounded clear enough when he condemned White nationalism and the January 6th attack on the Capitol. He had done that. But oddly, I thought, there was no discussion about how the Cowboy and the Congressman had just come from Belarus amid Russia's invasion of Ukraine.

There were plenty of Washington lobby shops lining up to help out Ukraine during this conflict, often for free. But Stryk and Taylor may have been two of the only people to offer their help to Belarus, which was cooperating with Russia. Just days after the invasion of Ukraine, Stryk submitted a letter of intent to lobby the U.S. government against sanctions on the Belarusian potash industry. Potash, which is a key ingredient in some fertilizers, was big business in Belarus, and some of their biggest producers had been dealing with U.S. sanctions ever since the State Department determined that its president, Alexander Lukashenko, had won reelection in 2020 by fraudulent means.

Belarus had been controversial before; now it was toxic. According to reporting from Politico, a lobbyist who had once worked for Belarus, David F. Gencarelli, had turned down multiple offers to do so again unless the country distanced itself from Russia. Stryk and Taylor had no such demands. If they could get a contract from the Belarusians, and then have it signed off on by the American government, they would be in for quite the payday.

"It's very touchy because I don't have a license," Stryk told me when I asked about the trip. "I really have no issues telling you. And I believe I'm within the legal confines of the DOJ and Treasury, but I'm nervous I may not be. FARA [Foreign Agents Registration Act] is being read very loosely right now. If there's a perception that I'm talking to a reporter or publication about a foreign national that could be taken as advocating... I think there are those that dislike what I do..."

Stryk told me the basic outline of the Belarus trip. He and Taylor met with the "highest levels" of the Belarusian government, he said, including Lukashenko's son. Just being there felt like a special opportunity, since the United States' own special envoy to Belarus, Julie Fisher, had been unable get a visa and enter the country. In fact, the State Department wasn't currently operating an embassy in Minsk at all.

When war broke out, Stryk and Taylor were caught off guard. I knew this to be true because they had called me from Belarus just hours before the invasion. On that call they had sounded punchy and optimistic. "I'm sitting in Belarus right now," Stryk had said when he called. "I am meeting with the senior leadership to hopefully provide a conduit between our governments, and the only way that is possible is because Donald Trump allowed a guy like me to go around the world and say, 'Look, hey, the U.S. government is open for foreign negotiations.'"

Taylor had chimed in. "The Trump administration has created people like Robert Stryk that understand, you know what, I can help out," the former congressman said. "Sure I'll make money because I'm an American capitalist, but I can also better my country's relationships. I can move foreign policy. I can create lines of communication—"

"The State Department is a very outdated organization," Stryk interjected. "If you're an ambassador, you have to have so many protocols. Not a sexist statement, but when a man gets together and has a drink and forms a personal relationship, you can find a way to somehow mitigate these issues."

They told me that they didn't believe Putin would really invade Ukraine. They had bad information on that one. The initial intel they got on how to escape the country wasn't much better. First they heard there was a bus. "Bullshit," Stryk said. Then they were told there was a train. "No train," he said. Stryk tried to get himself a private jet out of Minsk, but the airspace was closed. Eventually he found a guy who would drive them five miles from the Lithuanian border, and a Lithuanian driver who would meet them there and whisk them to safety.

"They probably thought we were CIA," Stryk said. "Later I got a call that we were being trailed by Russian intelligence."

The work was dangerous and it was pricey. Later in the spring when I caught up with Stryk by phone he told me he was on pace to spend, between travel and legal fees, upwards of $100,000 of his own money to try and get the contract. It would be worth it if they succeeded; the contract, he said, could make them millions. But it was no sure thing. He needed permission from the Treasury Department to work for Belarus.

"At this point we can't even negotiate money," he said. "But look, it's very lucrative. There's so much fucking money in it."

When I visited Alibi in early June, Stryk seemed tired, like the stress was starting to get to him. "I spent $100,000 getting the license and I might never get it," he said. "I can't use my God-given talents."

If Trump were still president, Stryk said, he would already "have the license."

This kind of talk was new. Ever since we'd met, Stryk had taken care to put distance between himself and the former president. Now, with Stryk's business prospects in Belarus in limbo, and Trump's political prospects seemingly on the rise, Stryk seemed nostalgic for the freewheeling days when Trump Guys were running Washington.

"I think Trump is probably needed again," Stryk said. "I think the country has got a social malaise, and chaos is good."

We were down by his fire pit again, but there were no flames. The climate had changed. It had been nearly six months since I'd first come out here and met Stryk. Back then he seemed truly ambivalent about Trump, regardless of how good the Trumpian chaos had been for him.

"I think we had Trump fatigue," Stryk said, referring to himself and "guys like" himself. "But now we are fully in. If you asked me today, I'd put a Trump flag in my yard right now. I would not have done it two years ago."

It was getting late, time for me to leave. But before I did I wanted to ask Stryk about another chaotic politician—someone who had run for office as a disrupter long before Trump ran for president. In all the time we'd spent together Stryk had been eager to discuss certain parts of his life, but had left out at least one story I'd been interested in.

"Can you tell me about the time you ran for mayor?" I asked him.

Stryk seemed surprised by the question, and the rarely hesitant host hesitated before answering. "It was hubris, arrogance," Stryk said. He didn't want to discuss it any further.

"And that's all it was," he said.

I thought it might be more than that. And if Stryk wasn't going to talk about it, I had to seek out people who would.

Chapter 27

The Tough Questions

Robert Stryk announced his candidacy for mayor of Yountville, a quiet town of 2,933 about two hours north of San Francisco, on a local-access show, sitting in front of a green-screen background that made him look like he was surrounded by a half dozen American flags. He wore a tailored black suit with a pocket square, and seemed a little nervous. His head twitched slightly as he responded to softball questions from the boisterous blond host.

"Don't you just think Yountville is an adorable little town?" she asked.

"It's an amazing town," Stryk agreed. "Some of the best restaurants in the world, some of the best wine in the world, and some really amazing people live there."

Most of the voters in this town were working-class folks. Many of them were residents at the veterans' home—one of the largest in the United States—and others worked at the various upscale hotels and restaurants (including two world-class spots, Bouchon and the French Laundry) that made Yountville a destination for the rich and powerful. It was 2010, and nobody was expecting any huge surprises. The locals had expected that perhaps the vice mayor—a resident of Yountville for more than a decade and member of the city council for four years—would be running unopposed.

Stryk had other plans.

His platform was nothing exotic: lowering taxes, getting the government out of the way of small-business owners, making sure that the locals on fixed incomes had affordable places in town where they could spend their money and feel like part of the community. He told the local press that he wasn't trying to "reinvent the wheel" but was following a path laid out by his role-model mayor, Rudy Giuliani. His newspaper ads promised he would balance the budget, put a freeze on outside consultants offering services to the town, end "free healthcare" to elected members of the town council, and eliminate redundant staff working for Yountville. He positioned himself as someone willing to "stand up and ask the tough questions."

People in Yountville had questions of their own, namely: Who *was* this guy?

Stryk had rubbed some people the wrong way. In 2009, he paid for an event at the Villagio Inn and Spa, a fancy spot in town, using a credit card that belonged to one of his lobbying clients, Vumii, an Atlanta-based security firm that sold thermal and night-vision cameras. The bill came to $1,077, and the card was declined. David Shipman, the managing director of the hotel, told the local press that he spent months trying to recover the payment from Stryk. The lobbyist claimed this was all one big misunderstanding, and said that as soon as he became aware of the issue, he paid in full out of his personal account. The dispute dragged on, and Shipman eventually told the *Napa Valley Register* that he "just got tired of dealing with the issue"; he told the sheriff's department that Stryk was no longer welcome at the hotel or any of the other properties he managed around town. Stryk became "enraged" when informed of the ban, according to an internal sheriff's report.

Shipman and his friends decided they wanted to know more about this mysterious interloper who would be mayor. And so they called a private investigator named Dawn King, of Dawn to Dawn Investigations.

King, a former FBI special agent, started pulling public records on Stryk. She found a résumé that included low-level work for former presidential candidates Bob Dole and Senator John McCain, and that he'd had staffing jobs for a couple of congressmen. His lobbying group had made good money for a couple of years—more than $1 million in 2008—but had made less than half of that the next year. Records also showed at least one other issue with the same Vumii credit card, Stryk having used it to pay a $4,000 bill covering rent for a Yountville town house, a charge that Vumii disputed. The sheriff's department had investigated but ultimately determined that the accusations of theft and fraud against Stryk were unfounded, and the matter had been settled without legal action. But it wasn't the only other example of a money dispute that King found in Stryk's past.

In 2003, Stryk's then business partner, John Greene, the former state senate president and attorney general candidate in Arizona, sued Stryk for allegedly misspending $40,000 of company funds. The lawsuit claimed that Stryk had run up tabs at Scottsdale nightspots, the Venetian hotel in Las Vegas, and fancy restaurants in New York City; it said he'd gone on a shopping spree at the Guess clothing store, taken a trip to Washington with friends for a soccer match, and used $3,800 to purchase a steer at an auction. The complaint specifically noted that Stryk did not share the meat from the steer with Greene and his partners. That lawsuit was thrown out on a technicality, and Stryk had threatened to file a $100 million countersuit for defamation.

On January 11, 2010, King reached out "telephonically"—according to contemporaneous notes—to a supposedly former employee of the lobbyist. According to this man, Stryk wasn't who he said he was. The former employee claimed Stryk was a "con man" who had stiffed employees, including $40,000 in unpaid wages the man said he was personally owed. The former employee told a story about Stryk spending $50,000 on a lavish vacation to France and then welshing on rent payments for his Washington, D.C., office, leading to the eviction of his lobby shop.

There wasn't a smoking gun, or proof to these claims, but it was enough to pique King's interest. She alerted Shipman, the Inn manager, who, hoping for more dirt on Stryk, offered to fly the man to California and put him up in a free room with a courtesy bottle of Napa wine for his trouble.

When the man arrived, King arranged a meeting in Shipman's office in the hotel. Because there was public interest in Stryk's mayoral candidacy, King also invited two members of the local press to join. One of them was Sharon Stensaas, the publisher of the *Yountville Sun*. She recalled being struck by how nervous the former employee seemed. "I remember that right away he started sweating profusely," she said.

The man talked about what a "scoundrel" Stryk was, but he didn't offer anything the group hadn't learned from public records. His whole vibe felt a bit *off*, according to a person who attended the meeting. He had a lot of questions for the group. Who had ordered this investigation in the first place? Why was the press so interested in Stryk's background? Was there something political going on here?

Afterward, Stensaas, the *Sun* publisher, said she received a call from Stryk, who revealed that he had sent his former employee as a mole. According to later reports from a local, right-leaning tabloid, the *Napa Sentinel*, the former employee was actually still a *current* employee for the lobbyist, working as his "director of intelligence," and had flown to California in order to "gain proof of the conspiracy" to discredit his boss. As soon as she hung up with Stryk, Stensaas called Shipman, the Inn manager, who proceeded to boot the Stryk mole from his complimentary room.

Getting rid of Stryk, however, wouldn't be that simple. The lobbyist turned politician was now in attack mode, and began using the industry toolkit on his Yountville enemies. He wrote a public letter to his supporters claiming that the investigation into his background was part of a "massive effort to discredit and spread lies" about him. He called the sheriff's department and asked that it investigate Shipman for libel and slander. "When I explained to Stryk that slander was a civil issue, he demanded I meet with him to file a report against Shipman," Napa County Sheriff's Officer Pascale Valente wrote in a report. "[Stryk] could not say what his complaint was, and advised me to 'figure something out' to file against him."

Stryk eventually accused the sheriff's office of being "corrupt" and turned his attention to Stensaas and the *Yountville Sun*. He made it known that Stensaas had been operating her newspaper without a license and demanded that they cease publication. (Instead, Stensaas paid some back taxes and had her license reinstated.) King said that she began getting calls from Stryk at all hours of the day (Stryk, for his part, suggested that the incessant calls probably came from the investigators *he* hired to look into King). The calls weren't threatening, exactly, but certainly not welcome. This wasn't a total surprise—when she had done her background check, she had found that Stryk had been charged in Maryland in 2009 with making "annoying phone calls." (Stryk would later say that the charges were dropped.)

Lewis Chilton, who owned a deli in Yountville and served on the town council, remembered meeting Stryk when he first moved into the area and being struck by how friendly and ambitious he was. Chilton recalled seeing him at a local event at the school, working the crowd and introducing himself to strangers at every table. It was wholesome retail politics. But then, sometime after that, Chilton started getting automated phone messages—robocalls—that asked questions designed to make the leaders of the town look bad. The messages implied not only that the town had a spending problem, but that its leaders may have been engaging in "possible theft."

"It's simply not the way Yountville politics has ever worked," Chilton said. "A bunch of people were upset."

The innuendos didn't end with robocalls. One day a website popped up called "Yountvilleexposed.com." It claimed the town was about to be known as the "corruption capital of Napa Valley." The site included phone numbers for King, Stensaas, and Shipman.

Beneath the questionable tactics, Stryk was trying to appeal to what could be interpreted as a populist agenda of sorts. The town, he said, was catering far too much to the rich and powerful part-timers and visitors, and not enough to the working-class folks who actually lived there.

"It's time for a Mayor who will stand up to the current leadership who believes that government is nothing more than a tool of the rich and elite to prosper," he wrote on his campaign website.

Tapping into the distrust of government and trying to convince voters that they are being screwed by an entrenched elite might be a viable political strategy for a national campaign targeting distant elites, but it didn't necessarily make sense in a tight-knit community like Yountville, where everyone knows everyone else. The town prided itself on decorum, said Lewis, almost to a fault.

"There have been campaign forums in the past where there's an elephant in the room about one of the candidates, maybe something about their past, and their opponents wouldn't dare bring it up," said Lewis. "It's a place that really prides itself on civility."

At a forum for mayoral candidates, some residents had confronted Stryk about his approach to politics in the town. During a Q and A, a Vietnam veteran in a white T-shirt and trucker hat pointedly asked Stryk about flyers and imitation newspapers that had been delivered to his house with "deceitful" and "misleading" information about Stryk's opponents.

"I stand by every piece of campaign literature I put out," Stryk said in response. "I stand by asking the tough questions in town."

At one point Rose Solis, the popular manager of the town's dive bar, Pancha's, rose to speak. "I think everyone in here feels the same way, which is threatened by you," she said. "Not scared. Just threatened by you. I think you should pack your things and leave Yountville."

On election night Stryk earned 177 votes, 17 percent of the votes cast.

"Last night," he told the *Yountville Sun* the next day, "the real losers were the people of Yountville."

And then, within a few months, Stryk was gone. John Dunbar became mayor. Yountville returned to its status as a sleepy tourist destination, where if there was any corruption to speak about, no one bothered speaking about it. But the townspeople think about Stryk often, both because they see his name in the news for totally different reasons, and because of just how strange their experience was with him. It was hard to shake off.

"The whole thing feels like it was a weird dream, and I have to remind myself that it really happened," said Lewis Chilton, the deli owner and former councilman. "Because it got so wild so quick. And then it just ended."

Chapter 28

Another Crack at It

Spring 2022

Robert Stryk was hesitant to discuss Yountville, but eventually he told me his side of the story. He told me that he'd moved to Yountville because his now-wife, who was then his girlfriend, was a wine person and had taken him there for a visit and he'd fallen in love with the place. But he eventually determined that the quaint beauty of the small town hid a dark side. He told me that shortly after he moved to town, he had overheard members of local law enforcement at the Villagio Inn making racist cracks about Black people, and that it made him "sick." He said that when he brought the matter up, instead of taking the matter seriously, law enforcement started to harass him. He decided he wouldn't take it lying down, so he ran for office.

That was when he learned about the "entrenched powers" of Yountville that would do everything they could to keep him from succeeding, he said. He believed the "Mickey Mouse" investigation into his past was proof of that conspiracy. What kind of small-town operation would fly his friend out to Yountville for "dirt" on him if they weren't hiding something?

Stryk believed he would have won the election and become mayor of Yountville if not for the meddling. He spent somewhere along the lines of $50,000 on the campaign. He had phone bankers and door knockers. But between the bad publicity and another Republican who jumped into the race (he believed she ran specifically to siphon votes from him), he lost. The experience, he said, reminded him that if he really wanted to be someone who fought the powers that be, it was best to try and do so "quietly behind the scenes."

"I've never been happier than to get out of that corrupt little town, but I think about it all the time when I go into these countries in need of reform," he said. "It's part of what made me who I am today."

When Stryk first returned to Washington after Trump's victory, he had been hailed as a success. The *New York Times Magazine* featured him in the "How to Get Rich in Trump's Washington" cover story, and over the years he had proved the article right. He had gotten rich. But as the Trump presidency was winding down, reports of turmoil started to leak out from the Sonoran Lobbying Group. By early 2020, six of the eight lobbyists working in Stryk's shop had jumped ship, leaving just him and his business partner Christian Bourge. They were losing clients too—at least fifteen foreign clients ended their relationship with Stryk—according to a report from Al-Monitor, a D.C.-based news website that covered the Middle East, leaving them with only six active accounts.

Stryk was finding new sources of income, but they were becoming more and more controversial. He signed contracts worth $2.2 million to represent Isabel dos Santos, the richest woman in Africa and daughter of Angola's former president, who had been accused of stealing millions of dollars. He also agreed to a $2 million payout from a U.S. law firm that had been hired by a top official in Nicolas Maduro's government—a deal that drew a strong rebuke even from members of his own party.

"No business in the United States should have any contact with Maduro's government, let alone willingly take money to lobby on its behalf," Senator Rick Scott of Florida wrote in a letter to the law firm Foley and Lardner. In his letter, Scott accused Maduro of being a "thug and a dictator" guilty of "murdering children and starving his people," and suggested boycotting his Washington lobbyists. The law firm canceled its contract with Venezuela.

"This is what happens when you get desperate for money," a former Stryk employee, Andrew Nehring, wrote in a now-deleted tweet. "You take money from Maduro's brutal regime to get him off lists he deserves/should be on."

There were still paydays available to lobbyists as the Trump years wound down, if you didn't mind the stink. There was, for example, George Nader, a Lebanese American businessman with ties to Trump's inner circle. Nader had been sentenced to ten years in prison on child pornography charges, and he gave Stryk's lobbying shop $4 million to seek a pardon. The pardon didn't happen, but the check cleared.

It could be a dirty game, but Stryk thought he deserved another chance to play. And as he got further and further into the Biden era, he resented that the old guard seemed to be making the rules again.

"I only got a four-year crack at it," he said. "I want another four-year crack at it. I deserve it, I earned it, I'm still here today. Those cocksuckers got forty years to do it and fucked this country up. I want four more years."

Chapter 29

I Will Spew You Out of My Mouth

Summer 2022

The last time I'd been to Ian Walters's home, in the early spring of 2022, he told me that his cancellation had started him on the path to self-imposed exile from politics. But the breakup with Matt Schlapp and CPAC had still been too fresh to fully understand how it had happened. When I visited him again in the early summer, he still wasn't entirely sure. But he thought that perhaps it had something to do with the loss of his father.

"He's been on my mind a lot," Ian told me after we'd settled into patio furniture in his front yard. He began by telling me the story of Ralph's death.

By the time Covid rolled around in early 2020, Ralph was already in bad health. He'd gained a lot of weight. He'd had a handful of heart surgeries and was suffering from breathing issues after a lifetime of smoking.

"I remember talking to him and Ralph was like, 'I can't get this shit, if I get this shit I'm dead,'" Ian said.

The whole Walters family took Covid precautions seriously, but after months in lockdown, they decided they needed to make a break for it. The pandemic had kept them apart from family for long enough, so he and Carin piled the kids into the car and drove to Bethany Beach, a Delaware beach town about two and a half hours northeast of Washington, for an overdue vacation reunion with their grandparents, Ralph and Millie.

It was perfect. They were right by the beach and the water was still warm enough to swim. Ralph, or Pawpaw to Hazel and Violet, wasn't in the best of health, Ian said, which made even the short walk to the water "a real burden" for him, "but god damn, he got out in the ocean" to splash around with his grandkids. It was still an unsettling time in the country—early enough in the pandemic that many people were living in lockdown—but things almost felt normal down at the beach. People were out, the kids were happy, and the grandparents loved seeing smiles on their real faces, not just on a phone screen.

On their last day, Ian was packing up the car when he heard a scream from upstairs. Ian sprinted in and found Ralph stuck between the toilet and the wall, having wedged himself there after a bad fall. They got him to the hospital, but they never got him out. He had a broken pelvis, which led to sepsis. He died days later.

The funeral was held at St. Anthony of Padua, a small Catholic church located in a D.C. neighborhood known as "Little Rome."

News of his death had drawn gestures of respect from notable Republicans. Vice President Mike Pence had tweeted, "With the passing of Ralph Hallow, our Country lost a Giant of American Journalism and I lost a friend." The *Washington Times*, in an obituary for Ralph, quoted Fox News host Tucker Carlson praising him as "a positive, optimistic, person always, right to the end." Conservative activist and lawyer Cleta Mitchell had weighed in, too, calling Ralph "the kindest, most warm-hearted person imaginable," a man who "did not suffer fools, braggarts, or idiots well." On the day of the funeral, Newt Gingrich and his wife, Callista, who was Trump's ambassador to the

Holy See, messaged an attendee to say they were watching the ceremony, via livestream, from Rome.

It was November 22, 2020. Two weeks earlier the networks had called the presidential race for Biden, and the MAGA movement was in freakout mode. "Frankly, we did win this election," Trump had falsely claimed, and all the president's braggarts, idiots, and fools— plus some members of the professional MAGA class—had fallen in line. Cleta Mitchell, for her part, would eventually emerge as an adviser to Trump in his efforts to overturn his loss in Georgia, participating in an infamous phone call in which the president pressed election officials there to "find" enough votes to put him ahead of Biden. Matt Schlapp had flown to Las Vegas, where he held a press conference with the state's former attorney general, Adam Laxalt, and said, "We have literally 9,000 people who voted in this election who don't live in Nevada." He didn't have any evidence to back up the claim, but Trump liked it, tweeting, "Nevada is turning out to be a cesspool of Fake Votes. @mschlapp & @AdamLaxalt are finding things that, when released, will be absolutely shocking."

For this, Ian had been called into duty. The fact-checking website PolitiFact wanted to know how Matt had come up with that number, and Ian was the person who gave them some spin: The number, he said, was extrapolated from a list that the Trump campaign had provided plus some of their own back-of-the-napkin calculations. PolitiFact found the argument unconvincing and rated the claim a Pants on Fire! on its "Truth-O-Meter" scale.

At the church in Little Rome, D.C., Ralph's friends from Official Washington gathered for a graveside service, including Matt.

It was the first time that Ian had seen Matt since Ralph died. Ian wasn't thinking much about election claims on this day, but Matt was deeply immersed in the nascent mythology of Trump's stolen-election narrative.

"I remember getting to the church," Ian told me. "And the thing he said was, 'Wherever Ralph is, he's got the access to really know what the real vote counts were, what really happened.'"

Ian rolled his eyes thinking about it. He was sitting in front of his house in a tank top, a handkerchief wrapped around his forehead, drinking coffee while his kids splashed in a nearby kiddie pool. It was the height of summer in Washington, coming up on the second anniversary of Ralph's death, but it still felt fresh to Ian. The pandemic had made it difficult to clock the passage of time. The days of isolation could feel endless, but it also felt like one endless day since Ralph had died.

With both Ralph and his birth father, Colin, gone (Colin died in 2003), Ian had become the family patriarch, and it was proving to be more difficult than he'd expected. The project to rehab the second house on a neighboring property, the one for his mother, Millie, had stalled out—his first set of contractors was really good at taking money, but not doing any work. This was particularly stressful since Ian was having some trouble on the jobs front. His friend had given him a lead on some work—a gig bashing Biden cabinet secretaries in the press. It was a job Ian might have liked, but he couldn't figure out where the funding for the project came from, and that was no longer something he felt comfortable with.

Money was tight and there was always something to do. He needed to get someone to trim back the dead branches on the trees by the house. He could spend all day in the yard and feel like he'd hardly made a dent. And it felt like he was spending hours each week driving to a nearby forest to release the woodchucks that his traps kept catching in his garden. I asked him whether the recent changes in his life were in any way related to the fact that he was now the only remaining father figure in the family.

"I feel it in a deep way," he said, walking through his yard to check on the woodchuck trap (empty). "It's like, let's get some shit done. Let's get this fucking house done. Let's rehab it and get my mom fucking moved in. Let's figure out what the next five years, the next ten years of our lives are—what the important things are."

After checking the traps, Ian and I walked to the garage, where Ian had a trove of artifacts he had recently recovered from Ralph's old study: photographs from the book party Arianna Huffington had hosted for him, which then–presidential contender Bob Dole had attended; old White House Correspondents' dinner programs, which Ian planned to throw away. He had also found an old letter that Ralph sent him when Ian was in college. Ralph told him to get his act together, which was a little painful to read, even now. But Ian knew he would keep it forever.

Ian also pulled out his phone to show me a video taken at Ralph's graveside service. It was a clip of Matt Schlapp's speech.

"He scrutinized every word, he thought about it, he invested himself in it," Matt had told the assembled mourners, expressing a bit of self-consciousness about attempting to eulogize a man with such an exacting BS detector. "I did what Ralph would probably expect me to do, I cracked open my Bible to the Great Author."

Matt looked down at a piece of paper in his hand. It was a Bible passage that he said he believed could have been "written just for Ralph," from the book of Revelation.

"'So, because you are lukewarm, and neither cold nor hot, I will spew you out of my mouth,'" he read, adding, "Is that not perfect for Ralph Hallow?"

Was it? Ian wasn't sure exactly what that passage had to do with his dad. But what Matt said next really gave him pause.

Matt addressed Ian directly. "Your dad was so proud of you. In moments where you couldn't hear or see, he would say the most tremendous things about your abilities," he said. "You were in a tricky position, he a journalist, you an anti-journalist. It was interesting to watch."

Anti-journalist?

Tricky?

"It's not tricky," Ian said, pausing the video and looking at me with his eyes starting to well. "That's my dad. I love him. And sometimes we fucking wrestle. Yeah, sometimes he's a journalist before he's a fucking dad. Yeah. And it gets rough. As dads and sons do, they can wrestle, and sometimes they don't get along and it can turn into a macho pissing contest. Sure. And certainly that was a part of our relationship."

It sure sounded . . . tricky, I thought to myself.

"Once we got over those type of tendencies," Ian continued, "it was a slice of heaven in my life for those years. Carin chilled me out, and she chilled him out. And boy, to see him around the baby. At a certain point he became Pawpaw. It wasn't tricky, it was a slice of heaven."

Ian pressed play and Matt finished the speech.

"I feel like we're missing a warrior," Matt had said in closing. "We have to take confidence that he would want us, more than anything else, to get beyond this period of mourning and to fight."

I peeked at Ian as he showed me the video and saw him grimace when Matt said the word "fight."

Fight, fight, fight.

"It's the pillar of the identity that he is going after," Ian said. "I dunno, I've come to think that it's kind of unhealthy."

Chapter 30

No, No, No, We're Doing Great

Summer 2022

Matt Schlapp lost his own father when he was a young man. They'd had a difficult relationship. Schlapp Senior had been an alcoholic, according to Matt—emotionally distant, not exactly a "fully formed human being who dealt with his demons." *That* had been tricky, and so Matt had been forced to seek mentorship elsewhere: adults in the neighborhood, professors in college, his tennis coaches back in Kansas, and eventually in the politics industry—where "everyone is equally fucked up."

That was where he learned the game. He didn't invent it; it was passed down.

"I played the game like everyone played the game—the game I was taught," Matt said.

We were sitting outside a coffee shop in Alexandria, talking about a previous version of Matt. Back when I first began writing about him, he had the reputation as being a Nice Republican.

A Nice Republican could make conservative arguments on PBS without making liberal viewers change the channel instantly. TV bookers could trust a Nice Republican to critique President Barack Obama without saying anything (too) racist.

"I used careful language," Matt said.

That was part of "the game." He knew not to criticize Obama "too harshly or people will assume you have racial animus." He came to believe Obama would "get a pass because he's the first Black president," and Matt would have to just learn to deal with that.

It was a relatively easy game to win, Matt said. All you needed was to know a little, look good enough in a suit, and have people like you.

"I've never known anyone to fail here," he said. "I think I'm the only one I know to actually fail in Washington."

He was talking about how he had been "canceled" for speaking his mind—how he had lost his clients and much of his business when even the "biggest dumb shit in the world" could be successful here.

And so Matt was done being a Nice Republican. "Over time, I guess, because people have been so harsh in their language toward me, I'm less concerned about what people think of me," he said. "I am less politically correct today than I would have been. I'm less willing to play the game."

Well. Less willing to play *that* game.

The new game was *fight fight fight*. And Matt was a Fight Republican.

A Fight Republican says things like, "D.C. can be the capital of Blue America and we will find the capital of Red America," and after an election that doesn't go his guy's way will say, "The presidency is literally in the breach."

Matt had been a key lieutenant in battles that sprang up after the 2020 presidential campaign.

"Pls get 4 or 5 killers in remaining courts," Matt had texted Trump's chief of staff, Mark Meadows, the day after the election. "Need outsiders who will torch the place. Local folks won't do it. Lawyers and operators. Get us in these states."

"I may need to get you and mercy to PA," Meadows responded.

Instead, he headed out to Nevada in search of fraudulent votes. He was part of an effort to cast the election as having been stolen, something the dwindling number of Nice Republicans around town couldn't tolerate.

"This is as un-American as it gets," the Republican super attorney Ben Ginsberg wrote in a *Washington Post* opinion piece about Trump's tactics to suppress voters. But Matt told me that these efforts were nothing new. It was an old game, one that had been passed down to him too.

Matt had, after all, been a participant in the Brooks Brothers riot that managed to shut down a hand recount in Miami-Dade County after the George W. Bush contest against Al Gore had been deemed too close to call. That event had turned ugly—though maybe not by today's standards. The *New York Times* reported that several people had been trampled, punched, or kicked when protesters tried to rush the door. The chairman of the Miami-Dade Democratic Party was chased down by a crowd that accused him of stealing a ballot. Maybe it had gotten a bit out of hand, but it wasn't off script.

"As I flew down there with Ben Ginsberg," Matt said, describing his trip to Florida with the then top lawyer for Bush's recount efforts, "he was the one telling me, 'Here's how they steal those things.'"

It was, Matt claimed, the first time he had ever heard about "stealing" an election, straight from the mouth of the Republican National Committee's own lawyer.

"And that's the word they used," Matt told me. "It wasn't Trump's word. It was RNC parlance the lawyers taught me. They will steal it if we don't get down there. I didn't know people stole elections before that; I didn't even use the term."

Personally, Matt said he didn't like to use the word "steal" when talking about what Democrats did in 2020. But only because he didn't think that was a strong enough word.

"'Stealing' is the wrong word because it was so orchestrated over a period of time, a big operation," he said. "Stealing to me is just like a pickpocket, like someone grabbed something when you weren't looking."

Matt, like all Republicans who talked like this, had never been able to prove any widespread voter fraud—or any illegal activity that could have changed the outcome of the election from Biden to Trump. But maybe that wasn't even the point; maybe the point was just to stay in the game.

I asked him if he really thought he had failed in Washington. I reminded him that he often bragged to me about feeling more influential than ever—he had lost the clients but gained some of the base and CPAC continued to be a central conservative gathering. It had, in fact, gone global, with CPAC Australia, CPAC Brazil, CPAC Japan, CPAC South Korea. In 2022, CPAC Orlando was followed by CPAC Hungary, CPAC Israel, and CPAC Texas—and quadrupled its revenue, bringing in $3.4 million from April 2021 to January 2022.

"No, I haven't failed," he said. "I was kind of humiliated publicly but I didn't fail. No, no, no, we're doing great."

He had been canceled; he was doing great.

"There's always a game, right?" Matt said. "And it doesn't change that much in the end."

Chapter 31

The Turn

Summer 2022

A few days after my visit to Alibi in June, Robert Stryk broke up with me.

"Hey Brother I have gotten uncomfortable with all of this," Stryk texted me. "I feel something is not right. So I wish you all the best but. I can't be involved anymore."

The text took me by surprise. I looked through our messages for clues for why he wanted out all of a sudden. Maybe it had to do with the fact that I'd let him know that I would be calling around to people who knew him. This was standard operating procedure, reporting-wise, but maybe this had spooked him? Or maybe it was because I'd asked him about Yountville, and he'd realized I'd be writing about stories other than just the ones he'd offered up. There was also a recent text exchange that had felt awkward. I'd declined to answer when he texted to ask what I thought about leaked reports that the Supreme Court would strike down *Roe v. Wade*. He wanted to know how I felt about the "hysteria" surrounding the decision. Instead I had deflected and asked him what he thought.

"I'm absolute on life," he'd said. "Pro-life and anti-death penalty. I get you are a liberal, but what do you think?"

I told him that I worried about how tense things were getting in the country.

"Nah," he'd said. "That's Democracy at its finest. Don't fall into the trap that Democracy is on the edge. The Mob likes to be loud."

None of this seemed like a reason to cut me off.

I tried to get a sense of why he no longer wished to speak with me, but was rebuffed.

"Ben," he messaged me, "it was a real pleasure and honor meeting you and I find you a really cool and fascinating fella but this is not right for family. I made a real mistake in speaking with you."

"Is there something I'm missing?" I asked. "Well, I admit I'm a bit confused, and certainly bummed to not get to keep chatting. But you always know how to reach me if you change your mind."

I kept reporting on Stryk, though. He might have decided not to talk to me anymore, but I still wanted to write about him. He was still an interesting figure in post-Trump Washington—even more so now that he was pursuing a lucrative lobbying contract with a Russian ally as Putin's army terrorized Ukraine. And so, without any future visits to Middleburg in my future, I set out to call people who knew Stryk, letting them know that he had been participating for this book before suddenly deciding that he'd rather not.

Stryk didn't seem to like that.

"I am disappointed as I have heard from a few folks that you are pissed and that you are out to get me bc I 'Ghosted' you," he messaged me, after I'd spoken to a few of his former coworkers. One of them had told me not to trust anything Stryk told me, that he was full of shit. Another said it was no fun being on his bad side. I had not, however, expressed any anger about Stryk cutting off ties. I had also, as far as I could recall, never used the term "ghosted" in my life.

"I am sorry if you feel that way I can't stop you from doing whatever you are doing but it definitely didn't help my concerns getting these messages," Stryk continued. "You will find that nobody really knows me as I keep to myself and very very small circle of friends."

Stryk sent more messages that day, explaining why he wanted to stop talking to me without really explaining it. It really did resemble a breakup, in the language, anyway.

"It's me not you," he texted after calling me a "good fella." He wanted me to know that he was working on himself, that he wanted to "do big things," and in order to do so, he needed to "humble [his] shit" and spend less time talking about himself. Still, he wanted me to know that he "really enjoyed our time together."

"You made me think about things which I will always thank you for," he said. "I love thinking and talking and you stimulated my brain."

The messages kept coming. Stryk was still under the impression that I had been telling people that he had "ghosted" me, which seemed to upset him.

"I am a huge fan of yours but to tell people that I 'Ghosted You' makes me feel that our many hours together at my ranch meant nothing," he said. "So that's disappointing to me but I guess in the end that's D.C. and the powers that be never want it to change and they are winning."

As far as breakups go, it was amicable enough. Stryk even left open the possibility of us talking again someday, saying he was working on something huge that, if he was able to get it done, could be the makings of a movie someday and that he'd tell me about it. But then things got weird.

Stryk began to text me asking if I was working with a reporter who had written about him before. I wasn't, but I had reached out to him in the course of my reporting and asked for contact information for people in Stryk's orbit.

"Is this a hard question for you to answer?" Stryk texted.

It wasn't a hard question, and I told him so: The answer was no.

"That's a lie," Stryk texted when I told him I was not working with anyone on this book. "You are not working alone."

Stryk had decided that since I would not own up to my supposed

use of the word "ghosted" or to my supposed partnership with a journalist who had written stories that Stryk didn't like, I was a liar. Maybe
worse.

"Ben you are a douche bag and a liar and that's ok," he texted.

"You are a liar. So have fun I don't give a fuck."

"You came to me home and you lied to me."

"I don't want you around my kids or family ever again."

"You are not a good dude. I know you need to feed your kids But
not lying about my family!!"

"I brought you to my Fucking house and you met my Son! What is
wrong with you!"

"And of course no Response."

"I am sorry you have kids."

"Good job, Ben."

"You have a predatory nature."

"Did you prey upon my kids when you came to my house?"

"You are a douche bag."

"And a liar"

"Of course no response you sicko."

*　*　*

There really wasn't much I could say to Stryk, response-wise. He had
basically accused me of being a child predator for absolutely no reason
at all.

"I'm trying to be diplomatic here because I understand that being
written about is a stressful thing and you have gone out on a limb talking to me—which I appreciate, truly," I had texted him, trying to give
him an out during his unhinged texts. "But I have to admit it's bothering me that you are calling me a liar. I am not a liar. I am not working
with any other reporter. I have a process, I try to be as fair as I possibly
can be, and that's just the truth."

Lying about his family? I hadn't even mentioned them. What did
his kids have to do with anything? I admit that I worried a bit for my

safety. If this guy really thought this stuff about me, would he want me taken off the streets by any means necessary? It was possible that this was just the case of Stryk having had a few too many drinks. He was living in England for the summer, and it tended to be late for him when the messages came in.

But I also wondered if he might be doing something more calculating with these messages. I wondered if it might be part of his playbook.

When Stryk thought that his participation in my book might be good for him, he worked the job like it was a public relations campaign. He cozied up to me, we bro-hugged and drank whiskey, just like he talked about doing with foreign leaders. He checked in on me frequently, texting and calling from overseas, reaching out on Valentine's Day to see if I'd gotten my wife something special, suggesting power brokers I should get in touch with for the book, sending me a picture from Mar-a-Lago, where he had gone to attend a screening of *2,000 Mules*—a conspiracy theory movie about the 2020 election.

Maybe when he started to get a sense that he might not like how he would appear in the book, the mission became more like trying to get a foreign country off a sanctions list. Was he trying to lobby—well, okay, bully—me out of writing about him at all?

It took only a little research to see that Stryk appears to have done something like this before. In 2020, for example, he had been called in by a friend of his, Domonic Foppoli, the mayor of Windsor, a small Sonoma County town, who had been accused by multiple women of sexual assault. Stryk had been brought in to do battle with one of the mayor's accusers and with the *San Francisco Chronicle*, which had been reporting on the story. Stryk told a reporter he had a sex tape of the accuser and would release damaging information. One *Chronicle* reporter started getting calls via WhatsApp from an account initialed "R.S.," who made derogatory statements about the reporter and refused to identify himself but denied being Robert Stryk. This person called back forty-three times over the course of two hours before the reporter blocked the number. Later, a reporter was forced to hang up on Stryk after reaching him by phone and listening to the lobbyist repeatedly call another reporter a "misogynistic expletive."

"Stryk's tactics in Windsor have struck some people as reminiscent of the 45th president," the *Chronicle* wrote in one story, "full of misinformation, repeated name calling and deflection."

Who was Robert Stryk, anyway? Based on the sum of my interactions with him and other people who had dealt with him, he seemed like a type that had become familiar in American politics. He could be doting and ingratiating. He could be exhausting. It was no fun to be on his bad side. He talked a big game. He hustled. He made things happen. He was apt to believe people were conspiring to stop him from getting where he wanted to be. The Trump era was proof that there was a version of Washington where a guy like Stryk would be taken seriously by people who were willing to spend serious money to advance their interests. Stryk had reached a level of success that could potentially keep him in the game forever. But another lesson from the Trump years was that no version of Washington is permanent, and that finding your way to the main stage is no guarantee that you won't end up in the sideshow.

Chapter 32

Frank Luntz, Dr. Phil, and *Roe v. Wade*

Summer 2022

When Frank Luntz invited me to speak about the importance of journalism to a group of high school students in late June, I leapt at the opportunity. The children are our future, after all. And even more important, Frank held these semi-regular discussions in his luxury penthouse apartment in downtown D.C. The one he hated. The one Kevin McCarthy had lived in.

The Speaker-in-waiting was not there when I arrived. But to my surprise, Dr. Phil was.

Phil McGraw, television therapist, was finishing his own talk (about the importance of television therapy?). He sat in front of a giant painting of an astronaut landing on the moon and next to a tiny statue of British Prime Minister Boris Johnson taking a shit on the floor—part of Frank's living room decor. I stood by a drawing of an American flag signed by every president since Franklin Delano Roosevelt (Trump's signature was by far the largest), leaned on a bar labeled "Frank's Sportspub," and listened in as a group of Black and

Hispanic students asked about the bombshell news that had broken only moments before.

If you were on the Supreme Court, with your legal expertise, and you faced the decision that they just faced, would you have voted to overturn it?

The world-famous TV personality stroked his world-famous mustache and responded in his slow Texas drawl.

"I would not have overturned *Roe v. Wade*," Dr. Phil said. "I'm an old guy; why would anyone give a shit about what I think a woman should do with her body? Why should I have any reason to tell a woman what she should do with her body? I just think that's insane."

I inched closer, over by a table with Biden-Harris face masks and a little statuette of Teddy Roosevelt. I caught a glimpse of a spiral staircase to the second floor, lined with Frank's colorful sneakers, and an actual motorcycle (painted red, white, and blue) at the top of the landing.

"I thought it was impossible," Frank told Dr. Phil, shaking his head. "I used to think it was just an issue that the left would use against the right to fight with people. I know it's a bad decision, it's actually a crummy decision, it's badly written, but I just assumed, for year after year for thirty years, that this would not happen. And now everyone is going crazy up on the Hill…Everyone's going batshit crazy."

"Well," Dr. Phil said in his slow Texas drawl. "All the constitutional experts knew it was a horrible decision technically, but I don't think anyone really thought they would really end it. Because commonsensically it didn't make any sense."

"Well, this could change the outcome of the 2022 election," said Frank.

"It could certainly affect the midterms," said Dr. Phil.

Chapter 33

Losing Traction

Summer 2022

Three days after the fall of *Roe. v. Wade*, I met up with Leah Hunt-Hendrix for coffee.

"I think, actually, on the one hand, it could be hopeful," Leah said about the Supreme Court decision. "The biggest problem with this year was that everyone assumes it's going to be a red wave and that has demobilized everyone. I think people are going to get mobilized."

Leah was trying to be optimistic, but she was falling back on talking points. She was feeling demoralized for other reasons.

"It's a tough time." She sighed. "I definitely feel like I'm under siege."

A day earlier, President Biden had endorsed Danny Davis, the eighty-year-old moderate Democrat running in Illinois's 7th district against Kina Collins, a thirty-one-year-old activist and one of Leah's candidates. Collins, like a number of progressives endorsed by Way to Win, was struggling to gain traction, which only exacerbated Leah's growing worry about her own reputation as a burgeoning Washington power broker. She was aware that donors were most interested in picking winners, and Leah found herself forced to make the kind of pragmatic decisions she despised. Her friend David Segal, for example, the guy who introduced Leah to her boyfriend and who was running for Congress in Rhode Island, had asked if she would write a fundraising email on his behalf. But Leah didn't think he was going to win, so she didn't think she could do it.

Leah found her fulcrum, as her father had advised; now her anxiety was about leverage.

"I'm probably losing traction," she said.

Her candidates were getting absolutely swamped with negative ads from AIPAC and DMFI, which meant Leah had to spend much more time fundraising than she would like.

"I'm worried that I'm not giving enough back to donors," she said. "I'm not offering community or a book club or anything. I have to raise so much more money to be successful that everything else is on the back burner."

H. L. Hunt's granddaughter was having money problems. Being from a wealthy family, even a family as wealthy as Leah's, doesn't necessarily mean having unlimited access to cash whenever you need it.

"My money situation is very complicated," Leah explained. "My mom has never wanted to give us very much money. When she dies, we will all start getting dividends, but we hope she doesn't die for a long time. There's all this money that's just sitting there. I'm trying to start fundraising from my mom."

Helen LaKelly Hunt was a giver. Her father's money had allowed her to live in comfort, but she considered it a burden. "All I know is, I didn't want money," she had told me in an interview. "I didn't care about money. I cared about poverty." She had given away chunks of her share of the family fortune, and helped other rich women do the same. She had started the Texas Women's Foundation and the New York Women's Foundation. She and Swanee had launched Women Moving Millions, a campaign that asked women to pledge gifts of $1 million or more, a community that had made commitments of nearly $800 million. Helen had built the kind of legacy in the women's movement that her daughter was now trying to build in progressive politics.

Leah's effort to raise funds from her mother, however, had been "very awkward."

"We had a meeting recently with her finance team," Leah said. "And then a couple weeks ago, she called me and was like, 'I've never supported your work, I'd like to give $2 million.'" A week later she changed her mind.

She said, according to Leah, "Maybe $50,000."

Things were a little strained with the crypto boyfriend as well. Leah and Marvin had been dating for a few months now, and Leah was starting to notice something about him that was rubbing her the wrong way.

"I'm pretty anti-elite," she said, sipping her matcha latte. "I didn't like growing up in elite circles or living in Silicon Valley. I've been happiest in New Mexico or Syria."

Marvin, however, was "super into money." He enjoyed the elite lifestyle in a way that Leah simply did not.

"He's totally self-made," she explained. "A first-generation immigrant from Iraq. Now he's hanging out with Marc Andreessen and I don't want to be with those people. I'm struggling with it, actually."

"Every meal we've had has been like a seven-course tasting menu," she continued. "I'm like, I can't. This can't be like how it always is."

Talking to Leah about money could be a bit strained. Being an oil heiress and political radical came with some inevitable contradictions. It was funny to hear her talk about being "anti-elite" and how she might be happier if she could just quit the fundraising game and go be a union organizer somewhere (technically, nothing was stopping her).

And yet Leah's earnestness was important—at least as an asset for the movement she had adopted. A lot of rich kids might say they care about poverty and solidarity, but very few of them make doing something about it their life's work.

"She's certainly one of the only people on the left organizing big money," said Morris Katz, a progressive consultant.

"When I first started a consulting firm and was looking for money," one progressive operator told me, "everyone kept telling me I had to talk to Leah. She's the nexus of the whole movement."

Lately, though, she had been daydreaming about quitting politics, or at the very least taking some time off. But at the moment there was still too much to do. She had seen a poll showing Mandela Barnes as the only Democrat in the Wisconsin Senate primary who could beat Ron Johnson. But in order to have a shot, Barnes needed to win the primary first.

The Senate was important. The smart money was on the Republicans to take back the House—Leah's work there had more to do with filling the party's bench with Maxwell Frosts, Greg Casars, and Andrea Salinases who could help pull Democrats to the left—but if her party managed to pick up a seat in Wisconsin, it would almost guarantee that they'd keep control of the Senate.

"Our specific goals are holding all the current Senate seats and adding two more to make Manchin and Sinema irrelevant," she said. "That's a high bar and why I've got to go all in this month for Mandela."

It was important to Leah to help show that a Black progressive could win in a statewide election in the Midwest—a place with its fair share of White voters, Trump Republicans, and middle-of-the-road Democrats.

Leah planned to write a fundraising memo and hit the phones: calling donors in her network, calling donors who had maxed out to Barnes's campaign but might have more to give to outside groups, calling groups on the ground to see what their needs were. And then?

And then she was going to take a vacation. Head to Spain and then Portugal, do some surfing, get her head straight. Having money wasn't all bad. Hopefully she could come back recharged and ready to fight. She was going with the boyfriend too. She had told her social worker to put a pause on the fostering process. She had decided to put off being a foster mom while she tried to make things work with Marvin. Portugal would be a test for *that* candidate.

"After that trip," Leah said, "if I decide I don't see the potential, I'll get back in touch with my social worker."

Chapter 34

Homeboy Does Not Cry

Summer 2022

I'm always happy," Sean McElwee told me one summer afternoon over lunch. "I live my life like I'm constantly swimming in warm water."

He had just broken up with his girlfriend of seven years.

In my time with Sean, I had never met his girlfriend, or even heard Sean talk about her. She was a freelance political consultant in New York named Bobbi. Bobbi was a Democrat, working mostly on the state and local levels. In 2015, a friend of hers matched with Sean on a dating app, and suggested that maybe he was more Bobbi's type. Bobbi found him a little weird on their first date—weird, but enjoyable. Bobbi enjoyed talking about politics with Sean, even if they didn't always agree. She was a normie Democrat, and he was going to Democratic Socialists of America meetups in Brooklyn—but their political arguments were civil, even fun.

Bobbi grew to love Sean, but she was still interested in pushing him to be a better version of himself. She would tell him when she thought he was playing too much online poker, which he seemed to be doing all the time, sometimes on multiple screens at once. The gambling wasn't the only thing she hoped he'd cut back on. She also suggested he should drink a little less booze and eat a little less takeout. She encouraged him to go to graduate school.

Sean's transformation happened slowly and then all at once. He went to Columbia University to get a master's degree in social science and quantitative methods. He went from a "normal guy" who would play a lot of video games into someone who couldn't stop talking about "discipline." He went all in on a weightlifting plan. He didn't stop gambling. But he cut out alcohol. He started cutting out meat. And then he cut out Bobbi too.

Sean said there had been tension in their relationship regarding his professional success. "I've already achieved more in my life than I thought I could," he told me. "I am definitely going to be the most successful person from back home." Bobbi couldn't handle his success, he said. It made him think about whether Bobbi was someone he expected to spend the rest of his life with. And when he realized she wasn't, he decided to fold the hand.

"I'm not particularly emotional about it," Sean said. "Or about anything, really."

Win some, lose some. The way Sean saw it, the breakup was just another opportunity to play a different kind of market.

"Me and David Shor are going to have a hot boy summer," he said.

Plus, he had plenty of other things to keep him busy. The Fetterman campaign had been thrilled with his work during the primary. DFP had been able to turn around polls quicker than the bigger guys, which allowed the campaign to continuously provide fresh data—publicly and whispered into the ears of journalists—that showed Fetterman with a commanding lead over Lamb. The polls were legit. Or at least legit enough for Sean to bet $3,000 that Fetterman would win the primary. The frequency with which DFP was able to turn out those good-news polls enabled Rebecca Katz and her team to cultivate a sense of inevitability around Fetterman.

That sense of inevitability was threatened four days before the primary, when Fetterman climbed into a car in Lancaster, Pennsylvania, and his wife, Gisele, noticed his mouth was drooping and his speech was slurred. It turned out the candidate was having a stroke. On primary day, Fetterman had a pacemaker installed. He won the election and Gisele gave the victory speech.

Fetterman had survived both the medical threat and the electoral test, but his stroke recovery added a dimension of uncertainty to the general election showdown with Mehmet Oz, the famous TV doctor whom Trump had handpicked for the race. The polling still looked good for Fetterman, stroke notwithstanding, but things were a bit too volatile for Sean to bet on it.

"I'm not prepared to predict one way or the other what happens there," he told me.

He had plenty of wagers elsewhere. Build Back Better was, maybe, back from the dead and Sean had $2,500 in his betting accounts for the chance to win more than $6,000 if Democrats managed to get the zombie version of the bill passed by September 2. Sean was really pulling for that one, and not just because of his personal investment. The Democrats needed a win, and Data for Progress was doing their best to help them get one.

DFP had been pushing out polls showing more than 70 percent of voters supported investing in clean energy, reducing prescription drug costs, and lowering healthcare premiums—goals found within Build Back Better. Sean had taken special interest in smaller-ticket legislation as well, like the bill to manufacture more semiconductor chips in the United States.

Bills like the U.S. Innovation and Competition Act wouldn't generate big headlines and major shifts in polls, but they were in line with Sean's enthusiasm for "achievable outcomes." Gone were the days when Sean would go to the mat for transformative yet politically infeasible legislation like the Green New Deal, a bill championed by Representative Alexandria Ocasio-Cortez and the Sunrise Movement. These days Sean was more likely to praise Joe Manchin, the stubborn centrist Democrat from West Virginia, than AOC, his former happy-hour guest from his socialist days.

Sean's new orientation made him a perfect fit in his role as a consultant for Guarding Against Pandemics, the organization run by Gabe Bankman-Fried, brother of the crypto billionaire. Gabe, who was a regular at Sean's poker nights, was a believer in only playing hands that he thought he could win. The bets that the Bankman-Frieds made on congressional candidates were puzzling to some. It could seem like there was little rhyme or reason to who they supported. But it made sense to Sean: They were picking candidates who could win. If they could help get a handful of people elected, it would make achievable outcomes—like allocating money for pandemic prevention—that much more achievable.

"If you want to reshape a political party in an ideological way, then you're not going to be very happy," he said. "But if you get into politics because you're, like, 'Oh, there are like seventeen seats that need to be leveled up in a real way,' well, that can happen."

This was the way to succeed in Washington, according to Sean. Keep swimming, slowly but surely, and hope the water never gets too hot.

*   *   *

"Homeboy does not cry," Bobbi, Sean's ex, told me. "I have seen it once, and I'm pretty sure it was fake."

That had been years ago, during an almost-breakup. This time, she said, Sean hadn't even pretended to be sad about it.

It had been a few months since they'd split when I reached her by phone. Their uncoupling had been amicable. Sean was the one who had given me Bobbi's number, and she was happy to talk. Now Bobbi was telling me about how, emotionally speaking, Sean wasn't "as human as your average person."

He could get angry. She'd seen that plenty of times over the years together. He'd improved on this front dramatically, she said, but there had been times when he'd come home from work, pissed about this or that, and take it out on her. Nothing scary, just general "dickishness" and "long-winded tirades, raised voice, punch-a-wall kind of thing."

But she'd never seen him particularly sad, and so it wasn't really surprising that he took the breakup in stride. Sean was an "optimizer," Bobbi said. Not always, but certainly in recent years. Sean used to have friends for the sake of friendship, but now every relationship in his life seemed like it had a purpose.

"If it's not obvious to you what your purpose is, dig a little deeper," she said. There was one exception, she said. Sean had always been incredibly close with his family, and was especially influenced by his parents. His father was retired Navy, and when Sean got his act together and started talking all the time about "discipline," it was as if he was quoting his old man. Sean spent much of his childhood home-schooled, and his mom was always his biggest supporter. She believed, Bobbi said, that her son was basically "God's gift." And it was a religious upbringing.

"Sean grew up as an evangelical," Bobbi told me. "No matter what his current thing is, he's an evangelical at heart."

He stayed in close contact with his parents. If anything kept him grounded, it was them. But outside of family, Bobbi said, Sean didn't stay in touch with anyone unless they served a specific "purpose or an agenda."

I'd gotten a sense of this from my time with Sean. When I asked Sean's buddies at poker nights how they knew him, the answer would often be that they barely knew him at all. When I'd ask Sean about his closest friends, he would invariably mention people in Democratic politics: in Schumer's office, at lefty think tanks, David Shor. I certainly served a possible purpose in Sean's grand plan for himself to become one of Washington's main characters.

Bobbi still served a purpose in Sean's life, even after the breakup. He had called her recently, she told me, and asked, "Am I an asshole?"

She had explained to him that, yes, he could be a jerk sometimes, but no, he wasn't an asshole. He cared about his family, and about people in general and about making the world a better place for them.

And she believed that. Bobbi shared with me a memory from the very beginning of their relationship, maybe two weeks in: They were hanging out in Sean's bed in New York City when he decided to play her something from one of his Spotify playlists. It wasn't mood music—at least not the usual kind. It wasn't music at all. It was a 1968 recording of Ted Kennedy's eulogy at Robert F. Kennedy's funeral.

"Each time a man stands up for an ideal, or acts to improve the lot of others, or strikes out against injustice, he sends forth a tiny ripple of hope, and crossing each other from a million different centers of energy and daring, those ripples build a current that can sweep down the mightiest walls of oppression and resistance," Teddy intoned.

Sean's move was corny, but Bobbi liked it.

"It was very obvious then, and a thing I will always respect and value about Sean, is that he is interested in changing the world and using political power to make people's lives better," she said. "And whatever ways he thinks is best, he will try."

And yet, Bobbi added, it wasn't that simple. She believed the Kennedy speech reflected his ideals, but she was pretty sure it spoke to another part of him too: a part that fantasized about someone giving a eulogy like that at his own funeral.

"Sometimes it is hard to tell to what degree those ends are serving him or himself and his own ego and own place in history," she said. "It's hard to tell the extent which his belief in doing really good things is stronger than his belief in his own influence and going down in history as having done something important."

Bobbi felt Sean was a net positive for the world. The work he did felt important to her. And she was proud that he had built an organization up from nothing, by himself, and that he surrounded himself with a young, diverse staff.

When he had ended things between them, she was not crushed.

Living with Sean, Bobbi had begun to have a difficult time feeling like her own person.

"He really likes to influence the way people think," she said. "It is really easy to get sucked up into that. And I think that was harming my own intellectual, professional, and personal growth. In a way that really prevented me from going after things that I really, really wanted."

She worried that she was not the only one getting Seanified by virtue of spending lots of time around him.

"You can kind of see it," she told me, "with his young staff."

* * *

Marcela Mulholland was thinking about getting on TikTok.

"I'm weirdly fascinated by Munchausen by proxy," said Data for Progress's twenty-five-year-old political director. "And there's this algorithm on TikTok just for Munchausen by proxy shit, just people telling their stories. It's great, but also I've decided I consume too much sad content because my interests are all politics and Munchausen by proxy so I'm trying to diversify."

Marcela seemed extremely comfortable with her boss, whom she had come to think of as a good friend. Her interests did, in fact, range beyond politics and Munchausen by proxy syndrome—an inexplicable phenomenon where a caretaker either fakes that a person, usually a child, is sick, or actively makes them sick, and which is generally regarded as mental illness or child abuse. She was also interested in spreading awareness about the dangers of urinary tract infections and figuring out her coworkers' attachment styles. (Her attachment style was mostly "anxious," she said. Sean's, she believed, was mostly "secure.")

Sean had taught Marcela that it was okay if a lot of people disliked you as long as nobody truly hated you, but people around Washington simply liked Marcela. Her job as political director was to be one of the more visible members of the Data for Progress team, and she was often the person responsible for smoothing things over with other political organizations and congressional offices when Sean's shtick became grating. She called herself the "spoonful of sugar that helped Sean go down."

She didn't mind. Sean had taken a big chance on her, essentially putting her in charge of her own think tank when she was barely out of college. Marcela was in briefings in the Senate and meetings in the White House. She'd even had a pleasant time meeting Neera Tanden, despite the alleged stink eye in 2019.

"Maybe I'm just naive and weak for schmoozy political people," Marcela said. "But she was very nice."

As for the schmoozy political person she worked for, Marcela appreciated that Sean had put together a diverse team. She was part of a vanguard of young progressives who seemed destined to be the future of the Democratic Party, while also being part of its present. Maybe she had been "modpilled," as she put it—awakened to the benefits of moderating one's politics in the name of making incremental (but real) change. But Sean had made a compelling case that the most progressive thing you could do was actually make progress. And Marcela had seen the data about what ideas were popular and which were not. And despite their awkward first encounter at happy hour, she had grown to trust Sean and seek his approval—not just on matters of politics.

"I started taking Lexapro," she told Sean one day during lunch at his favorite ramen spot. "I don't have peaks of anxiety, I have low-grade dread all the time. It's literally the American experience, but I was feeling really bad about taking it, like, am I weak?"

"No!" Sean said. "You're not weak."

"You don't think I'm weak for taking this? Honestly, Sean, I was embarrassed that you would think I was weak because I started taking it. Do you think I'm strong?"

"Yes."

Sean's rapport with his Gen Z employees was a valuable thing. There had been something happening at progressive organizations around town: Young staffers had been rising up and forcing organizations to reckon with issues of race, gender, and power structures within their own walls. Ryan Grim, the Washington bureau chief for The Intercept, wrote an article stating that it was nearly impossible to find a progressive organization that "hadn't been in tumult, or isn't currently in tumult."

But that wasn't a problem for Sean. Not yet.

"Me and Sean are like BFFs," she said. "Not in a weird way. I consider him a friend. He doesn't have friends, but we're friends. He's an older person that I trust and I want him to feel proud of me. And I was worried. He has a secure attachment style with optimized mental health, so he's not exactly someone who would indulge me in these things."

"Want to bet?" Sean said.

"See, this is what it's like," said Marcela. "I'm like Sean, I'm going through something serious, and he'll be like, 'You wanna bet?' Literally this is what he's like!"

Sean didn't respond.

"Can you give me a response?" Marcela said.

"I'm fine with it. Many of my staff are on Lexapro."

"Are you on Lexapro?"

"I am not," he said. "But it doesn't imply anything about me that I'm not. I don't want my not using it to make you feel ashamed that you do. You do good work. You're very disciplined."

"Are you going to cry?" Marcela said.

"No, I'm not going to cry."

Chapter 35

Everything Is Not Okay, Dude

Big breaks don't usually happen all at once. They happen as a result of many little breaks plus one more. And the cracks in Ian Walters's relationship with Matt Schlapp had been accumulating for some time.

In 2021, Paul Gosar—an Arizona Republican who had been a well-respected dentist in Flagstaff before going cartoonishly MAGA, calling the January 6th rioters "peaceful patriots" and President Biden an "illegitimate usurper"—spoke at an event thrown by White nationalist Nick Fuentes in Orlando the evening before he was scheduled to appear onstage at CPAC. It was basically the same as the Marjorie Taylor Greene situation, but a year earlier, back when Ian thought he still had Matt's ear. Ian remembered getting on a phone call with Matt and other CPAC staffers to discuss whether Gosar still should be allowed to speak at their conference. Ian thought CPAC needed to take a hard stand against Gosar. It was good politics, and also the right thing to do. On the same call, Ian also discussed some security issues at the conference hotel and the fact that there appeared be a "tracker"—someone hired to record political figures in hope of scoring something juicy that could be used against them—following Matt's every move with a camera.

"The only thing you're telling me of interest," Ian remembered Matt saying, "is that I've got a tracker."

Gosar spoke the next morning. That was a crack.

There were multiple cracks forming around the question of what kind of Republicans CPAC should be boosting as all-stars of the conservative movement. Ian was no moderate squish, or even a Never Trumper—he voted for him twice. And having the president of the United States as a regular at the conference was thrilling. But in addition to his role as communications director, Ian thought of himself a bit like a bouncer—tasked with keeping out riffraff—and he thought the mini-Trumps who had followed the president in the door were a problem. In June 2021, I went to lunch with Matt and Ian in Old Town Alexandria. It was a few months past Gosargate, and with just a few weeks until another CPAC—this one in Texas—Matt and Ian were wondering if they were about to be in for a repeat.

"We'll probably have Fuentes running his little alternative event," Ian said.

"He will," Matt said. "The question is, Does Marjorie Taylor Greene or Matt Gaetz do it too?"

Representative Matt Gaetz, a congressman from Florida and one of Trump's closest allies in the House, was a regular at CPAC. But at this point Matt was still on the fence about whether to start inviting the freshman congresswoman from Georgia.

"She seems like a genuine lunatic," Matt said.

Matt had problems with Gaetz as well, namely the fact that at the moment the congressman was the subject of an investigation: The feds were looking into whether he had paid for sex, whether he'd had a sexual relationship with a woman under eighteen, and whether he'd paid for women to travel across state lines for the purposes of having sex. Prosecutors didn't end up charging Gaetz with anything, but the news of the investigation had shaken loose other anecdotes about the thirty-eight-year-old congressman. CNN had reported that Gaetz had boasted to fellow lawmakers about the women he'd slept with, even showing them nude photos and videos of women on his phone.

"I think Gaetz is a bad guy," Matt said. "I just don't know if it's fair; it's just so easy for a Republican to get indicted, I don't know if it means anything anymore."

"He exudes 'Bad Guy,'" Ian chimed in.

"He's very popular with our party," said Matt. "I campaigned with him in Florida. He's a rock star."

"It's all way too unsavory for me," Ian said.

Crack.

Later that year, a right-wing website called National File wrote about a CPAC staffer's tweets in which the staffer had, among other taboos, praised Joe Biden during the 2020 campaign and "hyped COVID and pushed for gas mask use" after President Trump was hospitalized with the virus that October. Ian told me that a member of the ACU board wanted a swift response from the media team—that this story could be a problem among their base. Ian didn't think the website—described by the Daily Beast as a "conspiracy clickbait blog" with ties to Alex Jones's Infowars—deserved a response from him.

"All these people want is to be legitimized," he told me. Instead, he suggested sending a cease-and-desist letter from a lawyer, but Matt declined.

Crack.

Matt's eulogy for Ralph Hallow—where he had characterized the father-son relationship as "tricky"—that had also been a crack.

Ian agreed with Matt about some things. He didn't mind Matt's rhetoric about voter fraud and stolen elections. Ian also believed Democrats weren't always on the level on that front. Matt and Ian's breakup wasn't exactly about politics getting too personal. It was more the other way around—a case where the crumbling of a personal relationship helped lead to a big break in Ian's political worldview.

Part of it had to do with Matt being around the office so much after his post–George Floyd cancellation. Without much in the way of lobbying clients, it felt like Matt was always micromanaging Ian and Carin's work. Matt's "nice guy" shtick seemed to be fading, replaced with all that talk about "fighting." Some of this might have had to do with money. He hadn't lost his job, but it had become harder to support his expensive tastes, according to Ross Hemminger, the former CPAC spokesman who was also an employee of Cove Strategies, Matt's lobbying shop.

"Money became a huge factor for the Schlapps after he lost his lobbying clients," Hemminger told me in a phone interview. "They have five girls. And you've seen the house."

I had indeed seen it—the mansion on Mansion Drive.

"When I worked at Cove, he was always perusing online catalogs for, like, the best, most expensive, finest office furniture," Hemminger continued. "He hired this guy from this little town in southern Virginia to design light fixtures. Matt gets really into that stuff."

One way Matt helped make ends meet: He picked up a lobbying contract near the end of the Trump presidency—$750,000 to seek a pardon for Parker Petit, a former healthcare executive who'd served as Trump's Georgia finance chair in 2016, and who had been convicted of securities fraud. Matt got the money, but Petit never got the pardon.

TRUMP ALLY MATT SCHLAPP AND HIS FIRM GOT $750,000 FOR FAILING AT HIS JOB, trumpeted *Vanity Fair* in a headline.

"Schlapp didn't respond to inquiries about the other policy work he reported performing on the account," noted Axios.

"Will I survive this?" Matt asked Ian in a text at the time.

Ian thought Matt would survive. But in time he was less and less sure if their friendship would. Covid weakened the foundation dramatically. Matt's view on remote work was well known: He didn't approve of it. Carin had been pregnant with their third child, Blaise, during the pandemic, and it was still raging when he was born in March 2021. The Walterses had hoped to work from home more, and while it wasn't exactly forbidden, they felt like Matt was judging them—like they were being a couple of snowflakes.

Former ACU and CPAC colleagues I spoke with said they thought the fractures in Ian and Matt's relationship had to do with Ian giving advice that Matt didn't want to hear—including advice about trying to distance the organization from the grifters and performance artists that were taking over the Republican Party. "It used to be that Matt trusted Ian, and so we could all trust Ian to speak for Matt," said one former ACU colleague. But Matt's trust in Ian had clearly evaporated.

Carin had been ready to quit for a while. It wasn't about politics for her; it was about quality of life in the job. Being second-guessed by an underemployed Matt Schlapp? No thanks.

For Ian, the decision was more complicated. This job had been his life. It was an inheritance of sorts: Ralph had taken him to his first CPAC events. He'd met Carin at the organization. There were times when it had felt like a family—one that included Matt and Mercy—and which had given him a sense of identity. In Washington, he was CPAC Ian. If he were to leave it behind: Who would he be then?

* * *

Around the same time all this was going on, Ian became preoccupied with another person's identity.

In the spring of 2020, after a brief shutdown due to the Covid pandemic, the American Conservative Union began holding in-person events again. Carin hired up a new intern to help with the uptick in travel, and the intern would often bring around her boyfriend to pitch in. Who was this kid? For the purposes of Ian and Matt's story, it hardly mattered. What mattered was that the intern's boyfriend, The Kid, was the final crack in Matt and Ian's relationship. It was The Kid that finally broke Ian, that pushed him toward resigning, that made him decide to stop talking to Matt, and that eventually led to political epiphanies that maybe he should have seen a lot earlier.

Big breaks don't happen all at once, after all. And sometimes it takes something petty, something idiotic, to be the final crack that causes everything to come crashing down.

The Kid was just out of college, but he could have passed for a high school student. Nobody seemed to mind having him around. He seemed like a nice enough guy, happy to do gofer jobs.

But before long, The Kid's role in the organization started to feel strange to Carin and Ian. He began spending a lot of time in Matt's office, chatting with the boss like they'd worked together for years. Eventually there was talk about electing him to ACU's board. This seemed like a strange fit for a young guy with no clear role in an organization he'd only just started hanging around. But a rumor began to circulate as to why. Members of the ACU staff office had come to believe that The Kid was a member of an extremely famous, and extremely wealthy, American family.

Where exactly this rumor came from, nobody could say for sure. Maybe it had to do with the times he would refer to "The Family" in the office. One time, a colleague of Ian's had written The Kid an email and gotten a bounce-back message that said, "Thank you for connecting with [The Kid] in our family. Please note that you have been flagged as working with a politically affiliated organization therefore we must record all conversations that occur between you and [The Kid]." One colleague I spoke with remembered The Kid telling ACU staffers that he was an heir to his family fortune, and he bragged about having access to a fleet of luxury vehicles.

Talk of The Kid's supposed family connections was not confined to the rank and file. Carin said she heard about it from Dan Schneider, then the executive director of ACU—the No. 2 in the organization under Matt.

Once, in 2020, Carin had been tasked with throwing a donor event in North Carolina, only to be told to cancel: They couldn't get enough people to show up.

But then, a day or two before the event, Carin got a call that the reception was back on: The Kid's mom had said she would be there.

"She might not look like much, but that's just how those rich people are," Carin recalled Schneider telling her. (Schneider, when reached by phone, said this was "misinformation" but didn't stay on the line long enough to elaborate.)

At first, Ian and Carin didn't have a problem with any of this. They had catered to plenty of rich children with famous names at various CPAC events: a Schwab, a Bean from the L.L. Bean family. But then The Kid started stepping on Ian's toes. It was one thing to get to hang around the boss despite showing up yesterday, but it was starting to feel like every time Ian left a room, The Kid would come in after and start handing out work to Ian's team—as if someone had put him in charge.

Who did this Kid think he was?

Ian and Carin put in their notice. It was June 9, 2021. It was time. This wasn't the final crack, though. Ian and Carin thought there might still be a way to manage some part-time contracting work. They didn't want to be around all the time, but it didn't yet mean they never wanted to see Matt or Mercy again.

The next day, with nothing to lose, Ian decided he would have it out with The Kid. He brought a couple of his colleagues along as witnesses (who confirmed the account to me), and in an otherwise empty office, he asked The Kid what was going on. *Why are you undermining me? Why won't you make eye contact with me? Why are you managing my staff? Who gave you the authority?*

The Kid told him that Mercy Schlapp had given him the authority. And then The Kid said something that Ian could not believe: "He said, 'My family's lawyers have told me that I cannot communicate with you, because of what your family has been going through.'"

Ian's family had been going through something. A few months earlier, the *Washington Free Beacon*, a conservative newspaper, had broken a story about Ian's mother, Millie. She had, according to the story, diverted $40,000 from her employer, the National Rifle Association, to pay for Ian and Carin's wedding. The news had come out because Millie had been forced to testify in the NRA's ongoing bankruptcy trial. And while it became clear that Millie had paid back the money with interest, back in 2019, it was still an embarrassing episode for Ian and the family. But what did any of that have to do with The Kid and his family lawyer?

Ian ran into Matt as he was leaving the building that same day.

"Is everything okay?" Matt asked.

"What are you fucking talking about?" Ian said. "Everything is not okay, dude."

In the coming weeks, things got less and less okay. When Ian and Carin had put in their notice, they'd agreed to stick around for more than the customary two weeks—Matt needed their help putting on a CPAC event in Texas that was still more than a month away. But the news got out that they were not long for the organization, and things felt uncomfortable around the office. And later that month, Ian got a call from a colleague that made things even worse.

"She told me that [The Kid] was going around the office telling people that Carin and I were embezzling from the organization," Ian told me.

Ian went into preservation mode. He wanted to be sure everyone knew that this was not true. He told one of the organization's lawyers. And he went into Matt's office and told him that The Kid had to go.

"I hear ya," Matt told Ian, according to Ian's recollection. "I just need you to get me through Texas and we will take care of all these things."

Ian didn't want to wait for Matt. He and some of his colleagues started a text thread and did the kind of work they did for a living: They created an opposition-research file on the guy. They found the deeds for the cars he and his family drove. They seemed like a normal enough middle-class family; nothing to indicate great wealth. They found various family members, but couldn't find any branches that extended to the famous family tree.

Was Ian going down rabbit holes? Was he taking out his professional frustrations on this Kid—who, to be clear, neither Ian nor Carin had themselves ever actually heard talking about being an heir to a family or accusing them of embezzlement? Maybe so. Nothing was making sense to Ian anymore—his place in the hierarchy at work, his friendship with Matt, his place relative to his party and his country. But The Kid mystery—that at least seemed answerable. Ian described it to me as a "Rosetta Stone" for everything else. If the Schlapps had empowered The Kid because they thought his family was loaded, and he wasn't, that would be proof that Matt couldn't be trusted to make good decisions. If CPAC's office could be infiltrated by a pretender (assuming The Kid was, in fact, pretending anything), it would validate Ian's belief that the organization itself had become a home for grifters and performance artists.

Once Ian became convinced that The Kid wasn't an heir to any famous family fortune, he almost felt a sense of relief. He wasn't cracking up.

The Texas event hadn't happened yet, but he decided to tell Matt about what he'd found anyway. On Monday, June 28, Matt called and woke Ian up at 6:53 a.m. Ian took the call to the garage, where he chain-smoked Marlboros and detailed his findings to Matt. The call took a total of sixty-seven minutes.

"None of it fits," Ian remembered telling him. "He's not an heir. I found his parents. I found his grandparents. They live in a modest retirement home."

"Ian, well, why do you think I wanted to put him on the board?" Matt said.

"Because you thought he was loaded," Ian said.

"No," Matt said. "Dan said we needed to have more young people on the board."

Bullshit, Ian thought. This had to be more gaslighting. More revisionist history. He decided he never wanted to talk about The Kid with Matt again. He wasn't sure if he ever wanted to talk to Matt again, period.

Ian's reasons for fixating on The Kid may have been unique to him, but he wasn't the only person at CPAC who was skeptical of the guy.

He had the whole text thread working the case with him, and after the Texas event, one of his colleagues who'd worked on the opportunity file met with Matt privately to express his own concerns.

"I spoke to him very directly, very explicitly in private," the colleague told me. "I wanted him to know that it was unconscionable to me that someone who was misrepresenting himself would be so close to the organization, and trusted with so much."

He told Matt it would be hard for him to continue working at CPAC because he valued the organization and it would be destroyed if they kept letting untrustworthy people help to run the show.

He didn't get the reaction he'd expected.

"I was strongly rebuked," he said. "And I was told that I really should be fired for insubordination."

That staffer quit shortly after. So did nearly a dozen of his colleagues.

"No one would tell you that [The Kid] was the only reason," said the staffer. "But everyone would say that it was part of the reason."

Ian and Carin would be gone soon too. But they had given their word to help get the team through Texas, and they kept their word. They sprinted through the planning stages and headed down to Dallas in person, bringing the entire family, including their new baby boy, Blaise. It wasn't perfect—Ian had to spend more time than he would have liked telling reporters that the talk given by Representative Matt Gaetz was not a "sanctioned" CPAC event. But at least back then CPAC was seeking to distance itself from the embattled congressman.

One year later, at the next CPAC Texas, Gaetz would be a featured speaker. And Ian nowhere to be seen.

Chapter 36

If You Find Anyone Else Like Me, Let Me Know

Late summer 2022

When CPAC made its way back to Texas in August 2022, Ian and Carin Walters planned to head in the opposite direction and visit Carin's family in Minnesota. They decided to make a trip of it, to pack up the RV and visit some fellow exiles who had moved to the Midwest after quitting their ACU jobs. It was a relief not to have to worry about satellite hookups, press credentialing, and backstage buffet options, but there was still a lot to do before hitting the road. There was laundry to do, bikes to get up on the rack, and they needed to find a blender for the RV. A few weeks earlier, they'd had a tree guy trim back the branches on the giant oak tree out front.

Ian had been trying to do some shedding of his own.

"I'm sick of being CPAC Ian," he told me when I arrived.

It had been a few months since we'd sat on Ian's porch and talked about Ralph's death. Since then, he had only become surer that he'd made the right decision to walk away from Matt. A hearing from the January 6th Committee in late June featuring a young White House aide, Cassidy Hutchinson, had helped drive it home. Ian had watched that testimony in his living room, rapt as Hutchinson testified that Trump had known the mob heading to the Capitol had been armed, and yet did nothing to stop the violence. If Ian had still been working with Matt, his job would have been to help spin Cassidy as a disgruntled and untrustworthy source.

"Ms. Hutchinson approached @CPAC for help through our First Amendment Fund which has helped J6 political victims defend themselves," Matt had tweeted, and had retweeted by an account he'd help set up called @J6Facts. "I am pleased we did not assist her performance today. Relaying WH hallway gossip as fact does not qualify as first person testimony."

But Ian didn't see Hutchinson as a gossip. He saw her as brave. He tried to imagine where Hutchinson could go from there, what she could do next to make a living. Maybe that could help him figure out what he could do next himself.

When Ian decided to leave his job (one that came with a six-figure salary), he had options for a next chapter. He could have become a professional Republican heretic. There was nothing that liberal audiences loved more than a Republican turncoat willing to badmouth all their former friends. Just ask *New York Times* bestselling author Tim Miller, the former spokesman for Jeb Bush, who wrote a juicy insider account of how and why his party sold their souls to the MAGA movement; former George W. Bush communications director Nicolle Wallace, who rode her strange new respect from the left into an MSNBC anchor seat; or George Conway—husband of Trump senior adviser Kellyanne—who became a #Resistance hero for tweeting his every negative thought about his wife's boss and was now a regular pundit on cable TV.

Having grown up in Washington, Ian was very familiar with these moves. But he wasn't interested in any of them.

"I see all these groups as all part of the problem," Ian told me. "I wish I could just throw sand in all of it."

It would be perfectly reasonable to wonder why, then, Ian had bothered spending the past year talking to me for this book. Sometimes I'd wondered too. It had been really difficult to convince Ian to tell me his story. He worried about how he would be perceived by others, whether he might anger the wrong people. Ian told me he appreciated that I would take his story seriously and put it in a proper context. But there was another reason he opened up.

"Why am I doing this?" he'd said to me. "Because I need somebody to talk to."

He'd lost his fathers—Ralph and Colin—and his work version of a big brother, Matt. He had some friends, but he wasn't seeing all that much of anyone. There was no obvious home for someone like him in partisan Washington.

"If you find anyone else like me," he said to me now as we headed inside his house to watch the CPAC proceedings on TV, "let me know. It's lonely."

It was now after 11:00 a.m., and Ian had just woken up for the second time that day. He'd been up from 4:00 to 6:00, waking up to pee and then getting stuck doom-scrolling through Twitter. He wore boxers and an Orioles T-shirt. His long hair was a mess. He'd been up late drinking.

I arrived just in time for a lineup that could require a little hair of the dog—the kind of whack jobs that Ian had worked hard to keep away from CPAC but who now starred as main stage acts: pillow magnate and election denier Mike Lindell ("Over fifty-four countries have now been taken by the machines," he said), alt-right figure and conspiracy theorist Jack Posobiec ("Ah, Pizzagate Jack," Ian said), and of course, Marjorie Taylor Greene ("I'm a proud Christian Nationalist," she said).

"When I was a kid, 'Christian Nationalist' was just a term used by actual neo-Nazis," Ian said.

When Ian was on the job, defending CPAC against charges of racism or antisemitism or whatever other ism, he believed many of the attacks on the organization were in bad faith. Sure, CPAC had controversial speakers sometimes, but it wasn't necessarily an endorsement.

The conference used to be, at least in his opinion, a marketplace of ideas. But now they were only selling one thing. And it wasn't a product he wanted to be associated with.

"They're playing footsies with White nationalists," he said.

Even though he was happy to be out, the experience was making Ian nostalgic. His two daughters cuddled up with him on the couch, and he told them stories about the CPACs they had been to, reminding them of the take-out food they had eaten in conference rooms and the family they had made along the way ("Here's a picture with Aunt Kellyanne"). He scrolled through pictures on his phone, and found dozens of Matt.

"When should I delete these?" he asked Carin.

Carin told him it was time to get them off his phone, and that he could always back them up before deleting them for good. She had been patient with Ian's process. She'd heard him talk about how this was like a breakup, and how there was a ratio of years spent with someone to years apart that it would take to heal. It had been nearly twenty years of CPAC for Ian, five of them with Matt. She knew it would take at least a little more time to get over it.

Ian was still checking Matt's Twitter account more than he'd like to admit, and said he'd heard on good authority that Matt was checking his too, wondering aloud anytime there was a bad story about him or CPAC in the press if maybe Ian was behind it.

Matt's presence loomed as we watched the event on Ian's TV. Matt opened the show with Mercy onstage, conducted various interviews, and between each speech appeared in a commercial for some documentary called *Culture Killers*.

"This is the fight we were put on this earth to make," Matt said in the ad.

"Fight fight fight," Ian muttered under his breath.

* * *

Ian's mind had gone back to his stepfather, and how things changed after Ralph died. Ian had always sought Ralph's counsel and his approval. What would he have thought about Trump refusing to concede an election? About January 6th? About the Schlapps' embrace of it all and Ian's ultimate decision to leave? Ian told me that his dad had complicated feelings about Trump.

"If only this guy could stop stepping on his own dick," he used to say to Ian.

And yet, since he'd been a right-leaning journalist, much of his coverage about the president had been positive.

"Life is about trade-offs," he would tell Ian.

Still, Ian said he thought his father would have been completely turned off by the violence of January 6th. This was his city, after all, a place he had covered for decades. Surely he would be willing to hold an instigating president to account. Right?

Unfortunately for Ian, one of the things he had realized was that even if his father, the journalist, had turned on Trump and his MAGA movement, in at least one way, it would not have mattered. It used to be that Matt had been concerned about the coverage from longtime Washington reporters, regardless of ideology. The goal was to generate the best press possible. That was the point of Ian's job. But Ian came to realize that his job was as obsolete as an ink-stained wretch.

"The only audience Matt cares about now," said Ian, "is the audience of one. As long as Trump likes the show, nothing else matters."

* * *

Carin had taken the kids somewhere and Ian asked me if I cared to pop out for a secret cigarette. He'd quit, but there was that thing about old habits dying hard.

"During the first CPAC after January 6th, I got a call from a reporter friend of mine telling me I was arguing in bad faith," Ian said, taking a long drag off his Marlboro. That CPAC's theme had been all about election integrity, which, the reporter contended, was just a way to give Trump's stolen-election lie some professional talking points. Ian had bristled at the argument; the lineup was made up of all sorts of well-meaning Republicans who had been talking about this issue for years, folks from the Heritage Foundation and AEI, not just Trumpy conspiracy theorists.

"Of course," Ian said, "he was right. It took me longer than it should have to realize this. Here I was, idiot Ian, sticking his finger in the dike trying to hold back the water that was already overflowing."

Over the course of the past year, I'd asked Ian many times whether he ever regretted working for CPAC, or working for Matt. Ian was thoughtful, so he never scoffed at the question, but he also never really owned up to the role—small as it was—in helping create this moment in political history. Instead he would talk about the ways in which he'd tried to act as the guardrail for the organization—doing the work to keep out the bad actors, trying to give sensible advice. It was the same kind of thing people had said about going into the Trump administration: If I'm not there to be an adult in the room, imagine the kind of person who might take my place.

Certainly there was truth to this argument. But eventually the riff-raff weren't just sneaking into CPAC; they were speaking from the main stage. And eventually it wasn't just fringy conspiracy theorists arguing about fraudulent elections in Nevada; it was Ian, himself, on behalf of Matt.

I'd come to realize that Ian's story in its own small way was the story of the Republican Party. It was true that Trump rose to power with the help of some mega-MAGA enablers—the Schlapps, who saw an opportunity for influence; Stephens Bannon and Miller, who saw him as a vehicle for their nativist worldview. But there could never have been a Trump without millions of Ians—those who cast their vote for him twice before seeing what he'd been making plainly obvious for as long as he'd been in the political arena. Not all of them were overt bigots. But it's amazing what people are willing to overlook when things are going well for them.

In that way, the split between Ian and Matt fit the picture as well. In many cases, it can be easier to break up—with a person, a job, a party—over something personal, rather than ideological. The MAGA Universe was littered with people who turned on Trump only after he treated them terribly. Does anyone think Trump's ex-lawyer Michael Cohen would have gone from being willing to "take a bullet" for the boss to becoming a #Resistance podcast star and author had the boss just gotten him out of jail with a presidential pardon? It wasn't until Alabama Senate candidate Mo Brooks lost Trump's endorsement that he finally realized what people had been saying all along: "Donald Trump has no loyalty," he said. And it took a mob of people chanting "Hang Mike Pence" for the former vice president to start floating trial balloons about a possible 2024 challenge to Trump (if he were to run again).

There was a part of me that wondered if Matt had just continued being nice to Ian at the office, maybe Ian would still be working there. And maybe there was no point in guessing about that. Ian had left. And once he'd left, he realized that he was part of something he no longer wanted to be a part of. But there *was* the question of what had taken so long.

He paused and took another drag off his cigarette.

"I'm not a hero," he said. "If anything, I was too slow. Walking away was a concession of sorts. I lost."

We headed inside, and as the second day of events wound down, I asked Carin if she'd chat with me privately. She handed the three children off to Ian, who went into the other room to take a shot of whiskey and clear his head. She told me that it was hard for her to watch Ian struggle with losing part of his identity. She couldn't entirely relate—it was just a job for her; no one called her CPAC Carin.

"It's just tough because I don't know what I can do to help," she said.

But there was plenty of good too. The family had never been closer. They were better parents. They had the freedom to visit friends and family whenever they pleased. The garden had just produced a bounty of perfect tomatoes, and once they got that blender in the RV, they could make gazpacho for days.

As we talked, the weather outside shifted dramatically. What had been a sunny, humid summer morning had suddenly turned into a torrential storm. The rain whipped sideways and thunder clapped nearby, sending the kids scurrying into the room and leaping onto the bed in fear.

Another crash, this time preceded by the *crack* of breaking wood.

Ian shouted from the other room: "There's a branch on the roof!"

The CPAC livestream, which had been playing on the living room television, had frozen on a close-up of CPAC speaker Brandon Straka. Straka, a former Democrat who started a movement to get people to "walk away" from the party, had been at the January 6th riots, and was arrested shortly after. He did no time, having served as state's witness, and, perhaps in an effort to beat back charges of being a rat, had spent much of CPAC standing inside a makeshift jail cell, to draw attention to the supposedly unjust living conditions for insurrectionist prisoners. It was one of the stupidest things I'd ever seen.

The storm ended as quickly as it had started, and Ian and Carin headed outside to survey the damage. Out front, a twenty-foot branch had cracked off the oak tree and landed just feet from the front of the house.

"We are so lucky we had those tree guys trim the dead branches," Ian said to Carin. "Otherwise that would have been right through the window."

A smaller tree had fallen on the side of the house, clipping the roof, and only narrowly missing the electrical lines.

"Take a picture," Carin told Ian as she carried baby Blaise on her hip. "For insurance."

He snapped the photo, but there wouldn't be much need. The house hadn't been damaged. The power had stayed on.

"The only thing the storm managed to knock out was your livestream," I said as I headed to my car to leave.

"That's okay," Ian said. "I've seen enough CPAC."

Part 6

The Breaks

Chapter 37

The Big Blind

Six days before the election

It was mid-September, less than two months before the midterms, and Sean McElwee had bought a new poker table. He wanted to fit more people into his regular games. Tonight's crowd included a chief of staff for a moderate House member, a pollster for a major Democratic polling outfit, and an assortment of think tankers. Sean was drinking a nonalcoholic Guinness—part of a recent lifestyle change that also had him eating plant-based foods. This was how I learned that it wasn't necessarily the booze that made him say whatever was on his mind.

"All of the Zoomers that work for me are bisexual, and all of them have long Covid," he said. "I'll believe long Covid is real when someone who is not bisexual has it."

"You said that the last time we played poker," someone said from the other end of the table.

(Later, Sean said that this was just a joke, that he didn't even know the sexuality of his staff members.)

The veganism was for health reasons, but it also fit with the effective altruism philosophy that he had been flirting with. Broadly speaking, effective altruists were obsessed with doing as much good as possible with every decision they made—and many of them had decided that cutting animal products did more good for the world than harm to their own lives. Sean had been EA adjacent for a while now, but had recently leaned farther in—inviting people to a happy hour for EA celebrity author Will MacAskill, taking his staff to an EA conference that rolled through Washington, and handing out EA literature at social gatherings. Sean's attraction to EA made a certain amount of sense to the Washington version of Sean: It was a secular theory of goodness that was pragmatic.

Being part of the EA crew was also an effective way for Sean to pad his bank account—helping forge a connection with Sam Bankman-Fried, the crypto billionaire who, indirectly, paid for Sean's Guarding Against Pandemics consulting work. At one point in the night, Sean drew our attention to a little metal object he twirled between his thumb and forefinger.

It was Sam Bankman-Fried's fidget spinner, Sean said, left behind after a recent visit from the billionaire.

Besides all that, Sean had a new girlfriend who was into EA. Her name was Rachel and they'd been dating for three months.

"She's Eric Adams's vegan adviser," he said, showing the guys around the table a picture of her on his phone.

"As in she's a vegan and she advises him, or she advises him on how to be a vegan?" I asked.

"Both," Sean said. "She's a vegan and she advises the mayor on how to be vegan. She also advises him on how to make New York City more vegan."

"Isn't he a fake vegan?" one of Sean's poker buddies asked. (Adams, a former police officer, had touted himself as the first "plant-based slash vegan" mayor of New York City, but during his campaign some TV journalists on a tour of his apartment had found salmon in his fridge—a mini-scandal that the press had called "FishGate.")

"Look, I'm a Christian," Sean said, coming to the mayor's defense. "But I fuck up all the time on Christianity. But that doesn't mean I'm not a Christian. Much like how Eric Adams is a vegan even if he occasionally eats fish. It doesn't mean he's not a vegan. It just means he's a man."

Sean was feeling like a man. He and Rachel had just gone on a vacation to Rehoboth Beach, in Delaware, and it had gone according to plan. He had emailed her an itinerary of the things they would do: hot yoga ("I actually do yoga better than her"), a bike ride that would go past Biden's vacation home, a trip to the farmers' market ("Women love farmers' markets"), time at the beach ("I applied sunscreen to her back and it was moderately sensual"), followed by a dinner scheme that involved hitting four different restaurants and ordering one vegan dish at each of them as a way of juicing up demand for plant-based food ("Now all the restaurants think there are four times as many vegans as there are").

At the end of the evening, while sitting on the beach under the stars, Sean said there was one thing he had secretly added to his to-do list. He told Rachel he loved her, and then showed her an updated version of the itinerary as proof that he'd been plotting to say the words.

"How was the weekend after that?" someone asked.

"We fucked a lot," Sean said.

Sean said Rachel was the type of woman he could talk to for hours about everything from effective altruism to his love of super PACs. Sean's love of money in politics put him at odds with most liberals. It was why he called himself a "Clarence Thomas Democrat"—a reference to the case of *Citizens United v. Federal Election Commission*, in which Justice Thomas and the Supreme Court's conservatives banded together to lift the restrictions on how much non-individuals could spend on political campaigns. Many Democrats hated *Citizens United*, which empowered wealthy donors and organizations to plow cash into politics, often without much in the way of transparency. But Sean felt differently. He believed, he said, that more money in politics allowed for more issues-based advertising, made voters aware of the stakes of each election.

"I think it's one of the greatest decisions in Supreme Court history," Sean said.

"It's paying for our poker game!" said one of his poker pals. The poker pal asked Sean if he thought Democrats would hold the Senate.

"I would not bet on that," Sean said.

But he would bet *against* it. The two agreed to a $500 wager and added it to Sean's spreadsheet.

Placing bets like this—in person, with people he knew—had become Sean's best option for new action. A few weeks earlier, the Commodity Futures Trading Commission—the government agency that regulated markets—had issued a ruling that PredictIt would have to shut down by February of next year. Sean and everyone else could keep betting on markets that were already on the website, but PredictIt was barred from putting up new ones. PredictIt was fighting this ruling, but in the meantime, Sean would have to find some alternatives to new markets. There were places to bet online using cryptocurrency exchanges, which had piqued Sean's interest. But if nothing else, there was always the old-fashioned way.

"I just think we lose two of the three toss-up races," Sean said, explaining why he was willing to put money down on the Democrats losing the Senate. "Of Nevada, Arizona, and Georgia, I think we lose two of three."

He did feel like Fetterman, his candidate in Pennsylvania, was on track to win—even if his recent stroke had become a cause of concern.

"He can't string a sentence together," one of Sean's poker buddies said.

"That is worrisome," Sean said.

But he didn't seem worried. He was floating in warm water. He was in love. Democrats had passed their Inflation Reduction Act—a bill that probably did very little to reduce inflation, but which was a massive legislative victory for the party. It provided subsidies for the Affordable Care Act, lowered the price of prescription drugs, and represented the largest investment in combating climate change in the history of the country. Sean had been pushing out polls showing the bill's support, and for that work, he and his political director, Marcela, had been invited to the big White House shindig celebrating its passage. A few hundred activists and outside groups were there, including Leah and her boyfriend, Marvin.

That sunny afternoon on the South Lawn of the White House felt a bit like a graduation ceremony, where everyone could get a little love for their part in the two-year struggle to pass the bill. James Taylor was there to sing "Fire and Rain" and "America the Beautiful," and Biden removed his jacket (but kept on his aviator sunglasses) to give a speech about taking "aggressive action" to confront the climate crisis.

"Today offers proof that the soul of America is vibrant, the future of America is bright, and the promise of America is real," he said. Biden praised the impressive coalition of people who had come together to pass the bill and slammed Republicans for opposing it uniformly. The bill didn't have close to everything everyone wanted, but it was much better than nothing. And it was popular.

Fetterman was also popular, post-stroke symptoms notwithstanding.

"The polls are great," Sean said.

"You have to ignore the polls at this point," said the pollster for a bigger Democratic firm. "They're too good."

Chapter 38

October Surprise

Fall 2022

The Democrats' battle to keep control of the Senate was always going to come down to a handful of battleground states. There was the John Fetterman race in Pennsylvania, where Sean McElwee was polling for the giant's campaign. There was the Mandela Barnes campaign in Wisconsin, which was one of Leah Hunt-Hendrix's big bets. In Arizona, Democrat Mark Kelly, a former astronaut, was trying to fend off Blake Masters, a venture capitalist backed by the billionaire Peter Thiel. And in Nevada, Democrat Catherine Cortez Masto was running neck-and-neck with her Republican challenger, the former Nevada Attorney General Adam Laxalt.

But of all the races that could decide whether Democrats or Republicans controlled the upper chamber of Congress, Georgia was the wildest. The contest featured Senator Raphael Warnock, the senior pastor at Martin Luther King's former Baptist church, and Herschel Walker, the Georgia football legend personal friend of Donald Trump. Walker was, to put it bluntly, a terrible candidate. On a basic level, he had a habit of garbling his talking points in ways that made Trump seem like a policy wonk by comparison. He also had the kinds of skeletons in his closet that seemed potentially disqualifying even now, in a post–*grab 'em by the pussy* era.

Walker had been diagnosed years earlier with dissociative identity disorder, according to his 2008 memoir, which included a number of disturbing anecdotes like the time he was seized by the urge to shoot a man who was late delivering a car Walker had bought. An ex-wife said Walker had held a gun to her head and threatened to "blow [her] brains out." As the campaign progressed, there were reports of children Walker had fathered out of wedlock.

By mid-October, the Walker campaign was dealing with another skeleton. Roger Sollenberger, a reporter for the Daily Beast, reported that the vocally anti-abortion candidate had, in 2009, urged an ex-girlfriend to terminate a pregnancy and sent her a check for $700 to cover the cost. On October 17, Walker admitted to sending the woman the check, but denied it was for an abortion. Two days later, Matt Schlapp headed to Georgia.

Just as he had done for Trump after the *Access Hollywood* video broke, Matt decided to double down on his support for an embattled candidate, only this time the decision was easy. Trump had changed the definition of survivable scandals, and the race was just too tight for Republicans to even think about giving up. Plus, the candidate had the benefit of a political atmosphere that had shifted into the Republicans' favor. Any jolt Democrats felt after *Roe. v. Wade* fell seemed to have faded over the summer—voters appeared to be more concerned about crime rates and inflation rates, and pollsters were finding that they blamed Democrats for both. With pundits boldly predicting a "red wave" in November, it was easy to get Republicans—including Senators Tim Scott, Ted Cruz, and Lindsey Graham—to fly into a purple state like Georgia. Matt's turn to take the stage with Walker happened in a gun store parking lot in the small town of Perry, about a hundred miles south of Atlanta.

Matt wore a peach-colored checked shirt and gave a speech about how Democrats embraced "extreme policies" like defunding cops, open borders, the destruction of the fossil fuel industry, and "post-birth abortion."

"They're trying to make you feel like you're a minority," he said. "You're small, you're fringe, you're a hater, you're a bad person, you're a racist."

Carlton Huffman, a staffer for Walker's campaign, listened from about fifteen feet away. He understood a little bit about what Matt was talking about. Except he also might have known that if somebody called you out for being racist, they weren't necessarily wrong.

Huffman grew up in a conservative town in North Carolina. His grandfather, who was the town's longtime mayor, owned and operated a textile factory with around 500 employees. It was mostly an idyllic childhood for Huffman. But between the North American Free Trade Agreement sending manufacturing jobs to Mexico and an economy that struggled in the early 2000s, unemployment skyrocketed in his North Carolina town. Huffman started to feel anxiety about immigrants coming to town. He took a job working for Pat Buchanan, the anti-immigrant, "America First" politician. He contributed racist material to podcasts and blogs, writing about Black gangbangers, the displacement of White workers, and the need to maintain the country's European heritage. Huffman even lost a government job for working against the posthumous pardon for a former governor who had been impeached more than a hundred years earlier after leading a crackdown on the Ku Klux Klan.

He had been "MAGA before there was MAGA," he said, but by the time Trump descended the golden escalator at Trump Tower, Huffman was in a "profoundly different place" than he had been a decade earlier. The experience of losing his job and seeing his name associated with White supremacy was jarring, Huffman later told me. He said he went on a "journey" to try and become a better person. He spent more time with people of color. He tried to empathize with their suffering. In June 2020, during the racial justice protests that followed the

George Floyd and Breonna Taylor killings, Huffman went to a Black Lives Matter protest to show solidarity.

Huffman voted against Trump twice. On January 6, 2021, when Trump supporters stormed the Capitol, he texted Trump's chief of staff, Mark Meadows, to scold him for his role leading up to the insurrection. Still, Carlton Huffman remained committed to the Republican Party, and was working to elect Walker to the U.S. Senate despite his ties to Trump. He was still a conservative, and would rather have conservatives in the Capitol than Democrats. Even Trump couldn't change that.

On the day Matt came to town, Huffman was dispatched to the event from Atlanta to help out with crowd management and, later, to chauffeur Matt to his hotel. He had been on the political scene long enough to know who Matt was. Once, during the 2020 campaign, he'd even escorted Mercy when she visited Wisconsin. Mercy had been nothing but pleasant, but the Schlapps still left a bad taste in his mouth. Huffman hated how politics had become entertainment and saw CPAC as part of the problem there. He'd noted Matt's change from Bushie to Trumpist, and he was bracing for the possibility of being stuck in the car for a couple of hours with a MAGA asshole.

As he listened to the speech, he was relieved that Matt didn't say anything that offended him: no talk about political prisoners of January 6th or really anything "too Trumpy" at all.

Later, Huffman gave Matt a ride back to the Hilton Garden Inn close to the Atlanta Airport. Matt was perfectly pleasant, Huffman told me; he barely brought up politics at all, except for some effusive praise for Arizona gubernatorial candidate Kari Lake, widely seen as the leading heiress to Trumpism. After the ride, Matt was even gracious enough to invite him to get a drink later that night. Huffman accepted the offer. He may not have been a fan of Matt's politics, but he seemed like fine enough company. And even if they disagreed about Trump, maybe Matt could be helpful to Huffman's career.

What happened that night is something Huffman wouldn't talk

about publicly (or tell me) for months. Through a lawyer, Matt would deny Huffman's account, and the two men would go to court over it. Suffice to say it did change the course of both men's careers, and not at all in the way Huffman had imagined. (This account reflects what I was told by Huffman, which was consistent with what he reportedly told others; I gave Matt the opportunity to respond, which he declined to do.)

Matt had a fundraising dinner and a meeting with a donor, so it was late evening by the time Huffman met up with him for a drink at the Capital Grille in Buckhead, an uptown commercial district of Atlanta. Huffman had expected to talk about work and politics, but Matt seemed more interested in just shooting the shit. He also seemed interested in Tito's, the vodka he was drinking—quickly, in Huffman's opinion.

After a few rounds, Matt looked around the bar, and apologized to Huffman about it being so empty. Matt picked up the tab and suggested they go to another place for a drink, and Huffman suggested Manuel's Tavern. Manuel's was a classic dive, dimly lit and wood-paneled. It was also an old Democrat haunt and still hung portraits of JFK and FDR. Huffman ordered a Woodford and Coke and Matt ordered a Tito's.

After about ten minutes, Matt scooted a little too close and left his leg pressed up against Huffman's.

"What's that?" Matt asked.

He didn't really seem drunk. He wasn't slurring his words or anything. But he'd had seven or eight drinks at that point, by Huffman's count.

"That's my Sig Sauer," Huffman replied.

"What's a Sig Sauer?"

"It's my handgun."

Matt explained that he grew up in an urban part of Kansas and that he didn't have much experience with guns. This had struck Huffman as a bit odd—for a supposedly staunch supporter of the Second

Amendment to know so little about personal firearms. But he found it even odder when Matt looked at him and said, "Do you have a problem with looking at me?"

That remark made the hairs on the back of Huffman's neck stand up. Around then, Huffman suggested he drive Matt back to the hotel. They had to be up early the next morning for an event in Macon.

It was about a fifteen-minute drive from Manuel's to the Hilton Garden Inn. About ten minutes in, Matt put his hand on Huffman's leg. Huffman froze, unsure of what to do. As they approached the hotel, Matt's hand crept into Huffman's lap, grabbing him by the crotch and lingering there.

All Huffman could think to do was sit there, and not send Matt any signals that this was at all welcome. *Don't let him think you are enjoying this*, he thought. Out of the corner of his eye, he saw Matt's lips were pursed.

It must have only been a few seconds, but it felt like a lifetime. Matt withdrew his hand, and when they pulled up to the hotel, he invited Huffman up to his room. Huffman politely declined.

"He literally just fondled my junk," Huffman texted a friend. "Like. I'm over here shaking. He's pissed I didn't follow him to his hotel room."

He told his friend he wasn't sober.

"But I know I don't want some Trump ball washer to come on to me," he texted. "Or get grabbed against my will."

Huffman called three people he was close to and told them what had happened. He also filmed a video of himself describing the incident while it was still fresh.

"Matt Schlapp of the CPAC grabbed my junk and pummeled it at length," he said.

He felt shame. He hadn't wanted any of this to happen. *Had he let him do it?* Huffman cried himself to sleep that night. When he woke up, he decided there was no way he was going to drive Matt to the event in Macon. He got in touch with his supervisor on the Walker campaign, who couldn't have been more supportive. The supervisor suggested language for a message Huffman could send to Matt, which Huffman did: "I did want to say I was uncomfortable with what happened last night," he texted. "The campaign does have a driver who is available to get you to Macon and back to the airport."

"Pls give me a call," Matt replied. Matt tried calling twice but Huffman didn't pick up.

Huffman didn't want to talk to Matt. He decided he didn't want to go public about his experience, either. The Walker campaign had already been through so much, and was so close to winning. He didn't want to be a distraction.

Chapter 39

Once You Go Down, It's Really Hard to See How You Come Back Up

Four days before the election

I'm feeling good about the DFP polls," Sean McElwee announced to the table. "Which means I feel bad about the Democratic Party."

It was the Friday before the midterms, and he was presiding over a poker table populated by members of his regular crew: a progressive lawyer, a guy who did government affairs for an aerospace company but who seemed to have every congressional race's polling numbers memorized, a college dean, and Ari Rabin-Havt, the former Bernie Sanders staffer turned gives-no-fucks raconteur. Ari had spent much of the evening giving Sean shit over a recent Politico article that had featured Sean, pitting him and David Shor (the populists) against Leah Hunt-Hendrix (the bleeding-heart progressives, or "inclusive populists"). But Ari was less interested in the tensions about whether Democrats needed to moderate their stances or lean into progressivism than he was in the description of Sean in the article as being like an eight-year-old boy who had been blown up into an adult's body.

"Sean McElwee is a fat baby," Ari said.

"Twitter has successfully nagged me into losing a lot of weight, actually," Sean said. "Bullying works."

"And now you have Melissa Byrne bullying you," Ari said, name-checking a progressive organizer who had taken to Twitter recently to criticize Data for Progress's polling, which was showing nearly all of the key Senate races trending against Democrats. A certain segment of the Democratic activist and consulting class worried that publicizing bad numbers would become self-fulfilling.

Byrne had been on the Bernie 2020 campaign, and now worked as a consultant helping on the push to cancel student loan debt. A few weeks earlier, President Biden had announced a student loan forgiveness of up to $20,000. Republicans had quickly challenged the action in court, but Biden's move was a big deal—and Byrne's work, along with the work of many other progressives, had made it happen. It was a policy that could also be good politics—the sort of thing that could theoretically make a lot of people excited to vote Democratic in the coming elections. (Popularists and progressives might, however, disagree about the details. Shor, for example, believed loan forgiveness was popular only if "aggressively" means-tested so only people making less than, say, $75,000 a year qualified, while Byrne argued that a blanket forgiveness would achieve the most possible good.)

Byrne felt strongly that Sean's pessimistic polling threatened to kill any last-minute momentum a candidate might have, and could possibly keep voters from even bothering to show up for a race that they believed had already been lost.

"If I worked for @DataProgress I would simply not relate this knowing it could deflate dem side turn out," she had tweeted. "But hey, what do real world outcomes matter to folks in the data bubble?"

"I like her tweets more than most," Sean said. "The left is mostly like, 'I want to piss in Sean McElwee's mouth.' Where Melissa is more like, 'Sean's polls are voter suppression.'"

"She texted me almost exactly that," Ari said. He pulled out his phone and read aloud for the group, "'Why is Sean putting out research that creates negative news when we are trying to get out the vote?'"

* * *

It had been an eventful few months for Sean. He'd hosted a couple of birthday parties for himself, one in Washington and one in New York. At the Washington party, he'd handed out copies of *The Precipice: Existential Risk and the Future of Humanity*, a book that was quasi-scriptural in the effective altruism movement. At the New York party, Chuck Schumer had made an appearance. With a crowd gathered around the Senate majority leader, Schumer had asked Sean why he had gotten into the business of polling and Sean had told him it was because he wanted to be powerful.

And yet he had also been feeling wary of how others might judge how he was using his power. Nationally, things were looking bad for Democrats; Republicans were giddily anticipating a bloodbath. When things go poorly in an election, there's always lots of blame to throw around. Sean was getting the feeling that people were ready to throw some blame his way. He told me he'd even commissioned a study aimed at finding out whether polls showing candidates behind in their races really did have a negative impact on voter turnout—a study that, depending on the data, might be used to refute the kind of argument that Melissa Byrne was already making.

"I've been attacked by some Democrats for our polls," Sean had told me a few days before poker. "But I believe I'm accountable to reality. My job is to reflect reality and I think we'll be there. Ultimately I will be judged by how accurate my numbers are."

Sean was making a big bet. He had once told me that his ultimate goal was to one day be a president's pollster. He couldn't expect to get to that level if he just polled for progressives and only publicly released the surveys that fit a narrative. He had to cultivate a reputation as the most accurate guy in town, and having the paper trail to prove it. If Democrats lost big, but Sean's numbers were spot on, he could spin that as a win.

"It's a good advertisement for our product," he said about putting out accurate data, no matter what story they told. "Also, I believe in informing the public."

Sean knew the midterms could be ugly for the Democrats. And with less than a week out, he had invited me to a bakery around the corner from his office and told me he expected the Democrats to lose control of both chambers of Congress. He didn't want it to happen, but the odds were against them.

"I always knew we were swimming upstream," he told me.

But Sean? He was still floating in warm water.

"I think I'm going to make a lot of money on election night," he said with a smirk.

Sitting in the bakery, we went over a spreadsheet of bets that Sean had made with his poker buddies.

- $50 that Democrat Beto O'Rourke would lose his race for Texas governor by more than 10 points.
- $100 that Democrat Stacey Abrams would lose her bid for Georgia governor by 5 or more points.
- $200 that Democrat Gretchen Whitmer would win reelection as Michigan's governor by fewer than 7.5 points.
- $50 that Democrat Mary Peltola would lose her House seat in Alaska.
- $100 that Democrats would end up with fewer than 198 seats in the House.
- $200 that Democrats would end up with fewer than 197 seats in the House.
- $100 that Democrat Tim Ryan would lose to Republican J. D. Vance in the Senate race in Ohio.
- $500 that Democrat John Fetterman would do better against Mehmet Oz in the Pennsylvania Senate race than Ryan would do against Vance.

- $100 that Democrat Mandela Barnes would lose by more than 5 points in his bid for Senate in Wisconsin.
- $100 that Democrat Mark Kelly of Arizona would lose his reelection bid for Senate in Arizona.
- $100 that Democrat Catherine Cortez Masto would lose her reelection bid for Senate in Nevada.
- $500 that Democrats would lose the Senate.
- $500 (again) that Democrats would lose the Senate.
- $110 (again) that Democrats would lose the Senate.
- $1,000 (again) that Democrats would lose the Senate, to be paid to an "abortion fund" if Sean lost.

Those were just some of Sean's bets. It was impossible for me to know for sure the extent of his gambling. I wasn't even sure if *Sean* knew the extent of Sean's betting. He had sent me screenshots of various PredictIt bets over the months we'd been chatting, but he never gave me a full rundown (despite my many requests). All I had were random clues. He told me at the bakery that he had put more than $20,000 into PredictIt so far that year (and was up $4,000 at the time). What was clear was that the midterm outcomes would make or break Sean's year. Beyond his bets with the poker pals, he had placed PredictIt wagers on the Senate going Republican, Cortez Masto losing, and Kelly going down. (He showed me a wager slip for that one: He'd bet $1,276 and stood to get back $3,148 if Kelly lost.)

"Our current poll has him tied," Sean said. But things were trending in the wrong direction.

He'd also bet against Mandela Barnes, whom DFP had down by 6 percentage points. Sean put $1,700 on that one, and stood to get back $2,700 when Barnes lost, which Sean predicted would happen very quickly in the evening.

He had also placed a PredictIt bet on his client John Fetterman. He bet on him to lose.

"I think he's fucked," Sean said, taking a sip of his iced coffee.

For most of the summer and into the fall, Fetterman had had huge polling leads over his opponent, Dr. Mehmet Oz. But a few weeks earlier, Fetterman had had a shaky performance at his one and only televised debate of the general election. The lingering effects of his stroke had been obvious as he grasped for words and stuttered through answers. A lot of political watchers in Washington had decided that the performance would likely cut into Fetterman's now-dwindling lead; Sean was pretty sure the lieutenant governor's advantage was gone completely. He'd bet on Fetterman early. But now DFP's recent polling showed the Democrat in decline, and Sean had sold his shares on Fetterman's victory.

"Do you own any Fetterman stock right now?" I asked him.

"Let me see," he said, checking his phone. "I have fifty-three shares on 'No.'"

"Fifty-three shares that Fetterman will lose?"

"Yeah."

PredictIt bets, like polls, are just a snapshot in time. Sean could buy and sell whenever he wanted. He maintained he could always change his bets or dump all his stocks before Election Day. So, I asked him what it would take to change his mind in the coming days and get him to once again bet on a Fetterman win. He said if the final DFP poll showed Fetterman up, even by a point, he'd think about it. But he wasn't expecting that.

"I think he's at minus-one or minus-two," he told me. "Once you go down, it's really hard to see how you come back up."

* * *

Back at the poker table, on the Friday before the election. Sean had started talking about another betting market he'd been exploring, beyond PredictIt—suggesting more wagers that I didn't know about.

"I've been having to do all my gambling on crypto because they are banning PredictIt," he said, shuffling a deck to deal.

"Do you have a book?" the aerospace guy asked.

"Oh, like a bookie?" Sean said. "No, I used Polymarket…"

Sean explained: Polymarket was a site that allowed gambling on elections that was not legal in the United States. He had used a virtual private network (a "VPN") to hide the location of his computer, and used the site to make bets on congressional races. It was a fine enough alternative to PredictIt, he said, though it did have substantial fees required to transfer his money into cryptocurrency.

"Tell Leah to tell Marvin to fix that," the lawyer said, referring to Leah's crypto-lawyer boyfriend. "You guys notice that she's started referring to him as her 'partner'? I think they are getting serious. I went to his birthday party that she threw for him. And they're renting an apartment together in New York."

"Sean, you're pretty close to the Bankman-Fried guy, right?" the aerospace guy asked.

"Yup," Sean said.

The aerospace guy wanted to know how much untraceable money Sam Bankman-Fried had donated to Democratic causes during the 2020 cycle. Sean said he thought it was tens of millions.

"Why?" Sean asked.

"I assumed it was a lot," the aerospace guy said. "But I had no idea what the actual amount would be. God bless him. I don't get the EA stuff, but it's definitely good for the world."

Chapter 40

Dark and Stormy Democracy

Leah Hunt-Hendrix got the news from Marvin Ammori. She had just sat through an hourlong meeting with the Milwaukee mayor (for no reason other than because that's what rich people get to do when there's nothing else to do on Election Day), and she popped onto a downtown street with a grin.

"Did you guys hear what happened to SBF?" she said.

What *had* happened to Sam Bankman-Fried? It would take a while to fully figure that one out, but this much seemed clear right away: FTX, Bankman-Fried's crypto exchange, had imploded. A rival company was considering buying it for pennies on the dollar. The extent of Bankman-Fried's alleged fraud was not yet known, nor was the fact that more than $8 billion of customer funds had vanished. But by the time Leah and Marvin arrived at Mandela Barnes's election night party in Milwaukee, glued to the Twitter scroll of political and crypto news, it was clear enough that whatever clout the Bankman-Frieds had in Washington was in serious jeopardy.

"So I imagine he's no longer a billionaire?" Maurice Mitchell, the head of the progressive Working Families Party, asked Leah and Marvin at the Barnes watch party, about an hour before polls closed.

"I guess," Leah said.

"There was a tweet that he was worth $900 million," Marvin said.

"Oh. So a high-hundred millionaire," Mitchell said. "Must be tough."

"This is honestly the craziest day in the history of crypto," Marvin said.

"It's hard not to have schadenfreude about this," Leah said.

Leah and the Bankman-Frieds had been frenemies during the primaries, but when it came to Barnes's fate in Wisconsin, it was the Republican billionaires who had been her problem. Richard and Elizabeth Uihlein, founders of the Wisconsin-based packaging company Uline, and Diane Hendricks, a right-wing Wisconsin businesswoman with ties to Trump, had spent millions and helped their party flood the airwaves with ads painting Barnes as soft on crime, and as someone who "rationalized violence" against police officers. In one mailer, sent out by the Wisconsin Republican Party, a photo of Barnes had noticeably darkened skin. In recent months, Barnes's polling numbers had taken a dive. The latest survey from Data for Progress, for example, had him down 6 points the day before the election. No one here was calling this event a "victory party."

"Hmm, a 'Dark and Stormy Democracy,' that's a little grim," Marvin said, looking at a drink menu.

Marvin had come to Wisconsin not because he was involved with the race (though he was a progressive) but because he was still involved with Leah. He had, Leah told me, "passed with flying colors" on the test that was their trip to Portugal. The two had gotten along great, and Leah came to realize that maybe Marvin had been taking her out to those super-fancy restaurants not because he was obsessed with money but because he was trying to impress her. She began to believe that maybe they could make it work. She had told the social worker that now wasn't the best time for her to become a foster mom.

The Barnes party took place at Turner Hall, a four-story brick building that used to be a socialist meeting hall. Strings of white

Christmas lights hung from the ceiling, over a crowd of nervous Democrats. Leah and Marvin hung out on the second-floor balcony, the section for VIPs like Tammy Baldwin, the Democratic senator who wasn't up for reelection, and Karla Jurvetson, the uber-wealthy ex-wife of a Silicon Valley investor who had gotten in early on companies like SpaceX and Tesla. Jurvetson, a psychiatrist by trade, had a lot in common with Leah—the two women were friendly, and had gotten lunch earlier that day—with a notable difference: Jurvetson controlled her own money.

Leah's family money was another matter. Her pitch to her mother, Helen, had been successful, sort of. According to Leah, Helen had been worried that if she wrote a big check to her daughter, or her daughter's organization, it wouldn't be fair to the other siblings. So instead of a donation, Helen decided to just give all her children a bigger-than-normal gift that year. She wrote them each a check for a million dollars.

In terms of money Leah was able to raise from rich people who weren't her mother, it had been a pretty good year. Way to Win had raised and spent close to $80 million during the 2021–2022 election cycle by Leah's accounting—a ton of money, but nowhere near the $165 million the organization had raised amid the #Resistance fervor of 2018. Most of the 2022 midterm money went directly to groups on the ground—mostly 501(c)4s, the "social welfare" organizations that aren't required to list their donors. The super PAC associated with Way to Win spent $500,000 in Wisconsin, helping pay for TV ads and get-out-the-vote operations to help Barnes. Leah took me to see one such operation, Power to the Polls, the political arm of an organization run by local faith leaders called Souls to the Polls. They'd made a local community center their base of operations, and on Election Day it was jam-packed with hundreds of volunteers, mostly Black, loading into buses heading into low-income neighborhoods to encourage voting.

One of the big goals of Way to Win, Leah told me, was to find people who never voted and give them a reason to vote—not just appeal to the people already in the mix. This was what it really meant to be an "inclusive populist" instead of a "popularist." Leah told me that she could get frustrated by the Sean McElwees and the David Shors of the world, who looked at data and told Democrats to just focus on what was already popular.

"Pollsters can follow trends," she told me the night before. "But how can you *create* trends? Things that aren't popular until they become popular." That was the harder work.

It did bug Leah that her super PAC, Way to Lead, had raised and spent less than half of what Sam Bankman-Fried's super PAC, Protect Our Future, had spent on a single (failed) congressional candidate in Oregon—to say nothing of the millions Bankman-Fried had directed to other primary candidates, many of whom ran against Leah's progressives. But it wasn't the crypto crew that Leah was stewing about in Wisconsin (they seemed to be getting their own comeuppance). It was the Democratic establishment.

Leah believed the establishment—in particular the Senate Majority PAC, a spending operation with close ties to Democratic leader Chuck Schumer—had left Barnes for dead. This wasn't entirely true: The super PAC had spent $24 million *against* Barnes's primary opponent, Johnson (second only to the $41 million they spent against Dr. Oz). But it was true that as Johnson's polling average lead continued to grow against Barnes in Wisconsin, late-in-the-game spending from major Democratic donors went elsewhere.

Leah wanted to believe that Barnes could still win, but she had arrived in Milwaukee expecting him to lose. It helped to have someone to blame. What she didn't know was how close he was to winning.

It was about an hour before polls would close, and Barnes had arrived at his non-victory party. As he came through the crowd, Leah intercepted the candidate and gave him a big, warm hug.

"Do you feel like the Senate Majority PAC left you high and dry?" Leah asked him.

"Absolutely," Barnes said.

287

* * *

Money hadn't been an issue for John Fetterman. The Pennsylvania candidate's problem was narrative: the notion that his stroke and subsequent debate performance had killed his momentum. That once you start to go down, you never go back up. And on that matter, Rebecca Katz, his senior strategist, felt like Sean McElwee had left them high and dry.

She had brought in Data for Progress as pollsters specifically to help *control the narrative*, as they say in politics, by putting out polls that made Fetterman look good. That didn't mean rigging the results, but it did mean deciding which polls to make public and which ones to keep to themselves. As Election Day approached, Sean had publicly released some surveys that showed Democrats losing in swing states that went *against* Katz's preferred narrative—namely that kept voters and campaign staff from throwing in the towel. She began to feel like Sean was leaving Fetterman for dead. Making matters worse, Katz had heard rumors (not from me) that Sean had been talking shit about Fetterman's chances.

She sensed that Sean was making moves to control his own narrative: If Fetterman became a loser, he could be the pollster who saw it coming.

On the night before the election, Sean had released his final set of Data for Progress polls. They were terrible for Democrats. He had Republicans up by 4 points in the Arizona governor's race, where Republican Kari Lake, the former TV anchor, was waging a scorched-earth campaign against Democrat Katie Hobbs. Sean's Senate polls showed Republican Blake Masters leading Democrat Mark Kelly by 1 point in Arizona, Republican Herschel Walker leading Democrat Raphael Warnock by 1 point in Georgia, and Republican Adam Laxalt leading Democrat Catherine Cortez Masto by 2 points in Nevada. He hadn't released anything about Fetterman in Pennsylvania, but the broader story Sean was advancing was clear enough: Democrats were in trouble.

Katz was pissed.

"Yikes. Why the polls tonight?" she texted him.

"Nothing in PA. To be clear," Sean wrote back. He added, "I don't know a better night to release."

Katz wasn't sure why he'd felt the need to release them at all. He wasn't a news organization; he was a member of a team of Democrats who were trying to win elections. Fetterman's own pollsters had him down before the election, but the campaign kept that private. Katz even kept it from Fetterman, she told me, because she didn't want to upset him. Polls were snapshots in time; things could change. Pollsters could also be wrong.

* * *

The first thing Sean was wrong about was that Mandela Barnes did not get wiped out right away.

The polls closed at 8:00 p.m. Leah had been told by someone plugged into the campaign to expect the early numbers to favor Johnson heavily, and that if Barnes stood a chance, he'd have to claw his way back late in the game. But by 10:00 p.m., Barnes and Johnson were still running even. This had the crowd buzzing, and so did the televisions, which kept flashing returns from Pennsylvania showing Fetterman outrunning Oz.

At 10:15 p.m., I texted Sean, who was hosting a watch party at his New York apartment: "How's it lookin?"

"Becoming cautiously optimistic we'll miss the worst," he wrote back.

"Fetterman seems to be running better than expected, right?"

"Yes. It's looking very decent."

"Good for dems, bad for PredictIt spreadsheet?"

"I'm still up."

By 10:45, Barnes was still within 1.5 percentage points and Leah took note.

"I'm getting my hopes up!" she shouted over a crowd that was getting its hopes up too. "I would be so happy. I don't know what I'd do. I'd go on a rampage!"

I asked Marvin what that would look like.

"Never seen it," he said.

I texted Sean: "Im here at Mandela party. Any chance he wins?"

"Unlikely," he wrote back.

"People here are getting hopes up."

But this time Sean was right. Barnes kept it close all night, but eventually it became clear to the number crunchers in the room that the votes just wouldn't be there to close the gap.

"That was sobering," Leah said before leaving. "I'm okay. I'm okay. Yeah. I'm good."

I could tell that Leah was in the late-night process of trying to control her own narrative.

In a certain light, the night was a moral victory: Her guy had come within a single percentage point, way closer than people like Sean had expected. Then again, Tony Evers, the incumbent Democratic governor, had prevailed in his reelection bid; that meant that some people had voted for Evers but not Barnes, even though they were on the same ticket.

Did that mean that there was still just enough racism among Wisconsin Democrats to doom the Black candidate? Did it mean that Democrats might have picked up the seat if they'd run a candidate more like Evers—the White, seventy-one-year-old, moderate, milquetoast former school superintendent? Or did it mean that Washington Democrats hadn't spent enough money countering the Republican attack ads painting Barnes as an anti-police Black Lives Matter radical? Did his loss reflect some sad-but-true aspect of the electorate? Or was Barnes done in by bad assumptions about what could be *made* true with a little more money, a little more imagination, a little more work?

"It was all okay," she said. "It could have been worse. It wasn't a bad night. And it wasn't so bad for Mandela. It wasn't a mandate that a Black man can't win. There just wasn't any investment."

She thought about it and nodded her head.

"It was a pretty good night for progressives," she said.

Leah and Marvin decided to leave. It was late and she was tired. But even though a Barnes loss seemed inevitable, a lot of the crowd stuck around. There was still food and drinks and the televisions were turned on throughout the hall showing the crowd that Democrats across the country were proving a lot of naysayers wrong.

"Wow," Sean texted me.

"What happened?"

"Fetterman wins."

It wasn't official yet. But the Fetterman team was already preparing for it to be. Ten minutes earlier, top campaign staffers had huddled to discuss putting a podium on the stage to prepare for a victory speech. Katz and Fetterman had been hesitant to declare victory too soon. They looked to Jason McGrath, a top pollster on the team, for advice. McGrath had been one of the more bearish members of the Fetterman campaign, but gave the podium placement his blessing.

"Wait," Fetterman said. "*You* think I'm going to win?"

The day after the election, Sean called me from New York to debrief. He admitted that some of his bets had been misguided. On the other hand, the fact that Democrats were on track to keep control of the Senate was good! For the country, and for business.

"The results are good for me professionally," he told me. "So I'm hedged emotionally."

There would be plenty of work in Washington for a Democratic pollster in good standing. But where Sean stood, however, wasn't exactly certain. After Sean hung up with me, he texted Rebecca Katz.

"Do you have five minutes today?" he wrote.

"Sean," she wrote back. "What you did with those polls was terrible."

"We didn't release PA publicly," Sean reiterated. "I would love to apologize if you can find five minutes."

"Nope," Katz wrote back. "Unforgivable."

Chapter 41

What Side Am I On Here?

Late fall 2022

One week after the election, Sean McElwee walked through the rain in his neighborhood. He wore a puffy black Patagonia jacket and colorful New Balance shoes that had gone damp and gray. His hair was wet and matted down on his forehead. It had been a gloomy few days for Sean, but he was doing his best to spin the year as a win.

"We built up our credibility. Grew our team to twenty-three people," he said. "Our polling influenced a lot of policy discourse."

That may have all been true. But it was also true that many of Sean's bets this year had gone wrong. These included wagers made with his poker buddies:

- Senator Mark Kelly would lose reelection in Arizona. **Wrong.**
- Senator Catherine Cortez Masto would lose reelection in Nevada. **Wrong.**
- Mandela Barnes would lose by more than 5 points in Wisconsin. **Wrong.**
- Democrats would have fewer than 198 seats in the House. **Wrong.**
- Democrats would lose the Senate. **Nope.**

Sean had whiffed on key parts of the election, but so had plenty of people. And he'd even gotten some things right (Stacey Abrams *did* lose her bid for Georgia governor by more than 5 points). Sean also claimed that he had, at the last minute, dumped his shares on Fetterman's loss because he didn't want to be on the "wrong side of that coin" going into Election Day. The problem for Sean was that his big misses were doozies. Like betting on Sam Bankman-Fried. The entirety of Bankman-Fried's fraud still hadn't been fully revealed by this point, but it was pretty clear he'd fucked over a lot of people and that indictments were likely. It had gotten so bad, so quickly, for Bankman-Fried that Sean—who once told friends it was "cool as hell" to be advising the billionaire—wasn't even referring to himself as an effective altruist anymore.

"I'm a progressive person foremost," he said.

Sean was in sales mode as we walked through a dreary Logan Circle. He reminded me about how proud he was to help pass the Inflation Reduction Act, and explained that DFP's polling was actually pretty good in a lot of ways (like how more registered Republicans really did come out to vote) even if he'd whiffed on the actual outcomes. He was having a hard time getting through his pitch, though, because his cell phone kept buzzing, and he kept looking at it and quietly responding. Some college kids had been making fun of him relentlessly online for his bad prognosticating and his political gambling habit. They accused him of "insider trading," and one of them said that Sean had lost $50,000 on PredictIt. That number was made up, *New York* magazine would later report (and also, that's not what insider trading is), but the chorus of anti-Sean sentiment in the left-wing gossip mill was hard to ignore.

He apologized for being on his phone.

"I'm getting attacked a lot on Twitter," he said. "It gets in my staff's head."

He had bigger problems than he was letting on. In Washington, you can get away with a lot when you're right—swagger, loose lips, an ostentatious gambling habit. But now that Sean had been proven wrong about so much, it wasn't just the shit posters who had Sean in their sights. There was drama brewing with his staff at Data for Progress. I'd been spending time with Sean for more than a year, and I knew how bonded he was with his young protégés. Even now, as his reputation outside the organization was taking hits, he patted himself on the back for recruiting them to be part of the thing he'd built.

"I think where I have done the best in my life is..." He paused on the side of the street to check his phone again. "I think the strongest thing I have is I'm pretty good at finding talent."

And it was true: He'd bet on people and those bets had paid off. He'd help mold them into Washington players, and their success was his success. From nothing, Sean had built a political organization that was tied in with the White House and helped develop a young, diverse staff that was devoted to their work and who would go to battle for him.

That is, until they felt they couldn't anymore.

*   *   *

Three days later, Sean McElwee's senior staff asked him to step down.

There was no cinematic climax, McKenzie Wilson told me afterward, no one thing that made everyone decide it was time for him to go. It was everything: the midterm polls, the connection to Bankman-Fried, the betting, and the perception that a bettor like Sean might be tempted to tweak the DFP polls to improve his odds. "I know that's not the case," she said. "But it doesn't matter what I think."

What mattered was that the organization's credibility was bound to Sean's now-tarnished reputation. Clients had been calling with worried questions: *Was Sean using data we paid for, for his gambling?* When rumors of Sean's betting habits had spread online, Marcela and McKenzie's phones started blowing up with texts from everyone they knew in politics. The message was unanimous: *Get out before this ruins your reputations.* That made them feel bad. Representative Alexandria

Ocasio-Cortez had liked a tweet raking Sean for his gambling habit. That made them feel worse.

It was particularly personal for Marcela. Well before Sean became her professional mentor, Ocasio-Cortez had been one of Marcela's political icons. She had seen the New York congresswoman up close shortly after arriving to Washington as a fellow for the Sunrise Movement. It was November 2018, shortly after Ocasio-Cortez had been elected for the first time, and Sunrise was planning a sit-in at House Speaker Nancy Pelosi's office to push for the Green New Deal, a comprehensive climate plan. The night before the action, Ocasio-Cortez came to the church where the activists were spending the night. She had stood on a table and delivered a speech about how in politics there is nothing you can do more powerful than to "not give a fuck."

When Marcela saw that Ocasio-Cortez had liked an anti-Sean tweet, "That made me think, like, 'What side am I on here?'" she said.

For Marcela, all the red flags were much easier to see in retrospect: the first time they'd met at a happy hour and he'd been rude to her, the time in April when he'd said he was going to be stepping back to do more consulting, and all that gambling. Marcela had had reservations about betting on politics and expressed them to Sean. But Sean had told her it was fine, and his openness about it all had given her reason to believe he was right.

Just a few months before the election, Sean had hosted an event for up-and-coming Democratic staffers to celebrate the passage of the Inflation Reduction Act. The group of staffers—from the administration, from Congress, from outside groups—went around the table saying what they were excited about regarding the bill's passage. Sean told the group he was mostly psyched to be able to collect on some bets he'd made.

"I feel like an asshole because I went with it," Marcela said. "But when he says it in rooms of people and everyone just laughs, what am I supposed to think?"

The decision to ask Sean to resign was still difficult. He hadn't just built the organization; he'd helped build careers. No way Marcela would have gotten this far, this quickly—running a think tank, briefing members of Congress, and taking meetings at the White House—without Sean backing her. McKenzie felt the same way about running her own communications department, and so did Ethan Winter, who oversaw the polling as a "lead" analyst before the age of thirty. Sean knew a lot of people owed him, and after the midterms he'd been calling up team members on the phone, checking in, telling them he could fix things he'd broken. He'd met with Marcela and McKenzie separately, telling each of them that Data for Progress meant everything to him. He cried in both meetings. At home, McKenzie kept asking her boyfriend whether forcing Sean to leave was the right move. "Yeah," he kept telling her. "You have to burn the bridge because he threatened to burn the city."

Less than two weeks after the election, the staff decided to confront Sean during an already scheduled video conference meeting. Danielle, the top climate strategist and a de facto leader at DFP, would do most of the talking. She was worried that it could get confrontational, and so the night before the meeting, she got in touch with her boyfriend's mother, whose job overseeing a residency program at a hospital included firing doctors who were not meeting their ethical standards, for some coaching. She told Danielle to watch her demeanor, watch her tone. When the time came, Danielle spoke as calmly as she could, even though her heart was racing and she worried she might throw up. She told Sean that he risked permanently damaging the organization, and that if he didn't step down, the entire senior leadership was going to leave. It was clear that she wasn't bluffing; the team was all on the call. Sean folded right away.

"What's my severance?" he asked.

It was striking to Marcela that that had been his initial response. Then again, he lived an expensive lifestyle for a guy making $180,000 a year at a nonprofit.

"I mean, he has a very nice apartment in New York," Danielle said. "I would be asking those questions too."

Marcela and McKenzie each told me they'd expected Sean to put up more of a fight. He had shed tears to both of them—tears that Bobbi, his ex-girlfriend, said she saw only once in their seven years together, and which might have been fake. Marcela and McKenzie had been sure at the time that Sean's crying had been genuine, but like Bobbi, they'd grown skeptical.

"I think one of the things about this whole situation," McKenzie told me afterward, "is, I don't know what to believe anymore."

Marcela was having a similar existential crisis. She couldn't bring herself to repudiate her entire time working under Sean. She had come to believe in the importance of message control and trusting data. Maybe she had been "modpilled," but she was proud of the work she'd done helping pass the IRA and helping get candidates like Maxwell Frost in Florida elected. She had "drunk the Kool-Aid" that Sean was offering, but part of being twenty-five, she said, is "drinking lots of Kool-Aid and figuring out what flavor you like."

Now Marcela was twenty-six. And she wasn't sure if any amount of Kool-Aid was healthy.

"It makes me feel like I'm not fucking cut out for a job in this field," Marcela said. "It's so dark. And it's really scary."

Chapter 42

Washington in Winter

It was winter in Washington again, but there would be no holiday party at Chez Leah this year. Four years of fighting against Trumpism and two years of squabbling with fellow Democrats had left Leah Hunt-Hendrix feeling burnt out. She planned to get out of Washington for the holidays—to spend the end of December with Marvin Ammori's family in Michigan. Then she'd head to Italy for a little rest and relaxation, followed by a quick trip to the Canary Islands. And after that, she would move in with Marvin in New York. She would keep the house in Logan Circle; she wasn't ready to give up fighting for progressive causes and figuring out Washington's fulcrums. She planned on moving back in a year or two. But right now she needed a break. And she could afford to take one.

"One of the great things about being a funder is that even when you're burnt out, you can get money to people who still have energy," she said.

The Schlapps weren't going anywhere: Invites to their annual Christmas party went out shortly after the midterms. I got one, and—much to their surprise—so did Ian and Carin Walters.

It had been an anxious few months in the Walters household. Ian had been glad about the election. He saw the defeat of Trumpy candidates as a victory for sanity. But the health of our democracy had not been the big story out of Accokeek, Maryland. In September, they'd learned that Carin was pregnant with their fourth child—unexpected but happy news. The baby girl had an atypical heartbeat, which meant Carin needed to go on medication.

I'd asked Ian if he wanted to come with me to the Schlappening, but he had no interest in that, so I met up with him earlier that day. Ian had a gig playing keyboard in his friend's three-piece band at a holiday fair downtown. I watched him jam on classics like "Santa Baby" and croon on a Doris Day verse or two ("While I'm alone and blue as can be, dream a little dream of me…"). He wore a felt cowboy hat and seemed like he was having fun, though he was also at work.

"It's my main source of income at this point," he told me after his set.

As long as Carin could keep picking up freelance event-planning jobs, the family could stay afloat. But Carin was going to have to slow down soon, and Ian knew that meant he had to step up.

And so, over a double shot of Jameson at the bar by the holiday market, Ian told me he was thinking about dipping his toes back into the political game.

"Just a couple of short-term contract jobs," he said. "That way I can say 'I'm out' if it's no good."

The jobs were similar in nature to the work he'd done at CPAC. He'd be doing communications work for a couple of political conferences. One was a libertarian gathering, he said. The second would be for Ralph Reed's Faith and Freedom Coalition.

This surprised me. Ralph Reed was a Trump Guy. A longtime conservative consultant known for his role as the director of the Christian Coalition during the early '90s, he had worked with religious broadcaster Pat Robertson and helped mobilize forces in the 1994 congressional elections. Reed was a religious conservative who took great umbrage at Bill Clinton's sexual indiscretions, but would go on to write a book called *For God and Country: The Christian Case for Trump*. In 2017, I covered one of Reed's Faith and Freedom Coalition Road to Majority conferences. I watched Donald Trump receive standing ovation after standing ovation, then joined Reed for lunch along with some other reporters. I had asked Reed if he had any concerns about Trump's moral character and he'd replied, "I don't have any reservations at all."

I asked Ian if he had reservations about working for Reed. It seemed to me like he might be heading back into a similar situation he'd left with Matt Schlapp: spinning for a cause he no longer believed in.

"I believe in the way I operate, in the techniques I've developed to persuade people to listen to their better angels and do right by their fellow man," he said. He could simply tell the whole political system to screw off, he said. But if everyone like him left the conversation, then that would leave all the talking to the worst actors in politics.

I'd heard this rationalization before. It was Ian's answer for why he'd stuck around CPAC as long as he did. He was spinning again. And while it was just two of us talking at the bar, I got the feeling I wasn't the only one he was trying to convince. Maybe Ralph Reed was an old-school Republican guy who got caught up in the "whole MAGA thing, like a lot of people, for a moment," he told me.

I didn't buy it. If there was one lesson I expected Ian to have learned, it was not to go work for someone who had jumped on the Trump train the moment it became expedient to do so. But Ian was feeling good, all things told, about where he was at. Carin's pregnancy and the complications were stressful to deal with, especially without much money coming in. But had it all happened back during Ian's big break with Matt, he said he would have found it completely overwhelming. He was a more secure person now. He wasn't CPAC Ian anymore, but he still had a specific skill set that he could use to make money. He had a family to take care of, and that family was growing. He and Carin had spent the morning in a dark sonogram room. The technician had moved the probe over Carin's abdomen, and the screen showed them what they longed to see: The baby's heartbeat had begun to normalize.

*   *   *

I left Ian and headed Schlappward to the mansion on Mansion Drive, where I very quickly found myself in a conversation with Matt Gaetz, the Florida congressman whom Matt Schlapp had long ago described to me as a "bad guy" but a "rock star."

"Please don't write that I was wearing the same red blazer as Greta Van Susteren," Gaetz told me, referring to the Newsmax host who was standing nearby wearing the same red blazer.

The midterms had been an embarrassment for Trump and for Kevin McCarthy, the Republican House leader, who had been among the many, many Republicans who had predicted that a gigantic red wave would wash away Democrats. But a slim GOP majority in the House was not a bad scenario for Gaetz, who could now make McCarthy's life hell if the Republican leader didn't do what Gaetz and his fellow far-right trouble-makers wanted. Plus, it was looking like the congressman was not going to face federal charges for alleged sex crimes after all.

Gaetz and his wife, Ginger, walked through the kitchen, over to the dining room table, which was covered with finger foods—beef sliders, grilled cheese sandwiches, fried macaroni balls, crab dip.

"I don't have to report this because it's all appetizers," Gaetz explained, displaying a mastery of ethics rules that governed interactions with lobbyists and constrained a man of his station. "If this were a sit-down meal, that would be different."

The Gaetzes took their crab dip and grabbed a seat by the fireplace in the living room. Soon the congressman was explaining how Florida Governor Ron DeSantis had schooled him in the fine art of applying makeup for television appearances. ("He taught me how to contour; I taught him how to govern.") I made a mental note to check if sitting down with appetizers qualified as a "sit-down" meal under government ethics guidelines (it did not) and began making my way through the party.

Supreme Court Justice Brett Kavanaugh was here. After Trump

nominated him in 2018, Kavanaugh had willed himself through the confirmation process—despite a credible accusation that as a teenager he had sexually assaulted a high school classmate (which Kavanaugh denied)—in part by convincing Susan Collins, the pro-choice Republican senator from Maine, that he wouldn't mess with abortion rights. (Oops.) Over the summer, after it had leaked that Kavanaugh and his fellow conservatives were about to overturn *Roe v. Wade*, protesters had picketed the judge's house in the Maryland suburbs. A guy from California had shown up in Kavanaugh's neighborhood with a gun before turning himself in to police.

Standing by the dessert table, Kavanaugh seemed happy to be in a safe place to drink beer (he likes beer) surrounded by people who actually liked him. "We all have security," I overheard him tell a fellow party guest. "It's just something that happens in public office, something to adjust to."

Party guests were lining up to greet the justice and pose for pictures. Matt put his arm on Kavanaugh's shoulder and asked him if he felt popular here. Kavanaugh was popular here, but Republican candidates had paid for the Supreme Court's decision at the polls. As a candidate, Trump had promised to appoint anti-abortion judges to the Supreme Court. This helped win over religious voters and helped make him president. The backlash that ensued had been a major factor in the Democrats' successes in the midterms, which now made the ex-president look weak.

How weak was Trump? It was a good question, especially for the Mansion Drive crowd. A year earlier, Trump's strength—at least in terms of his grip on the party—had been undeniable. Now many of his handpicked candidates had been beaten in the midterms, and some Washington Republicans were accusing him of costing the party control of the Senate. Meanwhile, DeSantis, the Florida governor, was gaining on Trump in head-to-head polls among Republicans. For the first time in what seemed like ages, it seemed possible that Republicans might start hedging their bets.

"I do wonder if the country is ready for a little normalcy," said Michael Toner, the former chairman of the Federal Election Commission and, before that, chief counsel to the RNC, who was watching Newsmax in Matt's study. "Trump was a good fit for 2016, but maybe he's not as good a fit now."

Toner paused to look up at the TV, which was showing a segment on how Elon Musk was supposedly exposing past pro-Democrat bias at Twitter, the company he now owned. The upshot was that the tech company's previous minders had suppressed a story in 2020 about embarrassing material on a sketchy laptop once owned by Hunter Biden, Joe Biden's sketchy son. (The company was on guard against misinformation during the election season, and didn't want to risk the laptop being a fake. Which, as it turned out, it wasn't.) Much of the mainstream media had reacted with only vague interest—the fundamentals of the story were old news, and Musk was just another billionaire pleasing himself. But Trump was trying as hard as he could to make the "Twitter Files" a thing, calling it a "Massive Fraud" that allowed for "the termination of all rules, regulations, and articles, even those found in the Constitution."

"I wouldn't count him out, though," Toner said of Trump as the segment went to commercials.

Later, in the same study, I bumped into John Coale, a lawyer and husband of Greta Van Susteren (the television anchor who, by the way, was wearing the same red blazer as Congressman Matt Gaetz). Coale was sitting on a sofa in front of a painting version of a famous photo of the Brooks Brothers riot that featured a crowd of protesters including Matt Schlapp.

"I don't think you'll hear that much talk about him here this year," Coale said when I asked about Trump. "But next year..."

Caroline Wren, the Republican fundraiser, told me that anyone who thought Trump was toast wasn't thinking hard enough. The former president was still wildly popular with the base, and any challenger would have to face endless attacks from Trump and his allies—attacks that might not end even if Trump lost a primary, Wren said. "You think Trump is going to endorse anyone who beats him?"

One way or another, the Schlapps were well positioned to remain at the center of Republican politics in Washington. It was something Wren admired about them. "They are the most interesting people in Washington," she told me, "because they can get anyone on the phone from any part of the movement."

I ran into Daniel Lippman, the Politico reporter who had introduced me to Robert Stryk (thanks again, Daniel).

"Don't you two go causing any trouble!" Mercy Schlapp said after spotting us together. Nevertheless, Politico's *Playbook* ran an item the next morning saying that Justice Kavanaugh was at the Schlapps' house with the likes of Gaetz, Van Susteren, Stephen Miller (who had business before the Supreme Court), Sean Spicer, Erik Prince, former Trump cabinet secretaries Alex Acosta and Chad Wolf—and me. That item caused a bit of a row about ethics types in Washington, though I don't know if it troubled the Schlapps.

One of the more obscure party guests mentioned in the *Playbook* item, a congressman-elect from New York, would soon be the most infamous man in Washington. I spotted George Santos chatting with folks chatting by the fireplace. Within weeks we would all learn that Santos had lied about where he went to college and where he had worked, was under investigation by Brazilian authorities for allegedly forging checks, and had pretended to be Jewish. Later, he'd be accused of swindling a disabled Navy veteran out of $3,000 raised to provide lifesaving surgery for the veteran's dying dog. He was the kind of grifter Ian had worried about gaining purchase in Trump's, and Matt's, Republican Party.

I spotted The Kid alone in a hallway, off to the side of the dining room.

I had no idea if Ian was right about The Kid being a phony. I couldn't know for sure whether he'd insinuated he was part of that famous American family with the famous name. But I figured I'd ask him about it.

"Oh, yeah, my family invests in the company," he said.

I asked, specifically, if he was part of the family.

He didn't answer the question directly, saying only that his parents had a "holdings and investment firm, so, yeah," and then walking away.

It was a bit weird and uncomfortable, which was pretty much how I already felt just being at the party.

I spotted Matt standing in his backyard with Wren, drinking a martini. When I approached, Matt ducked back inside, saying, "We're trying to save the country!"

*   *   *

"I don't believe in war. War is a failure of men to sit down and negotiate and even say sorry. Me and you had a rough time; I'm willing to engage and apologize and give context."

Robert Stryk had called for the first time since he'd turned on me.

"I'm not going to defend my actions by any means."

He tried to explain what had happened the previous summer. He had been going through a rough time, he said. An illness in the family. People had told him I was calling around about him. He felt "disrespected." He wanted me to know that he never thought I was actually a child predator, that it was just bluster. He didn't explain, exactly, how that led to the name-calling, and I didn't push. Instead, we talked about politics and his lobbying work. Earlier in the year, Stryk had seemed all in on Trump. Now he seemed keen to put some distance between himself and the ex-president ("I don't know Trump," he reminded me), while also standing firm on his belief that Trump's foreign policy disruption was good for the world.

"He is the man who moved the embassy to Jerusalem, who created the Abraham Accords, who had great relationships with our trading partners," he said. "But it's very hard to juxtapose that with a guy who calls people names."

As for his attempts at wartime diplomacy, he explained that he hadn't been able to acquire a license to lobby on behalf of the Belarusians. Nevertheless, "Business has been the best it's ever been," he assured me. He told me he couldn't talk long because he was en route to Africa. He had just inked a deal, he said, a $5 million contract to help Africa's richest woman, Isabel dos Santos, the daughter of the former Angolan president, fight corruption charges against her.

He referred to me as "my friend," and before we hung up, he told me to reach out anytime. It was all very diplomatic.

Our talks resumed in early January, via a series of texts.

"Hey man I know Schlapp is a big part of your book as you told and also a good bud of yours. Does this make a mess of your book?"

"Seems that it would."

Carlton Huffman had told his story about his October evening with Matt to Roger Sollenberger, the same Daily Beast reporter who had broken the story about Herschel Walker allegedly paying for an abortion. The story was out. Huffman—who kept his identity private— showed Sollenberger the videos he'd recorded that night talking about the alleged groping, as well as his texts with Matt the next day. These included a text Huffman sent to Matt, stating that he was "uncomfortable with what happened last night" and recommending a different driver that might be able to take Matt to the next event; and a text Matt sent back (after reportedly trying to call three times in twenty minutes) that read, "If you could see it in your heart to call me at the end of day. I would appreciate it. If not I wish you luck on the campaign and hope you keep up the good work."

Huffman had told the Daily Beast that he'd told the Walker campaign about the incident at the time, and that campaign officials had been supportive. According to the story, a "senior Walker official" had "confirmed the details of the campaign's involvement as {Huffman} described it," including "a meeting between the staffer and legal counsel." The story also quoted a lawyer for Matt, who said his client denied "any improper behavior."

To Stryk, the meaning of all this was clear.

"Cautionary tale my friend. I hope you cover the arrogance of this. As these are the people who keep people like me out of the game bc we never had the connections or gave the campaign contributions," he wrote.

"The fallacy of it all," Stryk continued, "is that it's all one big 'Glass House' that could fall at anytime and why a Fella like me never met any of these folks, never went to the Trump Hotel and has never given one dollar to anyone bc it's one big house of cards that even you were sucked into."

After the news broke, I called Matt but he didn't pick up. He wasn't offering comments to any of the news outlets that were reporting the story. CPAC offered a statement, calling the reporting a "hit piece" aimed to disrupt their "first ever CPAC gala," which was set to begin on January 6, a day after the story dropped. The coming weeks continued to be disruptive. The Daily Beast would later publish a story quoting Huffman's wife in which she claimed that the alleged groping incident had led their marriage to unravel.

"If that situation never happened, I don't think we'd be getting divorced," she said.

Carlton Huffman would file a $9.4 million lawsuit against Matt and Mercy on four civil counts related to allegations of "sexual battery" and claims that the Schlapps and others tried to "discredit" him in a dishonest way. Matt would, for a time anyway, stop appearing on Fox News. (After Huffman's name became public over the course of his lawsuit against the Schlapps, the *Washington Post* reported that he had been accused by two women of his own sexual misconduct—allegations that local police said were investigated and closed, with no charges filled.)

Yes, Matt had been "canceled" before, but he'd never faced a public accusation quite like this.

He knew at least one person who had, though.

Years ago, Matt and Mercy Schlapp had made a decision about Donald Trump at a crucial moment. "When you're a star, they let you do it," Trump had said on the infamous tape. "You can do anything." The Schlapps had stood by him. And they kept standing by him.

Now, shortly after the publication of the first Daily Beast story, Matt headed to his gala in Florida, put on a tuxedo and a smile, and welcomed a small crowd to what he dubbed "CPAC Mar-a-Lago." He called Trump to his side, introducing the ex-president by the title he preferred.

"The President of the United States," he said. "Donald J. Trump."

Chapter 43

If People Think They've Seen the Last of Me...

Back in Washington, Sean McElwee was trying to save himself from cancellation. When the news first broke at the end of November that he had been asked to resign, I thought he might try to lie low for a while, but he was taking the opposite approach: He was talking to as many people as he could, filling his days with meetings, chatting with possible clients about consulting, touching base with donors and letting them know that while he had agreed to leave Data for Progress, he wasn't leaving town.

"If people think they have seen the last of me," Sean McElwee said, "they should know I'm a tenacious motherfucker."

He was in full-on *control-the-narrative* mode, speaking in pull quotes and projecting confidence as he munched on spiced nuts and sipped nonalcoholic beer at the end of a bar in Logan Circle.

He was explaining that his departure was the result of an overreaction by a young, progressive staff, who had grown frustrated by his pragmatic politics and then "got freaked out" by what people were saying about him on Twitter. Just a garden-variety Washington coup, nothing spectacular, attributable to the climate as much as anything (Zoomers, am I right?).

"I was talking to an executive director today and he was like, 'Yeah, I just assume I'm going to get kicked out at some point,'" Sean said.

Sean was confident that he'd survive this, no problem. Even his detractors thought that was likely too—Washington has always been a city of second chances. And maybe that would ultimately be the case for Sean. But it was quickly becoming clear that his was a unique case.

Less than two weeks after Sean and I met for a drink in Logan Circle, Sam Bankman-Fried was arrested in the Bahamas after the United States filed federal charges. A day later, on December 13, the U.S. attorney for the Southern District of New York unsealed an eight-count indictment against Bankman-Fried. One of those counts alleged he had been skirting political donation limits by funneling money through third parties—something known as "straw donations." Bankman-Fried and others, the indictment said, contributed to political candidates "in the names of other persons."

That evening, a lefty policy researcher and Sean critic named Will Stancil speculated on Twitter that one of those persons might just happen to be Sean. Stancil pointed out that Sean had given more than $70,000 to candidates in the 2022 election cycle. That was a lot of money for someone who only made $180,000 in salary from Data for Progress.

This was strange for a number of reasons. First of all, up until March 2022, Sean had never given a candidate for office more than $250. And he'd given that much only once. But after stepping up his outside work for Guarding Against Pandemics, he gave $2,900—the limit individuals can give to campaigns—to candidates like Maxwell Frost, Richie Torres, Greg Casar, and Bankman-Fried's personal project out of Oregon, Carrick Flynn. Many of these candidates received similar donations from other people in Sam Bankman-Fried's orbit.

I called Sean the next day to ask about it.

"I didn't get paid any money by Sam, so it couldn't be that," Sean replied. He said that he'd had a "very good" year consulting, including making "several hundred thousand dollars" from Guarding Against

Pandemics and that he wanted to "get on the ground floor on a lot of great, new Democrats."

"I've gotten used to people saying absurd things about me," he said. "And this is another one of those things."

Sean told me that no one had been asking him about this, so he wasn't too worried. But a week later, that would change. *New York* magazine, Politico's *Playbook*, *Rolling Stone*, *Puck*—they all had stories about chasing Sam Bankman-Fried's "dirty money," and they all focused on Sean. The reports included allegations that Sean had been doing something worse than just acting as a straw donor for Bankman-Fried. *New York* magazine said that Sean had allegedly pressured a member of his staff, Ethan Winter, to participate too. Ethan had made nearly $31,000 in donations, more than a quarter of his DFP salary. Sean had been in the middle of severance negotiations as this was coming out, but *New York* reported that the Ethan Winter situation had made things untenable and that Sean was fired immediately. (Ethan declined to comment on the matter when I reached out.)

When I got in touch with Danielle Deiseroth about this, she didn't want to get into the straw donor situation. It was still too fluid. But she told me it wasn't the only thing that had led to the sudden termination. Every day since she had stepped into the role as the new executive director of DFP, Danielle had found herself surprised by some new thing that Sean had been doing that was "undermining the goals of the organization."

The last straw, however, was when members of Data for Progress, and members of the advisory board for the Tides Foundation—the massive progressive incubator that sponsored DFP—found out about one of Sean's side hustles that he'd kept secret from them. Sean had, it turned out, created another polling organization, which he called Pioneer Polling. They had one client: the Crypto Council for Innovation, a trade association run by former Republican Senator Cory Gardner of Colorado. Up until Sam Bankman-Fried's implosion, the Crypto Council had included FTX as a member. But it wasn't exactly the SBF connection that drew the ire of the Tides Foundation. It was the fact that they believed Sean had used their own nonprofit polling infrastructure for a for-profit side hustle—a big no-no.

Had the team known about this at the time, Danielle said, he may have been asked to leave earlier.

"They would have felt betrayed," she said, "to a degree that is really unforgivable."

"It was the nail in the coffin," said McKenzie Wilson, the communications director.

By year's end, Marcela Mulholland hadn't forgiven Sean. But she was also having trouble fully removing herself from the Seaniest place on earth: Washington. When I talked to Marcela in mid-December, she worried about what becoming a Washington person might do to her. But by early January, she had decided to move there. She had been offered a job working on renewable energy at the Department of Energy. She had reason to believe this would be a different kind of experience—she longed for bureaucracy, she said, and the chance to get in the weeds on important issues. And at the very least, it gave her an excuse to move on.

"I'm starting at DOE this month," she texted me in early January. "So I can't speak about any of the Sean/SBF stuff anymore."

A few days later, she offered one last text: "Sean abused his power to enrich himself and advance the interests of a fraudulent billionaire. His behavior is inexcusable and an affront to the most basic progressive values."

The break between Sean and his staff was complete. Washington may remain fundamentally the same, but for Sean McElwee, it had changed. As all this was unfolding, I reached out to him to chat. For more than a year, there had been almost nothing that he wouldn't say to or in front of me: About being a "Clarence Thomas" Democrat because he believed money in politics was a good thing. About "not putting shit in texts" because if it's not written down, it's not illegal. About the bets he put down on his own clients. But now he'd gone bust.

"As you know, I'm not normally a closed book on this stuff," Sean told me over the phone in late December. "I've just never been in a situation like this."

But before he hung up, he had another thing to add.

"You know the craziest thing?" he said. "Before all this, I really thought everyone liked me."

Epilogue

I feel like, I just feel like I don't have the answers like I thought I did," Jamarcus Purley said. "I thought I had a greater sense of things, but I feel like there's something more I have to get to. Politics isn't doing it. I feel confused about what my role should be in the world right now. I know how I can survive and be happy on a personal level, but I'm thinking about what I could do to help my little sister, in general. I'm overwhelmed in that capacity. Homelessness is crazy here, where do I even fit in to all of this?"

Jamarcus had called from Little Rock, Arkansas, as the year came to an end. He'd moved home to Pine Bluff after his five-year stint in Washington only to find that his hometown felt more like a "ghost town." Without any opportunities, he'd hoofed it to Little Rock, where he was crashing with a friend from his post-college teaching stint for the program City Year.

Jamarcus was trying to "take a breath," he said. He seemed calmer than he'd sounded on the phone. He had been "humbled" by the experience of coming home, seeing the poverty up close and realizing that he had been gone too long from the real world. He was happy to be out of his fancy apartment building in a gentrifying Washington neighborhood. Living there had given him a "superficial" understanding of what people were going through.

He was a bit lost and consumed about what to do next, but he was okay with that. Living in Washington had made him feel like he had all the answers. At least now he was asking himself the right questions: Should he find work helping combat voter suppression? Should he become a teacher, maybe start by subbing at his old high school? Was business school really worth pursuing?

"All I know is that I'm optimistic," he said. "There's clearly a social revolution taking place around the world but also in the U.S."

Look at Pennyslvania Senator John Fetterman, Jamarcus said, the "epitome" of a politician who could only be elected when people were "really fucking tired of business as usual." Maybe the Overton window on "normal" was shifting in Washington after all.

Jamarcus was happy to be gone, but he was excited about some of the new faces that were arriving in his absence. He just hoped they could change Washington before Washington changed them.

* * *

"Maxwell, can I just have your head go down slightly?"

Click.

"And, Maxwell, can I have you move to your right? A little bit more. A little bit more. Okay perfect." *Click click click.*

It was January 3, 2023, the first day of Congress, and Maxwell Alejandro Frost was already taking orders. Almost all new Democrats in Congress are told at some point to keep their head down and think about moving a bit to the right, but these stage directions came from a *Vanity Fair* photographer who accompanied Frost for part of the day. She was joined, in Frost's brand-new congressional office, by a *Vanity Fair* reporter, and also a *New Yorker* writer working on her own story. A documentary crew had been filming Frost's every move earlier in the day, but they must have been taking a break.

This was a lot of exposure for a new member of Congress, but Frost was a special case. He was still just twenty-five years old ("I turn twenty-six in two weeks," he said), and the arrival of an actual young person to a House that had come to resemble an old people's home had captivated much of Washington. Some twenty-five-year-olds might have imposter syndrome on their first day in Congress, but this particular first day of Congress had made Frost look overqualified.

First of all, there was an *actual* imposter, Congressman-elect George Santos, who was moving into an office almost directly below Frost's in the Longworth House Office Building. Reporters had staked out Santos's office all day, lobbing questions about his various lies and possible ethics violations, which Santos—wearing a backpack and looking very much like a lost child on his first day of school—tried his best to ignore.

"That's been interesting to watch," Frost told me. Frost did not wear a backpack. He wore a navy blue suit, a sky blue tie with a tie bar, and a new, circular green pin on his lapel that gave him access to the floor of the House of Representatives. The pin was supposed to signify that Frost was a member of Congress. Only he still wasn't. Which brings us to the second reason young Frost needn't have worried about seeming underqualified for his new job: He still sort of didn't have one.

Despite hours and hours of repeated votes, Republicans had failed to nominate a Speaker of the House, and without a Speaker of the House, no members of Congress could be sworn in.

"It's a little case study of what the next two years are going to be like," Frost said. "They can't get their stuff together."

Getting himself to this House of Representatives in perpetual purgatory had taken a lot of factors: natural charisma and an impressive work ethic; thousands of grassroots organizers and small-dollar donors; endorsements and guidance from sitting members of Congress; and of course, that "coalition" of people who had gathered at a rooftop fundraiser for a man many of them believed could be the future of the Democratic Party.

Things had grown complicated with that coalition. Leah Hunt-Hendrix had hoped she could offer Frost a place to stay at Chez Leah when he first came to town. Frost had recently had an application to rent an apartment rejected for having bad credit (one of his many relatable Gen Z qualities), and Leah was in the Canary Islands so it should have worked out perfectly. But Leah's lawyers advised against it. He would be a member of Congress, not a candidate. There could be ethical concerns now.

The ethical concerns of the Sean McElwee and Gabe Bankman-Fried portion of the coalition were of a different nature. His team kept getting word that Sean was bragging around town about how helpful he'd been in getting Frost elected. And all that Bankman-Fried money had become an optics problem. Frost had already put out a statement distancing himself from Sam and Gabe Bankman-Fried, whose Protect Our Future PAC had donated nearly $1 million to his campaign.

"I never solicited their support," he said in the statement. "I don't want or need support from those scamming working folks."

Frost didn't want to talk much about all this on his first day in Congress.

"It's a real headache, I can say that," he'd told me early in the day, walking through a Capitol tunnel on his way to pick up his member pin. But without the various headaches—the endless fundraising, the tacit acceptance of dark money, forming a coalition with the various Washington hacks—he might not have been picking up that pin in the first place. The question for Frost, as it had been for every new-new thing to come to Congress, would be what would he do with that pin?

First, he would spend an entire day voting over and over again for a Speaker of the House. And when the House decided to call it quits and try again the next day, Frost would head to his non-Leah-friend's place where he was crashing and grab a shower. It was one of the most chaotic, most embarrassing days in the House of Representatives. Frost couldn't even technically call himself a member of Congress. But he had to do *something*, right? The plan before all this was to throw a party.

It was supposed to happen down by the Wharf, a waterfront shopping and entertainment district that recently underwent a billion-dollar renovation. They'd rented out a concert hall, where Frost's friends' band would play. It would be a celebration for the friends and family who had flown in from back home.

"The people who sent me here are from Orlando, Florida, from central Florida," Frost said. "At the end of the day, that's what matters. You have to stay grounded with your people." But because it was Washington and he was a congressman-elect now, there would be other people too. They were expecting, his spokesman told me, CNN's Jake Tapper, MSNBC's Symone Sanders-Townsend, celebrity chef José Andrés, White House staffers, and various members of Congress. That had been the plan. And what was the plan now that there currently were no members of Congress?

"The party's still happening," Frost said before leaving the Capitol. "It was always happening."

Acknowledgments

I've got to start by thanking Steve Kolowich. Steve has been editing me ever since we were in high school together, and everything he touches improves vastly. Without him this book would either not exist, or if it did, it would be a much worse read.

While we're on the subject of oldest, best friends: a big thank-you to Max Strasser. I probably wouldn't be a journalist if I hadn't stolen the idea from you back when we were teenagers working in our summer camp kitchen and passing our free time hanging out with the camp goats. Pssst: Thanks for always motivating me, calming me down, and cracking me up when I need it. It's good to laugh again.

Endless gratitude to the *Washington Post*, both for giving me a professional home that pushes me to become a better journalist, and for letting me play hooky for the better part of a year to write this book. Special shout-outs to Krissah Thompson, Liz Seymour, David Malitz, and Hank Stuever, four kick-ass leaders that the *Post* is lucky to have helping run the show.

Speaking of Posties, I consider myself incredibly lucky to have ended up in the Style section (which, I'll say for the millionth time, is a lot more than just fashion coverage), where I get to spend my days with the likes of Caitlin Gibson, Chris Richards, Monica Hesse, and Dan Zak. I'd say I'm lucky to be in your friend circle, but a 2-D circle doesn't do this friend group justice. It's really more of a sphere. One of the best parts about working at the *Post* is that I'm surrounded by people who are smarter than I am, and who are willing to share some of their smarts with me. This is why I made sure to have folks like Jose DeReal, Helena Andrews-Dyer, Jacob Brogan, and my brilliant former editor Rachel Dry take a look at various versions of the manuscript and help save me from myself.

Thanks, of course, to Sean Desmond—an editor extraordinaire who didn't take no for an answer when I kept telling him I didn't want to write a book. I'm glad I did, and I'm glad I got to do it with Sean and for a place as special as Twelve Books. None of this would have happened without the cajoling of my agent, Howard Yoon, who not only knows how to pitch a book, but was also incredibly helpful in figuring out how to structure one. (It turns out that it's different than just writing a bunch of long newspaper articles. Who knew?) I knew I was in good hands when professional-grade readers like Theo Emery, Jim O'Sullivan, Greg Hill-Ries, Eric Lach, Matt Flegenheimer, and John Hendrickson put eyes on my writing, and I was able to sleep at night knowing that all-star fact checkers Sean Lavery, Hilary McClellen, and Julie Tate were making sure everything was right. And then there was Evan McMorris-Santoro, my gut check when I couldn't trust my own gut. Two guts are better than one!

I never really expected, nor really wanted, to be a political reporter. I just knew I wanted to be a journalist, and my path to and through Washington was made possible by many journalists along the way. Stephen Tobey of the *Concord Journal* gave me my first byline, covering local sports for $15 an hour. Mark Feeney taught me the art of feature writing (and, by never giving me anything higher than an A-, taught me that I had improving to do!). Ron Fournier brought me to Washington. Terry Samuel and Matt Cooper let me actually try and have some fun while reporting on national politics, and Jim Oliphant gave me the best advice: Pretend you're writing for the *Washington Post* Style section. Thank you, too, to Eva Rodriguez for letting me actually write for Style, and to Marty Baron for, well, being Marty Baron. Coming to the *Post* has been a real career highlight for me, mostly because I get to work with—and look up to—journalists who can report and write circles around me: Philip Rucker, David Fahrenthold, Ashley Parker (special shoutout to her husband, Michael Bender, for helping guide me through the book process), Robert Samuels, and Wesley Lowery.

People always say that you shouldn't write a book unless you are deeply passionate about the subject, and I've always been a bit ambivalent about politics. I never cared much for the horse race of it all, and I never found myself particularly moved by a politician. When I first moved to Washington I promised my then-girlfriend, Rachel, that we would only be here for a year. It's been twelve years. But part of the reason we lasted so long was because Washington is actually a wonderful place to live, you just need to find your people. And I love my people here. Noah Bein, for being a true friend since college, and for giving me a reason to hang out at dingy bars and listen to Warren Zevon covers until the wee hours. My pals from my *National Journal* days—Shane Goldmacher, Tim Alberta, Scott Bland, Patrick Reis, and Alex Roarty—who, despite taking all my money at poker nights, are always the best company. You couldn't ask for a better crew of D.C. journalists to come up with than Alex Seitz-Wald, Lucia Graves, Benjy Sarlin, Suzy Khimm, David Graham, and Marin Cogan (and honorary member Thom Planert), or for better role models to look up to than Molly Ball, Jason Zengerle, Jason Horowitz, and Mark Leibovich. Another reason we managed to stick around so long was that we moved to Takoma Park and fell in with a great group of neighbors like Adam Jentleson, Britt Peterson, Dave Zirin, Michele Bollinger, Heather Hurlburt, Darius Sivin, Mimi Diez, and Joel Conlon.

Shoutout to all my summer-camp family. I know it's weird to be an adult and still think so much about camp, but here we are. Kate Seeger and Dean Spencer, thanks for making that place so special.

Emily Gordon, thanks for being my oldest friend and a freelance doctor on call whenever I see something weird on my kids' skin or feel an unexplained pain in my foot. And to Levi Albert for being my future lawyer.

Growing up, I was surrounded by so many writers—my Nana, my dad, my mom, my mom's many friends, my dad's friend—that I thought it was one of the only jobs in the world. Now I just think it's one of the only "good" jobs in the world (even if I hate it half the time). Thank you, Nana, for teaching me about writing when I was young, and continuing to offer sound advice (and story ideas!) now that I'm mostly a grown-up. I have to say it also rules having three younger brothers, all of whom figured out jobs other than writing. Eli, Theo, Sam, it would be annoying how much cooler your lives are than mine if I didn't love you all so much.

Also, I love my in-laws. *Not a joke*, to quote Biden. Donna and Larry are two of the best people in the world, and not just because they are responsible for creating the best person in the world (Rachel—with brother Doug a close runner-up). They are patient grandparents, and gracious hosts, and there's no one else I can imagine having to quarantine with for the first six months of a pandemic.

So much of this book is about inheritance. Not just money handed down from one generation to the next, but purpose, morals, humor, maybe some trauma. Pretty much everything good in my life I owe to my parents passing down a fraction of their smarts, their supportive and patient nature, their ability to make community for themselves and their children, and their humor. Thank you, Mom and Dad, for showing me how to be a good parent, even when I was a pain-in-the-ass kid. I'm only now figuring out how hard that must have been.

Which brings me to my boys! Ralph and Jack, you guys are amazing. I couldn't ask for better company when working from home. No one makes me laugh like you guys. It's no *My Father's Dragon* or *Where the Wild Things Are*, but I hope someday you will read this book and be as proud of me as I am of you. (Or maybe just a fraction of how proud I am of you.)

And to Rachel, if you read only one thing from this book I hope it's this: I love you so much. I couldn't do any of this without you. If you ever want to move anywhere for just a year, and then decide we should stay there for more than a decade, count me in. *Clink.*

Index

A

"Abolish ICE" guy, 33–35

A-bomb Kid, 99–101

abortion rights, 303

Abraham Accords, 306

Abrams, Stacey, 294

Acosta, Alex, 305

Adams, Eric, 266

Affordable Care Act, 85, 268

Al Franken, 145

Allard, Wayne, 80

Allen, Jon, 139

Almeida, Gisele Barreto, 183

America First Policy Institute, 19

America First Political Action Conference, 150

American Civil Liberties Union, 168, 179

American Conservative Union, 18, 138, 249

American Israel Public Affairs Committee (AIPAC), 115

American Mask Manufacturers Association, 123

Ammori, Marvin, 119, 284, 291, 299

Andreessen, Marc, 234

Andrés, José, 319

Animal Farm (George Orwell), 186

Armey, Dick, 194

The Art of War (Sun Tzu), 186

Assange, Julian, 15

B

Baines Johnson, Lyndon, 48

Baldwin, Tammy, 286

Ballard, Brian, 123–125

Ballard Partners, 123

Bankman-Fried, Gabe, 2, 116–117, 157–163, 166, 170, 239, 283, 318

Bankman-Fried, Sam, 2, 117–118, 166, 266, 284–285, 294, 311

Bannon, Stephens, 260

Barnes, Mandela, 16–17, 28, 115, 235, 270, 281, 284–285, 287, 289–291, 293

Barry, Marion, 44

Bassett, Stephen, 7

Bateman, Patrick, 133

Bautista, Millie, 44

Beach, Bethany, 215

Beeriodicals.com, 87

Beltway Republicans, 19

Bennett, Barry, 123–124

Berenson, Alex, 146

Bernie Bros, 32

Index

Biden, Joe, 1, 3, 6, 35, 103, 106, 123,
    141–142, 217, 223, 232, 247, 267, 269,
    278, 304
Biden's presidency, 1
Black Lives Matter, 16, 273, 290
Black Lives Matter movement, 145
Blaise, 50
Blanchard, Paul, 199
Blue & Gold Tavern, 33
Bobbi, 105, 236–237, 239–242, 298
Boehner, John, 99
Booker, Cory, 88, 176, 180–183
Bourge, 59
Bourge, Christian, 57, 212
Brown, Shontel, 3, 8
Buchanan, Pat, 194, 272
Buck, Ken, 146
Buckley, Christopher, 121
Buckley, William F., 45
Build Back Better, 6, 238
Build Back Better framework, 109
Bush, George H. W., 45
Bush, George W., 18, 20, 53, 67, 222, 256
Buttigieg, Pete, 32
Byrne, Melissa, 278–279

C
Callista, 215
Campbell, Kurt, 132–133
cancel culture, 144
Cannon Building, 71
Caputo, Marc, 138–139
Carlson, Tucker, 144, 215
Carson, Ben, 43, 123
Casar, Greg, 164, 311
Casars, Greg, 235
Ceauescu, Nicolae, 46
Center for Election Integrity, 19
Chauvin, Derek, 168, 177
Cheney, Liz, 62
Chilton, Lewis, 208, 210
Chomsky, Noam, 33
Chopra, Rohit, 27

Christmas party, 37–40
Citizens United v. Federal Election
    Commission, 267
Civil Rights Act of 1957, 93
Civis Analytics, 158
Clinton, Bill, 16, 36, 112, 192–194, 300
Clinton, Hillary, 15, 20, 36, 57
Clyburn, Jim, 68
Cohen, Michael, 261
Collins, Kina, 232
Collins, Susan, 303
Comcast, 145
Congressional Black Caucus, 3
Congressional Progressive Staff
    Association, 75, 187
Convent of the Sacred Heart, 113
Conway, George, 256
Conway, Kellyanne, 22, 50
Cooke, Jack Kent, 126
Coons, Chris, 5
Costa, Bob, 84
Cove Strategies, 23, 26, 145, 248
COVID-19 pandemic, 6
Covid response team, 4
CPAC, 42–43, 47, 49, 137–138, 140, 143,
    146–148, 150–152, 155–156, 214, 223,
    245–247, 249, 253–260, 262, 273,
    300–301, 308
Crenshaw, Dan, 5, 175
Crist, Charlie, 159
Cruz, Ted, 5, 137, 271
Crypto Council for Innovation, 312
Cuomo, Andrew, 30

D
The Daily Show, 141
Daniels, 56, 61
Daniels, Jacob, 55
Data for Progress, 1, 30, 34, 106–107,
    109–110, 117, 238, 242, 282, 285, 295,
    297, 312
Davis, Danny, 232
Dawson, Rosario, 183

Dear White Staffers, 72–75, 78, 89–90, 187
DeCasper, Jennifer, 78–82, 178, 183–184
Deiseroth, Danielle, 107, 297, 312
Delaney, John, 102
Demings, Val, 168
DeMint, Jim, 82
democracy, 31, 71, 103, 193, 225, 285, 299
Democratic Majority for Israel (DMFI), 115
Democratic operatives, 2–3
Democratic Party/Democrats, 2, 16–17, 28, 31, 34–36, 62, 68, 82, 109–110, 112, 115, 123, 159, 162, 164, 168, 170, 175, 179–180, 182, 222, 243, 268, 277, 279–281, 290, 293, 302
Dennard, Paris, 18
DeSantis, Ron, 4, 137, 302
The Desecrators, 143
Dole, Bob, 53, 206, 218
Dominion Voting Systems, 151
Duke, David, 82
Dunbar, John, 210
Duron, Veronica, 173–176, 180–181, 184
Duvall, Robert, 56
Dwight, 73–77

E
Eckhart, Aaron, 121
Ethan, 109
Euro Trash LLC, 41

F
Faith and Freedom Coalition, 300
Feinstein, Dianne, 66, 70, 91–94, 185, 187
Fetterman, John, 35–36, 184, 237–238, 280, 291, 316
The Fire Next Time (James Baldwin), 185
Fisher, Julie, 201
Floyd, George, 67, 145, 168, 177, 179, 247, 273
Flynn, Carrick, 311
Foreign Agents Registration Act (FARA), 200

Fox Business Channel, 33
Fox News, 146, 151
Fraternal Order of Police, 181
Fredericks, John, 149
Fried, Nikki, 159
Frost, Maxwell Alejandro, 163, 166–170, 298, 311, 316, 319
Frosts, Maxwell, 235
Fuentes, Nick, 150

G
Gaetz, Matt, 140, 146, 246–248, 254, 302, 304
Garamendi, John, 5
Garcia, Eric, 88
Gardner, Cory, 312
Garner, Eric, 178
Gay Straight Alliance, 107
Gencarelli, David F., 200
Getting the Love You Want, 111
Gibson, Bob, 196
Gidley, Hogan, 18–19
Gillibrand, Kirsten, 32
Gingrich, Newt, 194–195
Ginsberg, Ben, 222
Gisele, 238
Giuliani, Rudy, 127, 131, 194, 205
GiveWell, 117
Glover, Danny, 168
Gorka, Seb, 149
Gosar, Paul, 245
Gossip Girl, 113
Graham, Lindsey, 271
Green, Adam, 27
Green, Taylor, 245
Greene, John, 206
Greene, Taylor, 5, 62, 137, 148–151, 246, 257
Green New Deal, 238, 296
Grijalva, Raul, 84
Grim, Ryan, 15, 164, 244
Groser, Tim, 58
Guarding Against Pandemics, 117, 157, 163, 239, 311–312

Guarding Against Pandemics (GAP), 2
gun control movement, 168

H
Hallow, Ralph, 45–46, 214–215, 217–218, 247, 257
Harris, Kamala, 105
Harry, Prince, 174
  Spare, 174
#HasJustineLandedYet, 143
Hawk 'N' Dove, 84
Hawley, Josh, 137
Hazel, 50
Helen, 112
Hemminger, Ross, 147, 248
Hendricks, Diane, 285
Hendrix, Harville, 111–113
heuristics, 106
Hillyard, Vaughn, 150
Hilsenrath, Libby, 148
Hispanic Caucus Institute, 175
Hobbs, Katie, 288
Hoffman, Reid, 116
How to Change Your Mind, 174
Hoyer, Steny, 68
Hudson, Deal W., 151
Huffington, Arianna, 218
Hunt, Kasie, 84
Hunt, Nelson Bunker, 111
Hunt-Hendrix, Leah, 13–17, 26–28, 30–32, 111, 113–120, 163–170, 232–235, 270, 277, 284–286, 291, 299, 317
Hussein, Saddam, 102
Hutchinson, Cassidy, 255–256

I
Ian, 46–50
Imago Therapy, 113
#ImWithPablo, 86
Inflation Reduction Act, 296
Inhofe, Jim, 6, 84
Inslee, Jay, 108

International Association of Chiefs of Police, 181
Iran-Contra Affair, 45

J
Jackie, 48
James, Brendan, 32
Jeffries, Hakeem, 118
Jesus, 56
Jim Crow laws, 153
Joe, 47
John Birch Society, 111
Johnson, Boris, 230
Johnson, Ron, 17
Jolly, Stuart, 58
Jong-un, Kim, 7, 128
Jurvetson, Karla, 286

K
Kabila, Joseph, 59, 125, 130
Katz, Morris, 234
Katz, Rebecca, 36, 237, 289, 291–292
Kavanaugh, Brett, 302–303
Kelly, Mark, 270, 288, 293
Kennedy, John F., 14, 48
Kennedy, Robert F., 14, 241
Kerry, John, 123
King, Dawn, 205, 208
King, Jr., Martin Luther, 270
King Jr., Martin Luther, 14
Klain, Ron, 26, 35
Klepper, Jordan, 141
Kolbe, Jim, 53
Kool-Aid, 298
Kramers, 72
Ku Klux Klan, 82, 272
Kunce, Lucas, 119
Kushner, Jared, 91, 145

L
Lake, Kari, 273, 288
Lamb, Conor, 36
Latino Rebels, 83, 86–87, 91

law enforcement, 179, 181, 211
Laxalt, Adam, 216, 270, 288
legacy of wounding, 112
Legum, Judd, 145
Levin, Andy, 75
Lewandowski, Corey, 56, 123
Life Line, 112
Limbaugh, Rush, 46–47, 155
Lincoln, Abraham, 144
Lindell, Mike, 151, 257
Linen, James, 138–139
Lippman, Daniel, 23, 52
Lockheed Martin, 92, 123
Logan Circle, 13
Long, Billy, 22
Lopez, Alejandro Betancourt, 131
Lujan, Ben Ray, 105
Lukashenko, Alexander, 200
Luntz, Frank, 191–198, 230

M
MacAskill, Will, 266
Maduro, Nicolas, 59, 212–213
MAGA movement, 216, 256, 259, 261,
    272, 301
Malcolm X, 14
Manchin, Joe, 5–6, 238–239
Manriquez, Pablo, 83–89, 91, 99
Mapp, Karen, 66
March for Our Lives, 168
Martin, Billy, 48–49
Marvin, 163
Masto, Catherine Cortez, 270, 281,
    293
McAuliffe, Terry, 106
McCain, John, 53, 176, 206
McCarthy, Joseph, 13
McCarthy, Kevin, 197, 302
McConnell, Mitch, 88–89, 178
McCormick, David, 20
McDonald, Ronald, 191–192
McElwee, Sean, 1, 7–8, 30–32, 35,
    105–110, 117, 160–161, 163, 167, 192,
    236–244, 265–268, 270, 277–283,
    293–295, 310–314, 318
    in Democratic politics, 32
    jobs for GAP, 2
    rapport with Gen Z employees, 243–244
    salary, 2
McGinty, Katie, 36
McGrath, Jason, 291
McGraw, Phil, 230–231
Meadows, Mark, 221, 273
Mehlhorn, Dmitri, 116
Mellon, Andrew W., 126
Mellon, Paul, 126
Mercy, 44, 50
Merkley, Jeff, 55
Mexican Americans, 175
Miller, Sarah, 15, 260
Miller, Stephen, 20, 305
Millie, 217, 251
Mind the Gap, 158
Miss Universe Pageant, 139
Mitchell, Cleta, 215–216
Mitchell, Maurice, 284
MonicaPAC, 55
More Perfect Union, 15
Mother Jones, 140
Motion Picture Association, 23
Mulholland, Marcela, 107–109, 242–244,
    295, 297–298, 313
Mulvaney, Mick, 195
Murkowski, Lisa, 5
Musk, Elon, 304
MyPillow, 151

N
Nader, George, 213
Napa Sentinel, 207
Napa Valley Register, 205
National Journal magazine, 6
National Rifle Association, 44, 55, 251
Nayef, Muhammed bin, 130
Nehring, Andrew, 213
Newsmax, 21

New York Times, 91, 100, 111, 144, 222
New York Times Magazine, 123, 212
New York Women's Foundation, 233
Nice Republican, 220–221
North American Free Trade Agreement,
    272
Nunes, Devin, 61

O
Obama, Barack, 81, 196, 221
Obamacare, 176
Ocasio-Cortez, Alexandria, 33, 149, 164,
    175, 238, 295–296
Occupy Wall Street, 8, 114
O'Keefe, Ed, 88
Opportunity Zones, 180
The Oprah Winfrey Show, 112–113
O'Rourke, Beto, 280
Ortiz, Solomon, 175
Owens, Candace, 137
Oz, Mehmet, 238, 280, 282

P
Palin, Sarah, 55
Pasco, Jim, 181–182
Patch, Robin, 148
Pelosi, Nancy, 15, 68, 87, 118, 179, 296
Peltola, Mary, 280
Pence, Mike, 215
Percy, Charles, 100
Perlberg, Steven, 33
Phillips, John Aristotle, 99–104
Pine Bluffs, 66, 70
Pocan, Mark, 5
policing, 177–182
PolitiFact, 216
Pollan, Michael, 174
polymarket, 283
Pompeo, Mike, 137, 140
Popularism, 35
Posobiec, Jack, 257
PredictIt, 99, 104–105, 109, 123, 161, 169,
    281–282, 294

The Prince (Machiavelli), 186
progressive movement, 32
Proxmire, William, 100
Psaki, Jen, 6
psychedelics, 174
PTSD, 174
Purley, Jamarcus, 67–70, 75–76, 82, 89–94,
    184–188, 286, 315
Putin, Vladimir, 134, 139, 142, 150, 201

Q
Quinn, Tommy, 121–123

R
Rabin-Havt, Ari, 166–169, 277
racism, 94
racist, 153–154
Ralph, 45
Raytheon, 92
Reagan, Ronald, 138
Reed, Ralph, 300
Reid, Harry, 2, 15, 167, 191
Republican National Committee, 153
Republican National Convention, 28, 45
Republican Party/Republicans, 18–20,
    22–26, 28–29, 37–38, 62, 68, 82, 137,
    139, 154, 176, 182, 193, 212, 223, 269,
    279, 303, 305
right-wing populism, 15
Robertson, Pat, 300
Rodgers, Aaron, 174
Roe. v. Wade, 232, 271
Roe v. Wade, 231
Roofers Union, 166
Roosevelt, Franklin Delano, 230
Rose, Pete, 8
Rounders, 1
Rumsfeld, Donald, 102

S
Sacco, Justine, 143
Salinases, Andrea, 235
Salman, King, 130

Salman, Mohammed bin, 130
Sanders, Bernie, 3, 15, 166–167, 170
Sanders-Townsend, Symone, 319
San Francisco Chronicle, 92, 228
Santos, George, 305, 317
Santos, Isabel dos, 212, 307
Saudi Arabia, 129–130
Schilling, Bobby, 21
Schilling, Terry, 21
Schlapp, Matt, 17–18, 23, 25–26, 37–40,
    44, 49–50, 138, 143, 145, 151, 155,
    192, 214, 216, 218, 220–223, 245–246,
    248–249, 258–260, 271, 273–276,
    302, 304–308
Schlapp, Mercy, 17–18, 23, 25–26, 50, 151,
    305, 308
Schlapps, 18–20, 22–23, 25–26, 43, 146
Schnatter, John "Papa John," 140–141
Schock, Aaron, 41
Schuh, Becca, 32
Schulte, Todd, 27
Schultz, Wasserman, 85
Schumer, Chuck, 35, 75, 99, 158, 175, 279,
    287
Scott, Rick, 212
Scott, Tim, 42–43, 78, 80–81, 146,
    178–182, 184, 271
Scott, Walter, 178–179
Secure Elections for America Now
    (SEAN), 33
Segal, David, 118, 232
Shakir, Faiz, 15
Shelby, 61
Shipman, David, 205, 207–208
Shor, David, 34–35, 158, 240, 277
Simpson, Sturgill, 173
Sinema, Kyrsten, 3
soft power, 16
Solidaire Network, 114
Solis, Rose, 209
Sollenberger, Roger, 271, 307
Sonoran Lobbying Group, 212
Sonoran Policy Group, 53, 127, 129

Soros, George, 159
Southern Poverty Law Center, 150
SpaceX, 286
Spicer, Sean, 20–21
Stancil, Will, 311
Star Trek, 117
Steele, Michael, 153, 155
Stensaas, Sharon, 207–208
Straka, Brandon, 262
Stryk, Robert, 51–60, 125–135, 199–213,
    224–229, 306, 308
Stryk Global Diplomacy, 127
Summers, Larry, 27
Sunrise Movement, 108, 238, 296
super PAC, 163
Swanee, 16, 112

T
Talley, Brett, 7
Tanden, Neera, 108, 243
Tapper, Jake, 319
Taylor, Breonna, 177, 179, 273
Taylor, Elizabeth, 126
Taylor, James, 269
Taylor, Scott, 199–201
Terris, Ben, 79
Tesla, 286
Tester, Jon, 41
Texas Women's Foundation, 233
Thatcher, Margaret, 194
Thiel, Peter, 270
Thomas, Bill, 197
Thomas, Clarence, 31, 313
Thornton, Billy Bob, 130
Tiahrt, Todd, 23
Tides Foundation, 312
Toner, Michael, 304
Toomey, Pat, 35
Torre, Joe, 196
Torres, Richie, 311
To Tell the Truth, 100, 103
Trent, Corbin, 14
Tripp, Linda, 126

Trump, Donald, 3–4, 6, 14, 18, 26, 36, 51,
    55–57, 59, 103, 107–108, 128, 137,
    139, 141–143, 146, 149, 151, 154,
    193, 195–198, 201–203, 216, 221,
    223, 247, 259, 261, 270, 301–303, 306,
    308–309
Trump International Hotel, 61
Tshibaka, Kelly, 21
Tune Inn, 84
Turner, Nina, 3, 8
Twitter, 33, 143
Tyler, Steven, 130

U
Uihlein, Elizabeth, 285
Uihlein, Richard, 285
U.S. Innovation and Competition Act,
    238

V
Valente, Pascale, 208
Vance, J. D., 140
Vanity Fair, 101–102
Van Susteren, Greta, 302, 304
Varela, Julio Ricardo, 86
Verizon, 145
Violet, 50
Vogel, Ken, 131
Voight, Jon, 60
Vumii, 205–206

W
W. Bush, George, 53
Wag the Dog theory, 141
Walker, Herschel, 270–272, 276, 288,
    307
Wallace, Nicolle, 256
Walmart, 145

Walters, Carin (Carin Hudson), 44, 47–50,
    152, 155, 215, 219, 249–254, 259,
    261–262, 299–301
Walters, Colin, 44–45, 217
Walters, Ian, 40, 43, 47, 49–50, 152–155,
    214, 217–218, 245–246, 254, 258–260,
    262, 299
Warner, John, 126
Warnock, Raphael, 93, 270, 288
Warren, Elizabeth, 27, 109
Washington, 8–9, 14
Washington Free Beacon, 251
Washington Post, 6, 91, 100, 222
Washington Times, 215
Way to Win, 16
Wehby, Monica, 55
Weiner, Anthony, 84, 145
West, Dr. Cornel, 114
Whitmer, Gretchen, 280
Whittaker, Leigh, 72
WikiLeaks, 85–86
Wilson, McKenzie, 31, 107, 109–110, 295,
    297–298
Winter, Ethan, 107, 297
Wolf, Chad, 305
Women Moving Millions, 233
Working Families Party, 164
Wren, Caroline, 304

Y
Yarmuth, John, 5
Yglesias, Matthew, 26–27
Youngkin, Glenn, 106
Yountvilleexposed.com, 208
Yountville Sun, 207–209

Z
"zero tolerance" policy, 33

About the Author

Ben Terris is a writer in the *Washington Post*'s Style section with a focus on national politics. He lives in Maryland with his wife, Rachel, and sons, Ralph and Jack.